MANCHESTER
MEDIEVAL
LITERATURE
AND CULTURE

VISIONS AND RUINS

Manchester University Press

Series editors: Anke Bernau, David Matthews
and James Paz

Series founded by: J. J. Anderson and Gail Ashton

Advisory board: Ruth Evans, Nicola McDonald,
Andrew James Johnston, Sarah Salih, Larry Scanlon
and Stephanie Trigg

MANCHESTER
MEDIEVAL
LITERATURE
AND CULTURE

Manchester Medieval Literature and Culture publishes monographs and essay collections comprising new research informed by current critical methodologies on the literary cultures of the Middle Ages. We are interested in all periods, from the early Middle Ages through to the late, and we include post-medieval engagements with and representations of the medieval period (or 'medievalism'). 'Literature' is taken in a broad sense, to include the many different medieval genres: imaginative, historical, political, scientific, religious. While we welcome contributions on the diverse cultures of medieval Britain and are happy to receive submissions on Anglo-Norman, Anglo-Latin and Celtic writings, we are also open to work on the Middle Ages in Europe more widely, and beyond.

Titles available in the series

Visions and ruins

Cultural memory and the untimely Middle Ages

JOSHUA DAVIES

Manchester University Press

Published by Manchester University Press
Altrincham Street, Manchester M1 7JA
www.manchesteruniversitypress.co.uk

British Library Cataloguing-in-Publication Data
A catalogue record for this book is available from the British Library

ISBN 978 1 5261 2593 4 hardback

First published 2018

The publisher has no responsibility for the persistence or accuracy of URLs for any external or third-party internet websites referred to in this book, and does not guarantee that any content on such websites is, or will remain, accurate or appropriate.

Typeset by Out of House Publishing
Printed by Lightning Source

Contents

Figures

Acknowledgements

In the very early stages of this project I received important advice and encouragement from Clare Lees, Bob Mills, Jenny Neville and Bernard O'Donoghue. I thank all of them for their help. Much later, as this work came together, I benefited greatly from presenting material to audiences. I thank Noelle Gallagher, Anke Bernau and David Matthews for inviting me to Manchester; Patricia Dailey for inviting me to Columbia; Cath Nall for inviting me to present at the London Old and Middle English Research Seminar; and Amy Evans and Robert Hampson for inviting me to the London Contemporary Innovative Poetry Research Seminar.

I thank Bernard J. Muir for supplying an image of the Exeter Anthology of Old English Literature and for permission to reproduce it; the British Library for permission to reproduce images from the Luttrell Psalter and Thomas Gray's *Odes*; the British Newspaper Archive for permission to reproduce a page from *The Graphic*; and Historic England for permission to reproduce Henry W. Taunt's photograph of the effigy at Dorchester Abbey.

I am very grateful indeed to Elizabeth Price for allowing me to reproduce a still image from her film, *The Woolworths Choir of 1979*, and to Michael Landy and Thomas Dane Gallery for their permission to reproduce *Saint Jerome*. Flora Bowden helped enormously with the other images.

It gives me great pleasure that this book has been produced between Manchester and London. In Manchester, I'd like to thank the Series Editors, Anke Bernau and David Matthews, for their support and critical acuity, the staff at the Press for their help and patience and the anonymous readers for their time, energy and insight. In London, I'd like to thank my teachers, friends and colleagues at King's. I'd particularly like to thank Clare Lees (again!), who has provided so much advice, support and inspiration over the years. Pat Palmer read far too many early drafts and always responded with insight and encouragement. Carl Kears provided focus and reassurance just when it was needed. Working with Sarah Salih on another project gave me a sense of how I might see this book through. Rachel Homer, Richard Kirkland, Sarah Lewis, Jo McDonagh, Clare Pettitt, Lara Shalson, Ed Sugden, Mark Turner, Lawrence Warner, Julian Weiss, Bea Wilford and Patrick Wright all offered valuable advice and assistance. Elsewhere, I'd like to thank Caroline Bergvall, Denis Ferhatovic, Karl Fugelso, Liz Herbert McAvoy, Susan Irvine, Chris Jones, Richard Maguire, Hal Momma, Gillian Overing and Laurence Scott.

My family – Davies, Bowden and Haygarth (especially, I have to say, Alice and Elizabeth) – gave me distraction, support and sustenance. The Chickmans and the Tucker-Dawsons offered refuge in Asturias, Essex, Kent, Lochailort and Nottingham, and I'd also like to record my appreciation of Paddy Molloy and Hannah Montague, Ed Eustace and Fiona McDermott, and Ken and Joann Davis, who told me what I needed to hear when I needed to hear it.

Finally I'd like to thank my mum and dad, Marion and Rhys Davies, for their endless support and encouragement, and Flora Bowden, who made it all so much easier and makes it all worthwhile. This book is for them.

Introduction

> Memory is the matrix of all human temporal perception.
>> Mary Carruthers, *The Book of Memory*[1]

This book is a study of cultural memory in and of the British Middle Ages. It is about ways of knowing the past created by individuals and groups in medieval Britain and how those texts and images have been adapted and appropriated in the modern West. Like the medieval and modern material with which it works, this book's methodology is associative. It traces connections – often explicit, sometimes intuitive – across time, place and media to explore the temporal complexities of cultural production and subject formation. So while the methodology of this book is defined by historicist readings of the texts with which I work, this book is also a study of untimeliness, an investigation of cultural productions bereft of their original context.

The line drawn between the Middle Ages and modernity carries great cultural significance. For some critics it marks the birth of the individual,[2] for others the birth of the nation,[3] for some the beginning of historical consciousness.[4] As Margreta de Grazia writes, there is an 'exceptional force' to 'that secular divide' between medieval and modern which 'determines nothing less than relevance'.[5] But exactly what prompted the break, and exactly when it occurred, is mysterious. Indeed, historians have offered numerous dates for the end of the Middle Ages. For Hans Blumenberg, the transition between the Middle Ages and modernity could be marked precisely with Petrarch's walk up Mont Ventoux on 22 April 1336, which he described as 'one of the great moments that oscillate indecisively between the epochs'.[6] Jacob Burckhardt agreed that Petrarch was 'one of the first truly modern men'.[7] Other possible dates include the discovery of the 'new world' in 1492; the Dissolution of the Monasteries in the 1530s; the end of the

Byzantine Empire in 1453; the death of Richard III at Bosworth Field in 1485; and Stephen Greenblatt has recently offered the Italian humanist Poggio Bracciolini's reading of Lucretius' poem *De rerum natura* in 1417.[8] But there is little consensus beyond the fact that the Middle Ages did – at some point – end and that this break in time altered, somehow, human life and culture profoundly.

Visions and Ruins, however, examines continuities and connections as well as breaks and fractures. The scope of this book is determined by the duration of cultural forms rather than historical period. It explores some of the ways in which the presence of the Middle Ages has been felt, understood and perpetuated, as well as the cultural possibilities and transformations this has generated. It is prompted by the paradox that, on the one hand, Western modernity is predicated on the idea that the Middle Ages has passed and that the time of the medieval was somehow inferior, more barbaric and less civilised than modernity, while, on the other hand, modernity is characterised by continual returns of medieval cultural forms and conditioned by medieval institutions. The Middle Ages is therefore both inside and outside modernity, as both abjected other and necessary origin. The tensions of the paradox are expressed in the work of cultural memory, which records and perpetuates diverse and often contradictory ideas of the Middle Ages. *Visions and Ruins* traces some of the trajectories of cultural memories of the Middle Ages in the modern word, while at the same time exploring the production of cultural memory in the British Middle Ages. This double focus enables an examination of texts that may be separated by long stretches of time but which share desires, anxieties or sources alongside one another, in sometimes uneasy proximity. The texts we encounter in this book work creatively with time and history. They insist that the past might be, or become, present.

Structures of feeling and networks of memory

Definitions of cultural memory are necessarily broad and flexible, as the practices encompassed by it are multiple and diverse, but it does have what Jan Assmann terms 'fixed points'. As Assmann writes, 'These fixed points are fateful events of the past, whose memory is maintained through cultural formation (texts, rites, monuments) and institutional communication (recitation, practice, observance).'[9] Cultural memory is the realm in which communities come to terms with the past and remake it according to their present needs. It forms part of what Raymond Williams calls a 'structure of feeling', a concept which draws attention to what he describes as 'meanings and values as they are actively lived and felt'. Similarly, to think about cultural memory is not to think about the past as history, that is, as a record of past events, but to think about how those past events are represented and experienced, understood and imagined. Part of the value of Williams' term lies in the fact that it brings together the individual and collective, the personal and the social, as it marks out a territory of shared knowledge and experience and gestures towards the historicity of such structures. As he writes, the phrase attempts to define 'a social experience that is still *in process*, often indeed not yet recognized as social but taken to be private, idiosyncratic and even isolating, but which in analysis (though rarely otherwise) has its emergent, connecting and dominant characteristics, indeed its specific hierarchies'.[10] Memory, too, is always personal and social. It is lived and learned, understood according to socially inscribed structures but always mediated by individual experience. So the productions of cultural memory in the Middle Ages encountered in this book range from poems, monuments and chronicles to political acts and rituals, while cultural memories of the Middle Ages range from 'common-sense' understandings of the medieval past as a place of violence and backwardness or a site of ideological purity, to private personal acts of devotion to a medieval event, individual or text, to public gatherings that use a medieval or medievalist site or monument as their locus.

Cultural memory depends on a desire to make the past present, but how exactly that is achieved and what the results of that work are, is by no means predictable.[11] In his essay 'The Return of the Middle Ages', which has become a foundational piece of work in medievalism studies, Umberto Eco recognised the diversity inherent in the idea of the Middle Ages and offered a taxonomy that identified what he called 'ten little Middle Ages', including the 'barbaric', the 'romantic', the 'philological' and the 'decadent'.[12] Eco's paradigm is productive but, over the course of this book, I do not seek to rationalise, limit or generalise the diverse meanings attributed to or generated by engagement with medieval culture. Instead I attempt to locate productions of 'the medieval' within contemporary structures of feeling. The category of 'the Middle Ages' invites generalisation because it is itself a generalisation and invites oversimplification because it is itself an oversimplification, but the differences between expressions of 'medievalness' matter, as Eco recognised. With this in mind, I draw comparisons tentatively and seek instead to initiate conversations between texts. The texts I read alongside one another constitute networks of memory and reveal the transfer and transformation of ideas, desires and anxieties. I read my texts not as straightforwardly evocative of a particular time and place, but as embedded in historical process and discourse in diverse and multiple ways, as part of the structures of feeling that define, and are defined by, particular moments in history, but with the potential to move and belong in and across different historical moments. Therefore, I understand the historicity of the texts with which I work to be mutually constitutive, rather than determined by habits of periodisation. As I trace exchanges between texts in this expanded temporal field, I follow Maura Nolan's suggestion that 'relationships between and among epochs must be understood as multiple, with many temporalities at work in a single age'.[13] As we will see, while iterations of the Middle Ages are always informed by the precise context of their production, in the same historical moment it is possible to find contradictory representations of the Middle Ages. The Middle Ages, as the plural noun suggests, is always multiple. Western modernity, in contrast, as Amitav Ghosh notes, is characterised by 'enormous intellectual commitment to the promotion of its supposed singularity'.[14] The texts with which I work are ambivalent and inconsistent.[15] They initiate conversations in as well as across time and generate ideas of the future as well as ideas of the past.

Medieval futures

For Jacques Derrida, memory is best understood not as an engagement with the past but as an attempt to fashion the future. He writes that, 'Memory stays with traces, in order to "preserve" them, but traces of a past that has never been present, traces which themselves occupy the form of presence and always remain, as it were, to come – come from the future, from the *to come*.'[16] According to Derrida's thinking, memory is creative rather than representative and 'projects itself toward the future' rather than the past.[17] The Italian historian and philosopher Boncompagno da Signa made a similar point in his *Rhetorica novissima*, completed in 1235, when he wrote that 'Memory is a glorious and wonderful gift of nature, by which we recall the past, comprehend the present, and contemplate the future.'[18] For both Derrida and da Signa, memory is an instrument by which we navigate time, a means of fashioning the future.

It is dynamic, subjective and creative. This book explores some of the ways in which cultural memory constitutes, in Derrida's phrase, 'the presence of the present' in the Middle Ages and how those works of memory have been perpetuated and transformed. As I examine representations of the past in the Middle Ages and their continuing presence at later moments, I reveal how works of memory draw people as well as temporal moments together, define personal and collective identities, and mark some people, places and times as alien.

Of course, the Middle Ages is itself often characterised as Western modernity's other. Elizabeth Scala and Sylvia Federico, for instance, argue that it is 'the necessity of the Middle Ages, of the idea of the medieval, that makes a very discourse of modernity possible'.[19] As Andrew James Johnston explains, this means that 'the Middle Ages does not precede modernity but becomes the effect of a certain self-construction of the modern, which gives itself identity by delimiting a "before" that is everything the modern is not'.[20] The structures of modernity rest upon the idea of the Middle Ages. For instance, one of the most influential critical formulations of memory studies, Pierre Nora's groundbreaking theorisation of 'lieux de mémoire' (sites of memory), depends upon a developmental narrative that positions 'hopelessly forgetful modern societies' against a simpler pre-industrial pre-modern world in which there was some sort of natural connection between people and their past.[21] Nora writes of 'the irrevocable break marked by the disappearance of peasant culture, that quintessential repository of collective memory' and claims that, 'Such a fundamental collapse of memory is but one familiar example of a movement toward democratization and mass culture on a global scale.' For Nora, the 'lieux de mémoire' of modernity are but a pale imitation of the premodern 'milieux de mémoire, real environments of memory'.[22] Nora's analysis of cultural memory relies on a nostalgic vision of the Middle Ages as a simpler 'before', without the alienation and complexity of modernity.[23]

Because of the complex discursive work the idea of the Middle Ages is put to, it is very difficult to situate it in a singular and stable moment in time. The Middle Ages, to use Raymond Williams' words again, is always 'still *in process*', even as it is taken to be fixed, still and monolithic. This is a point made eloquently by Michael Camille in his study of the gargoyles of Notre Dame. Camille argued that it is impossible to view 'the art of the Middle Ages without looking past and through the nineteenth century' and went on to suggest that the complex chronologies of medieval material 'should not preclude our wanting to understand the Middle Ages as a distinct historical period; we find, however, that it is hardly ever as distinct or as separate as we might want to think, but always flowing into other periods, haunting other epochs, emerging where we least expect it, in romanticism, surrealism, and even postmodernity'.[24] Encounters with medieval culture are always mediated. While formations of medievalist cultural memory are often characterised by an idea of the realness, stillness, distance and difference of the Middle Ages – as in, for instance, Camille's example of romanticism – there is no way to access a pure, real, enduring Middle Ages. The presence of the Middle Ages in modernity is defined by its diversity, its cultural and temporal complexity.

Camille's thoughts echo important aspects of Dipesh Chakrabarty's work on historiography. Chakrabarty unpicks developmentalist views of history and argues that all times are necessarily plural, that different cultures and societies have their own unique and productive ways of organising time, as he reveals the political foundations of totalising models of history. Chakrabarty uses the term 'time-knots', derived from the Bengali word 'shomoygranthi', to describe how people, cultural productions and societies are able to resolve apparent contradictions between past and present. Chakrabarty writes:

> It is because we already have experience of that which makes the present noncontemporaneous with itself that we can actually historicize. Thus what allows historians to historicize the medieval or the ancient is the very fact these worlds are never completely lost. We inhabit their fragments even when we classify ourselves as modern and secular. It is because we live in time-knots that we can undertake the exercise of straightening out, as it were, some part of the knot.[25]

Camille and Chakrabarty offer ways to think through how the signifiers of the past become 'the presence of the present', but also how various pasts are threaded through each temporal moment. How, in Geraldine Heng's terms, 'the past can also be non-identical to itself, inhabited too by that which was out of its time'.[26] The work of memory is always of both the past and the present. Similarly, acts of medievalist cultural memory are defined by the movement of cultural forms through and across time. It is always of the present and also noncontemporaneous. It is always untimely.

Cultural memory and the untimely Middle Ages

While 'untimely' may suggest a lack, fault or deficiency, I read it, with Elizabeth Grosz, as potential. As Grosz writes, glossing Friedrich Nietzsche, 'The untimely is that which is strong enough, active enough, to withstand the drive of the present to similarity, resemblance, or recognition.'[27] This is the Middle Ages that is encountered in this book, urgent rather than out of date, a site of cultural potential rather than stasis, a means of imagining the future as well as imaging the past. The untimely is not without, or outside, history, however. In Alexander Nagel's words, 'History is effective and real, even as chronology is bent and folded.'[28] As Carolyn Dinshaw has demonstrated, a focus on the transhistorical attachments and radical temporalities of medieval and medievalist texts reveals what she describes as 'a heterogeneous *now* in which the divide between living and dead, material and immaterial, reality and fiction, present and past is unsettled'.[29] Attention to the flows and knots which define medievalist texts emphasises the complex interactions between temporality, history and memory which define subject formation.[30] It reveals that although cultural productions may be embedded in historical process, this does not mean they can be limited to a single historical context. While a text may be defined according to modern habits of periodisation, it may also offer new ways of understanding the past.

In her study of artistic influence and tradition, *Quoting Caravaggio: Contemporary Art, Preposterous History*, Mieke Bal uses the term 'historical attitude' to describe the ways in which the visual artworks she examines speak to and with the Baroque.[31] Similarly, I do not suggest that the texts examined in *Visions and Ruins* are representative of a particular period, style or genre, but rather a mode of thinking, an attitude, which is at once historically situated and insistent that the connections which can be created or detected between past and present matter. Like Bal's work, *Visions and Ruins* 'attempts to trace the process of meaning-production over time (in both directions: present/past and past/present) as an open, dynamic process, rather than to map the results of that process'.[32] This means that *Visions and Ruins* presents a discontinuous, nonlinear history that moves across as well as through time as it traces the constellations that form, and which have formed around, the medieval and medievalist texts it examines. The duration of cultural forms – and the manner in which the meanings of those forms alter according to their context – is the central organising principle of this book rather than historical period. By emphasising duration rather than period I am able to recognise some of the breadth and diversity of the archive of the Middle Ages.

The four chapters of this book each revolve around a single vehicle of cultural memory. Chapter 1 examines the image of the ruin, Chapter 2 takes public monuments as its focus, Chapter 3 the idea of the nation and Chapter 4 interrogates representations of the body. Each chapter is structured around a close reading of a medieval text or group of texts and works out from that material to interrogate how it represents the past and how it has been used in or speaks to modern representations of the Middle Ages. Chapter 1 focuses on the Old English poem *The Ruin*, a text that meditates upon the material remains of a long-passed civilisation and has often been read as typical of the nostalgic poetry of the Anglo-Saxons. The poem is commonly taken to be a depiction of early medieval Bath and, as I examine the ideas of time, memory and history that the poem presents, I analyse what its disciplinary history can reveal about the desires and practices of modern critics as well as of the poem itself. *The Ruin* is a 'time-knot' that brings together the Roman and the Anglo-Saxon, the medieval and, in its continuing life as a read, studied and translated text, the modern. The poem's interest in how the signifiers of the past are incorporated in the present and its thoughtful, playful and purposeful engagement with chronology and temporality allow me to frame the ideas of time, history and networks of cultural memory which will be elucidated in the remainder of the book. I contextualise the historical attitude I detect in *The Ruin* by examining the image of the ruin in various early and late medieval texts and, developing this analysis, interrogate the distinctions and contradictions between historicist analysis and the logic of periodisation. My reading also takes account of the translation history of *The Ruin*. While a great deal of work has been done in the past few years on the creative histories of Old English literature, *The Ruin* has largely escaped critics' attention and the work that has been done has focused on poetic and literary translation and appropriation.[33] By examining the two dominant strands of this history side by side, that is, scholarly and poetic translation, I seek not to play one off the other but to reveal the interaction and interdependence of the two traditions and the complex networks of influence that define the twentieth- and twenty-first-century existence of Old English texts. As I demonstrate, even the most experimental version of *The Ruin* of the twentieth century – Peter Reading's 'Fragmentary' – was written under the influence of the work of Michael Alexander, author of the canonical *Earliest English Poems* and holder of the Berry Chair of English Literature at the University of St Andrews. Similarly, when the filmmaker Julien Temple used *The Ruin* to illustrate images of the post-industrial ruins of Detroit he adapted the work of Siân Echard, a professor at the University of British Columbia. Here, and throughout *Visions and Ruins*, history and memory brush up against one another in productive and provocative contact.

These examples demonstrate the complexity of the relationship between the academy and the artist. Throughout this book I make distinctions between what I label 'creative' and 'critical' responses to medieval culture. Broadly, I categorise works as critical if they claim to offer insight or access into medieval material, while the work I categorise as creative takes a self-conscious step away from the medieval and can be understood and appreciated without reference to the medieval material with which it engages. The distinctions between the work of Reading and Temple on the one hand, and Alexander and Echard on the other, illustrate the distance between these practices. However, it is easy to overstate the differences between these works and the distinctions are not always clear: critical work is not without creative value and creative work is not necessarily without critical insight.[34] I therefore use the term 'medievalist' to describe work that takes an interest in medieval culture without making claims regarding intent, skill or knowledge. As the *Oxford English Dictionary* suggests, as a noun 'medievalist' designates someone who shows 'sympathy' to the medieval.[35] As I use it as an adjective, it suggests a similar emotional or intellectual engagement. The medievalist material we encounter in *Visions and Ruins* ranges from Thomas Gray's Pindaric Ode to the Cædmon Memorial, from E. M. Barry's Victorian Eleanor Cross to Michael Landy's kinetic sculptures of medieval saints. While all these works can be understood and appreciated without detailed knowledge of the medieval material with which they work, I suggest they nevertheless offer rich insights into aspects of medieval culture and how the medieval has been defined and understood in the postmedieval world.

Developing the ideas of appropriation, translation and networks of influence outlined in the opening chapter, Chapter 2 unpicks the medieval and modern histories of the Eleanor Crosses, the memorials erected by Edward I following the death of his wife Eleanor of Castile in November 1290. While the crosses might be read with Nora as 'sites of memory', they did not and do not provide uncomplicated access to the past. Examining the ideas of time and history created by the monuments and interrogating their social and political contexts, I argue that the crosses create a cultural memory of Eleanor attuned to national and racial fantasies and heavily invested in ideas of religious and secular authority. As I trace the cultural histories of the crosses, however, I also outline the fluctuations of cultural memory and the complexities and contradictions of the idea of the Middle Ages in early modern and Victorian Britain. Over their long history, the Eleanor Crosses have been celebrated, abjected and ignored. Their non-linear history records a range of invented histories of the Middle Ages, even as it marks out one trajectory of its reception. As Eric Hobsbawm suggested in his work on the invention of tradition, the Eleanor Crosses are a complex historical phenomenon that offer only a pre-mediated connection with the past and only establish their meaning and authority through their repetition.[36] As with *The Ruin*, it is the repetitions and reiterations of the Eleanor Crosses that constitute their ability to offer continuity with the past. Their meanings, and their locations within contemporary structures of feeling, have fluctuated dramatically, but I argue that this lack of a stable essence or singular, continuing, meaning reveals their cultural value rather than undermines it.

Chapter 3 develops the tension between essence and effect and continuity and rupture to explore what I term 'medievalist double consciousness'. In their study of medieval historiography, Paul Freedman and Gabrielle Spiegel used the term 'dual consciousness' to explain the manner in which the Middle Ages signifies as both 'a place and time of non-origin (that is, the dark period constructed in and by the Renaissance) and that of origin (the origin of the modern state)'.[37] The dual consciousness of medievalist work is well demonstrated by the Eleanor Crosses and *The Ruin*, which both show how medieval and medievalist cultural productions can speak simultaneously of past and present, as other and subject, non-origin and origin. Freedman and Spiegel's phrase carries a rich and suggestive echo of W. E. B Du Bois' concept 'double consciousness', a term he coined to speak of the experience of black people in the USA and Europe who found themselves at once inside and outside Western culture.[38] While Freedman and Spiegel's term reveals how 'the medieval' is often figured as simultaneously inside and outside modernity, their echo of Du Bois' thinking encourages an examination of the way medieval studies and medievalist structures of feeling speak to racial and ethnic, as well as historical and cultural, origins. In a marked difference to Du Bois' original thinking, medievalist double consciousness is projected rather than directly experienced and felt. It is a means of producing difference, a way of creating and describing a problem, an act of bad faith that marks some bodies, people, practices or institutions as not quite belonging in either the past or the present. This is never more powerfully expressed, as Patrick Geary, Reginald Horsman, Clare Simmons and others have demonstrated, than in discourses of nationhood.[39] Because the idea of the Middle Ages relies on a sense of closure, despite its endless reiterations, medievalist thinking is a powerful means of closing down the possibilities of the future, of marking feared or undesired aspects of the contemporary as non-contemporary, as being out of time.

In the third chapter, then, I explore a group of texts by the English poet Thomas Gray, the Hungarian poet János Arany, the Icelandic scholar Grímur Jonsson Thorkelín and the Danish poet, historian and educator Nikolai Frederik Severin Grundtvig that exhibit medievalist double consciousness as they engage and promote ideas of the nation. As well as their interest in the nation, the texts share a fascination with the figure of the public poet, or bard. As I demonstrate, Gray's 1757 poem 'The Bard' sits at the centre of modern perceptions of premodern bards. Like the Ossian poems circulated by James MacPherson from 1760, Gray's bard is an invention, a figure of cultural memory that expressed a fantasy of wholeness and exclusion. I trace the influence of Gray's bard in Britain and Europe, across creative and critical works produced during the nineteenth century, to explore how medievalist cultural memory operates in tandem with nationalist thinking. In these texts, the idea of the Middle Ages functions less as a marker of historical time than a means of producing difference. The network of memory established by Gray's poem engages medieval culture as well as modern and, in order to unpick the constructed pasts of the bards, I frame my discussion with an examination of a performative act of cultural memory by Edward I and Eleanor of Castile that speaks eloquently to Gray's text and reveals one example of how historical and social difference was produced in late thirteenth-century England. As in the previous chapters, the material encountered in Chapter 3 reveals shared concerns across time. It explores how ideas of the past are used to generate ideas of community and exclude some people, ideas and traditions from the future.

Unlike the first three chapters, Chapter 4 does not follow a chronological order. Instead, discussions of medieval and modern works are woven together to unpick conversations among texts, in and through time. This chapter is prompted by two twenty-first-century pieces of art: Elizabeth Price's immersive video installation *The Woolworths Choir of 1979* (2012) and Michael Landy's *Saints Alive* (2013). Both of these works turn to medieval culture in order to examine the untimeliness of the body and in this chapter I trace their sources and explore how their work speaks with, and to, medieval representations of the body. The chapter begins with a study of a group of thirteenth-century martial effigies that feature in Price's film and goes on to use the Middle English poem *St Erkenwald* to explore Landy's interest in hagiography.

The effigies insist on the continuing presence of the body while there is a palpable anxiety throughout *St Erkenwald* about the unknowability of the past, the unreliability of memory and the unresolvable contradictions that exist between past and present. Price and Landy both engage productively with these concerns and, like the medieval texts that define their work, explore intratemporal connections through the movement of the human body. My reading of these works is informed by Aby Warburg's work on gesture in early modern art.[40] Warburg investigated gestures as, in Giorgio Agamben's words, 'a crystal of historical memory',[41] and unpicked the times, histories, memories, desires and beliefs contained in their representation. While *St Erkenwald* and the effigies privilege similarity, Price and Landy work hard to allow the difference of the past – and different readings of the past – to flourish rather than become subsumed in the present and acknowledge that the past, like the future, is potential. The thirteenth-century effigies, however, offer a powerful account of the continuing presence of the body that defies traditional habits of periodisation. This chapter takes the desires of the effigies seriously and explores the consequences of allowing the untimely to structure thought.

The texts I investigate in this book reveal the Middle Ages to be a complex assemblage: a period of history, a cultural category, a way of being and a way of doing, but also a way of forgetting, because to mark something as medieval can be to mark it as uncivilised, undeveloped, undesirable, naïve, irrelevant and unworthy of attention. The Middle Ages can be, as Theodor Adorno suggested of modernity, 'a qualitative, not a chronological, category',[42] and the archive of the Middle Ages is defined by its diversity rather than its consistency. This book attempts to recognise some of that diversity and map some of the diverse work cultural memory is put to in the Middle Ages and modernity. Medieval culture is open and relational. It is not merely a resource but a means of structuring cultural practice and knowledge, a way of defining, and undermining, habits and assumptions. So while ideas of gender, race, sex, politics, power and culture are always embedded in the idea of the Middle Ages, they are not stable. Rather, they are constituted differently in different structures of feeling and in each formation and communication of cultural memory. The texts encountered in this book demonstrate exchanges of cultural energy and influence between past and present but also offer new ways of knowing the medieval past and the contemporary moment.

Notes

1 Mary Carruthers, *The Book of Memory: A Study of Memory in Medieval Culture* (Cambridge: Cambridge University Press, 2008), p. 238.

2 See David Aers, 'A whisper in the ear of Early Modernists; or, reflections on literary critics writing the "History of the Subject"', in David Aers (ed.), *Culture and History, 1350–1600: Essays on English Communities, Identities and Writing* (Detroit: Wayne State University Press, 1992), pp. 177–202.

3 See Kathleen Davis, 'National writing in the ninth century: A reminder for postcolonial thinking about the nation', *Journal of Medieval and Early Modern Studies* 28 (1998), 611–37.

4 See Lee Paterson, 'On the margin: Postmodernism, ironic history, and medieval studies', *Speculum* 65 (1990), 87–108.

5 Margreta de Grazia, 'The modern divide: From either side', *Journal of Medieval and Early Modern Studies* 37 (2007), 453–67, p. 453.

6 Hans Blumenberg, *The Legitimacy of the Modern Age*, trans. Robert M. Wallace (Cambridge, MA: MIT Press, 1985), p. 341. See further Andrew Cole and D. Vance Smith (eds), *The Legitimacy of the Middle Ages: On the Unwritten History of Theory* (Durham, NC: Duke University Press, 2010).

7 Jacob Burckhardt, *The Civilisation of the Renaissance in Italy*, trans. S. G. C. Middlemore (Harmondsworth: Penguin, 1990), p. 193.

8 Stephen Greenblatt, *The Swerve: How the Renaissance Began* (London: The Bodley Head, 2011). See also the essays collected in 'Book review forum: *The Swerve: How the World became Modern*', *Exemplaria* 25 (2013), 313–70 and Laura Saetveit Miles, 'The ethics of

inventing modernity: Stephen Greenblatt's *The Swerve*', *In the Middle*, 30 May 2016, www.inthemedievalmiddle.com/2016/05/the-ethics-of-inventing-modernity.html, accessed 24 October 2017. For a survey of the problems and possibilities of periodisation see Elizabeth A. R. Brown, 'On 1500', in Peter Linehan and Janet L. Nelson (eds), *The Medieval World* (London: Routledge, 2001), pp. 691–710; Eric Hayot, 'Against periodization; Or, on institutional time', *New Literary History* 42 (2011) 739–56; David Matthews, 'Periodization', in Marion Turner (ed.), *A Handbook of Middle English Studies* (Chichester: Wiley-Blackwell, 2013), pp. 253–66; Ted Underwood, *Why Literary Periods Mattered: Historical Contrast and the Prestige of English Studies* (Stanford: Stanford University Press, 2013); and the essays collected in David Matthews and Gordon McMullan (eds), *Reading the Medieval in Early Medieval England* (Cambridge: Cambridge University Press, 2007) and Jennifer Summit and David Wallace (eds), 'Medieval/Renaissance: After periodization', *Journal of Medieval and Early Modern Studies* 37 (2007).

 9 Jan Assmann, 'Collective memory and cultural identity', *New German Critique* 65 (1995), 125–33, p. 129. On cultural memory studies see Astrid Erll, *Memory in Culture*, trans. Sara B. Young (Basingstoke: Palgrave Macmillan, 2011) and James Fentress and Chris Wickham, *Social Memory* (Oxford: Blackwell, 1992). On medieval cultural memory see Elisabeth van Houts, *Memory and Gender in Medieval Europe, 900–1200* (Basingstoke: Macmillan, 1999); Matthew Gabriele, *An Empire of Memory: The Legend of Charlemagne, the Franks, and Jerusalem before the First Crusade* (Oxford: Oxford University Press, 2011); and Elma Brenner, Meredith Cohen and Mary Franklin-Brown (eds), *Memory and Commemoration in Medieval Culture* (Farnham: Ashgate, 2013).

10 Raymond Williams, *Marxism and Literature* (Oxford: Oxford University Press, 1977), p. 132.

11 On the performative nature of memory see Liedeke Plate and Anneke Smelik, 'Performing memory in art and popular culture: An introduction', in Liedeke Plate and Anneke Smelik (eds), *Performing Memory in Art and Popular Culture* (New York: Routledge, 2013), pp. 1–23, p. 3. For a similar definition of memory practice in medieval contexts see Howard Williams, *Death and Memory in Early Medieval Britain* (Cambridge: Cambridge University Press, 2006), p. 3.

12 Umberto Eco, 'The return of the Middle Ages', in *Faith in Fakes: Travels in Hyperreality*, trans. William Weaver (London: Vintage, 1998), pp. 61–85. See further Kathleen Davis and Nadia Altschul (eds), *Medievalisms in the Postcolonial World: The Idea of 'the Middle Ages' outside Europe* (Baltimore: Johns Hopkins University Press, 2009); Tison Pugh and Angela Jane Weisl, *Medievalisms: Making the Past in the Present* (London: Routledge, 2013); David Matthews, *Medievalism: A Critical History* (Cambridge: D. S. Brewer, 2015);

and Louise D'Arcens (ed.), *The Cambridge Companion to Medievalism* (Cambridge: University of Cambridge Press, 2016).

13 Maura Nolan, 'Historicism after historicism', in Elizabeth Scala and Sylvia Federico (eds), *The Post-Historical Middle Ages* (Basingstoke: Palgrave Macmillan, 2009), pp. 63–86, p. 67.

14 Amativ Ghosh, *The Great Derangement: Climate Change and the Unthinkable* (Chicago: University of Chicago Press, 2016), p. 103.

15 See Paul Strohm, *Theory and the Premodern Text* (Minneapolis: University of Minnesota Press, 2000), p. 81, where he writes that no text 'can be temporally self-consistent'.

16 Jacques Derrida, 'The art of memories', in *Mémoires: For Paul de Man*, trans. Cecile Lindsay, Jonathan Culler and Eduardo Cadava (New York: Columbia University Press, 1986), pp. 45–88, p. 58. Emphasis in the original.

17 Derrida, 'The art of memories', p. 57.

18 Boncompagno da Signa, 'On memory', trans. Sean Gallagher, in Mary Carruthers and Jan M. Ziolkowski (eds), *The Medieval Craft of Memory: An Anthology of Texts and Pictures* (Philadelphia: University of Pennsylvania Press, 2002), pp. 103–17, p. 105.

19 Elizabeth Scala and Sylvia Federico, 'Introduction', in Scala and Federico (eds), *The Post-Historical Middle Ages*, pp. 1–11, p. 4.

20 Andrew James Johnston, *Performing the Middle Ages from* Beowulf *to* Othello (Turnhout: Brepols, 2008), p. 19.

21 Pierre Nora, 'Between memory and history: Les lieux de mémoire', *Representations* 26 (1989), 7–24, p. 8.

22 Nora, 'Between memory and history', 7.

23 For a critique of Nora's nostalgia see Anne Whitehead, *Memory* (London: Routledge, 2009), pp. 141–3.

24 Michael Camille, *The Gargoyles of Notre Dame: Medievalism and the Monsters of Modernity* (Chicago: University of Chicago Press, 2009), p. xi. See also Bettina Bildhauer and Anke Bernau, 'Introduction: The a-chronology of medieval film', in Anke Bernau and Bettina Bildhauer (eds), *Medieval Film* (Manchester: Manchester University Press, 2009), pp. 1–19.

25 Dipesh Chakrabarty, *Provincializing Europe: Postcolonial Thought and Historical Difference* (Princeton: Princeton University Press, 2008), p. 112.

26 Geraldine Heng, 'The invention of race in the European Middle Ages I: Race studies, modernity, and the Middle Ages', *Literature Compass* 8 (2011), 315–31, p. 322.

27 Elizabeth Grosz, *The Nick of Time: Politics, Evolution, and the Untimely* (Durham, NC: Duke University Press, 2004), p. 11.

28 Alexander Nagel, *Medieval Modern: Art Out of Time* (London: Thames and Hudson, 2012), p. 14.

29 Carolyn Dinshaw, *How Soon is Now? Medieval Texts, Amateur Readers, and the Queerness of Time* (Durham, NC: Duke University Press, 2012), p. 37.

30 See further Kathleen Davis, 'Time', in Jacqueline Stodnick and Renée R. Trilling (eds), *A Handbook of Anglo-Saxon Studies* (Oxford: Wiley-Blackwell, 2012), pp. 215–34.

31 Mieke Bal, *Quoting Caravaggio: Contemporary Art, Preposterous History* (London: University of Chicago Press, 1999), p. 4.

32 Bal, *Quoting Caravaggio*, p. 9.

33 See Fred C. Robinson, '"The might of the north": Pound's Anglo-Saxon studies and *The Seafarer*' and 'Ezra Pound and the Old English translation tradition', in *The Tomb of Beowulf and Other Essays on Old English* (Oxford: Blackwell, 1993), pp. 259–74 and pp. 275–303; Nicholas Howe, 'Praise and lament: The afterlife of Old English poetry in Auden, Hill, and Gunn', in Peter S. Baker and Nicholas Howe (eds), *Words and Works: Studies in Medieval English Language and Literature in Honor of Fred C. Robinson* (Toronto: University of Toronto Press, 1998), pp. 293–310; Chris Jones, *Strange Likeness: The Use of Old English in Twentieth-Century Poetry* (Oxford: Oxford University Press, 2006); and Daniel C. Remein, 'Auden, translation, betrayal: Radical poetics and translation from Old English', *Literature Compass* 8 (2011), 811–29.

34 On the problems of distinguishing medievalism from medieval studies see David Matthews, 'Medieval studies and medievalism', in Ruth Evans, Helen Fulton and David Matthews (eds), *Medieval Cultural Studies in Honour of Stephen Knight* (Cardiff: University of Wales Press, 2006), pp. 9–22.

35 'Medievalist, n.', *OED Online* (Oxford: Oxford University Press, 2013), www.oed.com/view/Entry/115640?redirectedFrom=medievalist, accessed 24 October 2017.

36 Eric Hobsbawm, 'Introduction: Inventing traditions', in Eric Hobsbawm and Terence Ranger (eds), *The Invention of Tradition* (Cambridge: Cambridge University Press, 1983), pp. 1–14.

37 Paul Freedman and Gabrielle Spiegel, 'Medievalisms old and new: The rediscovery of alterity in North American medieval studies', *American Historical Review* 103 (1998), 677–704, p. 679.

38 W. E. B. Du Bois, *The Souls of Black Folk*, ed. Henry Louis Gates, Jr and Terri Hume Oliver (New York: Norton, 1999), p. 11.

39 See Patrick J. Geary, *The Myth of Nations: The Medieval Origins of Europe* (Princeton: Princeton University Press, 2002); Clare A. Simmons, *Reversing the Conquest: History and Myth in 19th-Century British Literature* (New Brunswick: Rutgers University Press, 1990); and Reginald Horsman, *Race and Manifest Destiny: The Origins of American Racial Anglo-Saxonism* (Cambridge, MA: Harvard University Press, 1981).

40 On the importance of Warburg's work in cultural memory studies see Erll, *Memory in Culture*, pp. 19–21.

41 Giorgio Agamben, *Infancy and History: The Destruction of Experience*, trans. Liz Heron (London: Verso, 1993), p. 138.

42 Theodor Adorno, *Minima Moralia: Reflections from Damaged Life*, trans. E. F. N. Jephcott (London: NLB, 1978), p. 218.

1

Ruins and wonders: The poetics of cultural memory in and of early medieval England

In the beginning there is ruin.

Jacques Derrida, *Memoirs of the Blind: The Self-Portrait and Other Ruins*[1]

When is the now of a medieval text? How might a text be situated in, or free from, historical process? These are the questions posed by Benjamin Thorpe in the preface to his edition of *Cædmon's Metrical Paraphrase of Parts of the Holy Scriptures, in Anglo-Saxon*, a foundational work of Anglo-Saxon studies first published in 1832. Although he justified his edition by referring to Cædmon as 'the Father of English Song' and sidestepped the tricky question of the evidence for Cædmon's authorship of the texts he presented, Thorpe was nevertheless worried about the reception of the volume.[2] In a direct plea to his audience, Thorpe writes that, 'Those readers who may rise disappointed from the perusal [of this book] should reflect, that he [Cædmon] is our earliest poet; that he lived (himself a herdsman,) when all around him was barbarism; and that these his mangled remains are all that Time has spared to us.'[3] Thorpe's worry was that Cædmon's putative poems, or Thorpe's translations of them at least, would not thrive in the nineteenth century. Despite the work he had put into editing and translating the texts, Thorpe offered them to his readers as ruins. The texts, as Thorpe tells it, are doubly compromised, first of all by their context (they were written when all around Cædmon was 'barbarism' and carry too much of that barbarism to flourish in the modern world) and secondly by historical process ('these his mangled remains are all that Time has spared to us'). Even as he brings them into the present, the texts are mere fragments of memory, defined by an idea of an original, whole, lost history.

A similar sense of ruination colours Bede's account of Cædmon's *Hymn* in his *Ecclesiastical History*. After telling the story of the miraculous composition of the *Hymn* and making clear its cultural significance, Bede included a Latin version of the poem before warning that his translation is necessarily inaccurate, 'neque enim possunt carmina, quamuis optime conposita, ex alia in aliam linguam at uerbum sine detrimento sui decoris ac dignitatis transferri' (for it is not possible to translate verse, however well composed, literally from one language to another without some loss of beauty and dignity).[4] Like Thorpe, Bede worried about what could not be transferred from past to present and it is unclear exactly why he included only a translation of Cædmon's Old English *Hymn*.[5] His mini-treatise on translation emphasises 'detrimento' (loss) and generates a sense that the past is passed and all that is left is ruin: 'mangled remains ... that Time has spared', without the 'decoris ac dignitatis' of the original.

Together, Bede and Thorpe provide an answer to the problem they identify. While they both lament the unknowability of Cædmon's life and text, their own work demonstrates that, although historical context does matter, the moment of composition is not the only moment that defines the meaning of a text. Although we will never know, thanks to Bede, how the Old English versions of Cædmon's *Hymn* relate to the words he spoke in his dream, we can trace the life of the text from the early copies in Cambridge, University Library MS Kk. 5. 16 and St Petersburg, National Library of Russia, MS Lat. Q. v. I. 18, to the many other copies made across the Middle Ages, to Francis Junius' *Cædmonis monachi: paraphrasis poetica Genesios* of 1655 and Thorpe's edition of 1832, and the modern translations and appropriations of Cædmon's life and *Hymn* by Ann Hawkshaw, Christopher Fry, Paul Muldoon, U. A. Fanthorpe and Maureen Duffy among others.[6] For Denise Levertov, Cædmon was a 'clodhopper', pulled, reluctantly, 'into the ring of the dance';[7] for Seamus Heaney, he was 'the real thing' but his 'real gift was the big ignorant roar / He could still let out of him'.[8] This network of cultural memory is not exterior to the meanings of the early medieval Cædmon. There is, as Bede and Thorpe make clear, no uncompromised, reliable, singular Cædmon to return to, and for the reader in the twenty-first century, Cædmon is a complex figure whose life and influence, real and imagined, cannot be restricted to a single context. But all is not lost, all is not ruin. Or, rather, even ruins are full of meaning, because even as they regret that the history of Cædmon's *Hymn* is lost, Bede and Thorpe contribute to, even constitute, the cultural memory of the poet and the poem.[9] To borrow Tom Boellstorff's

language, as Bede and Thorpe worry about the non-presence of
certain historical moments they fail to notice what is 'copresent'.
Even as they worry that the past is over, Bede and Thorpe dem-
onstrate some of the ways in which it lives on as cultural memory.

Bede and Thorpe struggle, in Boellstorff's language, to 'con-
ceive of copresence without incorporation'.[10] The difference of
the past, they suggest, cannot reside in the present, even as they
illustrate one of the ways in which it might. The questions I will
explore in this chapter lie in the shadows of these anxieties. How
might various times be present in a medieval text? How do medi-
eval texts and their histories challenge normative structures of
time, and what new ways of knowing the past and present do
medieval texts offer? The locus of these questions in this chapter
is the Old English poem known as *The Ruin* – the most sustained
early medieval meditation on ruination, cultural memory and the
copresence of time to survive. Like Cædmon, *The Ruin* stands at
the centre of what Rita Felski describes as a 'cross-temporal net-
work', which reaches across the Middle Ages and through moder-
nity.[11] This network incorporates critical and creative practice and
reveals that far from being 'incarcerated in the past', the histories
and meanings of medieval texts offer up rich case studies of what
Felski calls 'transtemporal movement and affective resonance'.[12] In
this chapter I will trace these movements and resonances from the
early medieval manuscript to twentieth- and twenty-first-century
translations, adaptations and appropriations of the text. In Bruno
Latour's terms, this network of memory doesn't simply transport
'effects without transforming them'. Rather, each point in the net-
work can 'become a bifurcation, an event or an origin of a new
translation'.[13] What this trajectory reveals is, first of all, the culti-
vation of cultural memory in Anglo-Saxon England and, secondly,
how early medieval forms of cultural memory have lived on and
formed, and been formed and reformed by, cultures of moder-
nity. Like *The Ruin* itself, these translations reveal the possibility
of intimate intersubjective relations between past and present and
offer examples of translation as a hopeful practice, one committed
to ethical engagement with the past, present and future. In these
works, translation does not replace the source text. It writes with
rather than over. The relations between source text and translation
are not singular and linear but folded and multiple. Their starting
point, and my starting point too, is the copresence of the past and
the potential of cultural memory to give form to affective relations
through and across time.

Approaching the Old English *Ruin*

The Ruin anchors its reflections on time, memory and community on the material remains of Roman rule in Britain and describes 'wrætlic' (wondrous) buildings, 'gebræcon' (broken by) mysterious 'wyrde' (events) and imagines the lives lived before, during and after the place 'wong gecrong / gebrocen to beorgum' (fell into ruin, shattered into heaps).[14] This meditation on materiality and temporality is qualified and confirmed by the very pages on which the poem survives, as it is recorded on three very damaged folios of the late tenth-century Exeter Book and twelve of its thirty six manuscript lines have been lost (see Figure 1.1). The fragmentary state of *The Ruin* has created a rare unity between its material condition and subject matter which contributes to its 'affective resonance'. This means that while, as Chris Abram notes, 'it is almost traditional to describe it as a ruin itself',[15] for some critics such as Michael Swanton, 'The ruined state of the poem, far from obstructing our appreciation of it, only corroborates the truth it imports.'[16] Indeed, the two earliest editors of the poem were both struck by the harmony between material form and meaning.[17] In his edition of 1842, Thorpe commented that 'although (like the fallen burgh which it so vividly and graphically describes) a ruin, enough remains to show that, in its entire state, it must have been one of the noblest productions of the Anglo-Saxon muse',[18] while William Conybeare, writing in 1826, described the poem as 'a fragment … superior, both in picturesque description and in the tone of moral feeling which pervades it, to the great mass of Saxon poetry'.[19]

The aspects of the poem privileged by the editors – its relationship with 'the fallen burgh which it so vividly and graphically describes' and its 'tone of moral feeling' – speak of its affective power. But despite its ample demonstration of the power of art to speak across time, many critics have read the poem as an invocation of a lost past. Helena Znojemská suggests that the poem is fascinated with 'the transitoriness of human life',[20] while, for Nicholas Howe, *The Ruin* is a profoundly 'static' poem, and he notes that 'no one speaks or acts in it, the site moulders away across the turn of generations, the scene is haunted with a meaning that can be articulated only through precise description'.[21] James F. Doubleday suggests that, 'Implicit in *The Ruin* is a philosophy of history, a way of looking at historical events', and for Doubleday and many others, that philosophy is eschatological or nostalgic.[22] For other critics, the value of *The Ruin* lies in the putative identification of

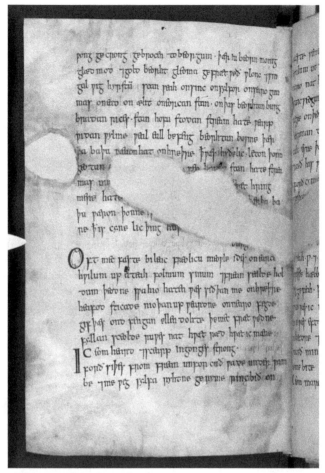

1.1   Folio 124v of the Exeter Book

the buildings the poem describes as the ruins of Roman Bath.[23] As I will explore later in this chapter, these aspects of *The Ruin*'s interpretative history, which insist on a singular, ruined past, echo common strands of modern discourses of the Middle Ages.

There are also significant echoes between these readings of *The Ruin* and the worries of Bede and Thorpe with which I began. What unites these critics and historians is an insistence on a return to the moment of the text's conception and a desire, in Paul Strohm's words, to 'read through' the text 'to its supposed historical "meaning"'.[24] There is an underlying assumption that time can be neatly divided up into singular and coherent historical periods, that time and meaning are singular. However, as with Cædmon's *Hymn*, *The Ruin*'s relations with time and history are complex and multiple. The poem weaves temporal moments together to demonstrate how past and present intermingle in the production of cultural memory and its reception history further enriches its meanings and temporal possibilities. *The Ruin*, like Cædmon and his *Hymn*, illustrates how, as John Frow suggests, 'The historicity of texts is not a matter of the singular moment of their relation to a history that precedes them, because that moment is in its turn endowed with meaning in a succession of later moments, as well as in the lateral movement of texts across cultural boundaries.'[25] Although 'mangled' by its journey through time, *The Ruin* has lost none of its 'decoris ac dignitatis'.

The Ruin

The manuscript filed under classmark MS 3501 in the Library of the Dean and Chapter of Exeter Cathedral is commonly known as the Exeter Book and contains some of the oldest extant vernacular poetry from Anglo-Saxon England. It is assumed that the book came to the library as a gift from Leofric, whose time as Bishop of Exeter straddled the Norman Conquest, although it is also generally agreed that the anthology was made *c*. 965–75 and that the texts themselves were composed some time before this. It is very unlikely that the anthology's mysterious origins will ever be fully explained. Before his death in 1072 Bishop Leofric had a list of his donations to the Cathedral drawn up and the Exeter Book is identified as the item described as 'i·mycel englisc boc be gehwilcu(m) þingu(m) on leoðwisan geworht' (one big English book concerning miscellaneous subjects composed in verse).[26] The book has not, however, been treated with care for most of its life. As Bernard Muir writes,

> the condition of the manuscript suggests that it has survived only because it could be put to practical use in the scriptorium: it was used as a cutting board (as the slashes on its front leaves show); a messy pot (perhaps of glue) was placed on its exposed first folio on at least one occasion; a fiery brand was placed upon its exposed back with apparent indifference; and sheets of gold leaf were often stored between the folios, leaving a sparkling residue of gold on many of its leaves.[27]

The greatest damage to the manuscript was done by the fiery brand that burnt through parts of the last fourteen folios and made many individual texts, including *The Ruin*, incomplete. The Book's history is therefore marked in its pages, however little we know of that history.

As with the other manuscripts that survive from the Middle Ages, the recovery of the Exeter Book is also the story of the journey from antiquarianism to academia. In 1705 Humfrey Wanley provided a description of the Book as part of his contribution to George Hickes' *Linguarum vett. Septentrionalium thesaurus grammatico-criticus et archæologicus* and in 1830 Nikolai Grundtvig made the first full transcription of the manuscript.[28] In 1842 Thorpe published his transcription and translation of the manuscript and just under a century later, in 1932, R. W. Chambers, Max Förster and Robin Flower published a facsimile edition.[29] George P. Krapp and Elliott van Kirk Dobbie worked from Chambers, Förster and Flower's facsimile for their edition of the manuscript that was published as volume 3 of the Anglo-Saxon Poetic Records in 1936.[30] The most recent book edition was published by Bernard Muir in 2000 and an electronic edition was published by Muir in 2006.[31]

So the textual and material history of *The Ruin* is marked by unaccountable events and mysterious lacunae and its precise Anglo-Saxon contexts are unknown too. This is fitting, as the poem itself is a meditation on how the signifiers of the past are incorporated or not in the present. Although it begins with a description of a ruined Roman wall, rather than providing a detailed description of the site, the poem focuses its attention on the processes by which the scene of destruction was created:[32]

> Wrætlic is þes wealstan   wyrde gebræcon,
> burgstede burston;   brosnað enta geweorc.
>
> (1–2, Wondrous is this wall-stone – events broke it, the battlement burst; the work of giants decays.)

In these opening lines the alliteration brings into contact the agent of destruction, 'wyrde' (events, although more commonly translated as 'fate'), the speaker's response to the scene of destruction, 'Wrætlic' (wondrous), and the object which is, in the imagined scene and the poetic line, their point of connection, the 'wealstan' (wall-stone). The consonance between these words undercuts the dynamic temporality of the line. Although the scene exists in the present (the wall is wondrous, not was), it is defined by the past and there is only a brief moment between the description of the wall and the acknowledgment of its destruction. The reader's attention is turned to the past and 'gebræcon' (broken by) not only marks the end of the first line and the destruction of the wall, but introduces the 'b' sound that dominates the second line. These sounds – 'burgstede burston; brosnað' – resound to mark the passage of time as the destruction continues. Repetition of the 'n' sound ('wealstan', 'gebræcon', 'burston') confirms this sense of progression, only for 'geweorc' to recall the alliteration of the opening phrase and again recall the origins of the object.[33] As Howell Chickering suggests of *Beowulf*, in these lines the reader can hear 'time passing in language'.[34] But time does not unfold in a strictly linear manner. Instead, moments are woven together to create a rich sense of the recursive patterns of time and memory. Rhyme and alliteration draw connections between lines and between various moments of the building's existence. But the poem does not explain where these buildings are, or who lived among them. Moreover, as Alain Renoir puts it, the poem 'has a speaking voice but no speaker': no internal experience, philosophical teaching or consolation is offered.[35] It gives no thought to the causes of destruction, even if it is fascinated by its process. The poem is less interested in creating a detailed image of the building than investigating what meanings it holds in the present and held in the past and how those meanings are and were generated.

As the scene is described in greater detail ever more attention is given to how this image of the past was created, but interpretation is always deferred:

> Hrofas sind gehrorene,   hreorge torras,
> hrungeat berofen   hrim on lime,
> scearde scurbeorge   scorene, gedrorene,
> aeldo undereotone
>
> (3–6a, Roofs are fallen, towers wrecked, doorways destroyed, rime on the lime, roofs are gaping stripped, perished, eaten away by age)

The sense that the past is being brought into contact with the present is confirmed by the very sound of the words as they roll into one another. Echoes and rhymes between 'gehrorene', 'hreorge', 'scorene', 'gedrorene' and 'undereotone' give the passage a sense of recursiveness, of circling back on itself.[36] This thoughtful, playful and purposeful engagement with temporality is confirmed by the oral delivery of these lines, which is slow and laborious, and the past participles focus attention on how the present is produced by and in the past. The text teaches the reader that past and present weave together, that time is always hybrid. Like the 'hrim on lime' (4, rime on lime) that is layered upon the wall of the ruin, in this poem time is richly textured. The poem is littered with what Jonathan Gil Harris describes as 'untimely matter'.[37] Like its language and form, the buildings the poem meditates upon are defined by their relations to various temporal moments: moments of construction, occupation, destruction, contemplation and composition. The manuscript, too, is untimely in that it cannot be limited to a single context. The moments of the making of the manuscript, the damage, the critical history of the volume, not to mention the unknowable origins of the poem itself, all contribute to the ideas of time, history and memory it generates. *The Ruin*, like the 'weallstan', is polychronic and multitemporal.

The poem is particularly interested in imagining the communities associated with the ruins. The central passage of the poem, which runs from lines 25 to 37 and therefore falls between the two burn marks, appears to distinguish between multiple historical moments and describe the inhabitation of the buildings by different groups:

> Crungon walo wide,   cwoman woldagas,
> swylt eall fornom   secgrofra wera;
> wurdon hyra wigsteal   westen staþolas,
> brosnade burgsteall.   Betend crungon
> hergas to hrusan.   Forþon þas hofu dreorgiað,
> ond þæs teaforgeapa   tigelum sceadeð
> hrostbeages rof.   Hryre wong gecrong
> gebrocen to beorgum,   þær iu beorn monig
> glædmod ond goldbeorht   gleoma gefrætwed,
> wlonc ond wingal   wighyrstum scan;
> seah on sinc, on sylfor,   on searogimmas,
> on ead, on æht,   on eorcanstan,
> on þas beorhtan burg   bradan rices.

(25–37, Far and wide the slain perished, days of pestilence came, death took all the brave people away; their places of war became deserted places, the city decayed. The rebuilders perished, the armies to earth. And so these buildings grow desolate, and this red-curved roof parts from its tiles of the ceiling-vault. The place has fallen to ruin shattered into heaps, where once many a man glad of mind and goldbright, gleaming adorned, proud and merry with wine shone in war-trappings; gazed on treasures, on silver, on curious gems, on wealth, on property, on precious stones, on this bright city, this glorious place.)

Three distinct scenes, or historical moments, can be detected in this passage. The first describes the 'wera' (26, people) whose occupation of the buildings ended in 'woldagas' (25, days of pestilence). Following this, the poem records that the 'Betend crungon' (28, Rebuilders perished), too. Finally, the third scene turns to 'beorn monig / glædmod ond goldbeorht gleoma gefrætwed' (32b–33, many a man glad of mind and goldbright, gleaming adorned) and describes the lavish jewellery and riches that they enjoyed. It is difficult to ascertain the exact chronological order of these scenes and the precise degree of overlap between the communities. It is also ambiguous as to whether the 'beorn monig' (32, many a man) enjoyed the wealth of the city before or after the 'woldagas' (25, days of pestilence) brought the occupation of the 'wera' (26, men or people) to an end. Throughout, however, the poem refrains from passing judgement on any of the occupants or drawing a moral from the events.

Those 'wera' do, nevertheless, seem to be the earliest occupants of the site. The Bosworth–Toller dictionary of Old English defines 'wer', the singular of 'wera', as 'a man, a male person', but notes that 'in the plural the word seems sometimes to include women as well as men'.[38] The poem identifies the latter group meanwhile as 'beorn'. Unlike 'wer', 'beorn' carries overtones of what the University of Toronto's Dictionary of Old English describes as 'martial vigour'[39] and Bosworth–Toller acknowledges this by offering a broad definition that includes 'prince, nobleman, chief, general, warrior, soldier'.[40] It is an identity defined by action. The difference between these nouns – which is not possible to replicate in Modern English – is clarified by their usage. For instance, the poem commonly known as 'The Gifts of Men' writes of a 'beadocræftig beorn' (man/warrior skilled in fighting)[41] and in the *Dream of the Rood* the speaker refers to the warrior-like Christ as 'beorn' and recalls how 'Bifode ic þa me se beorn ymbclypte' (I trembled when the man/warrior embraced me)'.[42] A good indicator of the differing cultural meanings attached to these terms is that while Ælfric often employed 'wer(a)', he never used 'beorn(as)'.[43] 'Beorn' was a cultural identity freighted with significance and status. This is important, as it has often been suggested that the past communities imagined by the poem are Roman, that the

Anglo-Saxons did not distinguish between historical moments or that the poem is mistaken in its association of earlier Anglo-Saxon communities with Roman buildings.[44] The use of 'beorn', which carried with it such clear Germanic overtones and stands in contrast to 'wer', undercuts this reading. This terminology suggests the poem imagines both Anglo-Saxon and non-Anglo-Saxon communities occupying the ruins and demonstrates that the past imagined by *The Ruin* is not singular and homogenous, but formed of diverse, overlapping moments. It is, though, the Anglo-Saxon-esque 'beorn(as)' who define the site. There is a hierarchy of presence. This is a vision of the past, and an understanding of history, that operates on Anglo-Saxon terms.

In a final circular movement that concludes its speculative meditation on the cultures of the past, *The Ruin* turns its attention from the communities who lived among the ruins and returns to the material remains themselves. Despite the damage to these lines (in the last six lines of the edited text, twelve complete words remain), it is clear that the poem ends in the present tense. As with the 'wealstan' of the first line, the focus is on how historical material comes into contact with the present. The poem describes a bathhouse and there is a suggestive echo between the flow of the hot streams and the fluidity with which the poem imagines the passage of time:

> Stanhofu stodan,   stream hate wearp
> widan wylme;   weal eall befeng
> beorhtan bosme,   þæt þa baþu wæron,
> hat on hreþre.   Þæs wæs hyðelic (þing).
> Lēton þonne geotan (............................)
> ofer harne stan   hate streamas
> un(................... ....)
> (o)þ þæt hringmere   hāte (............
> ....) þær þā baþu wæron
> Þonne is (........... ....
> ....)re.   Þæt is cynelic þing –
> hū s(e ....)burg(...)

> (38–49, Stone courts stood here, where hot streams flowed
> in a broad surge; everything enclosed by the wall
> in its bright bosom, where the baths were,
> hot at the heart. That was right.
> They let pour (.......................)
> over grey stones hot streams

un(..................... ....)
that round pool hot (..............
.......................) where the baths were
Then(.................... ....
.....................)re that is a royal thing,
how (the.............. ....)city (...))[45]

Like the complex temporality the poem imagines, the 'widan wylme' (39, broad surge) of the water takes place in a 'hringmere' (45, round pool). The manner in which the poem assembles the social worlds it depicts – its images of the past – is equally fluid. Partly due to the damage to the manuscript, it is as difficult to distinguish what or who is being described at certain points as it is to distinguish between past and present. It is unclear exactly what the 'cynelic þing' (48, noble thing) is, just as the poem does not identify who it is that 'þonne' (they) are when it is written that 'Leton þonne geotan' (42, They let it pour). This creates a richly textured temporal world, a world in which time does not flow in a strictly linear manner but, through the effects of the poem's metre, style and palaeographic history, different temporal moments swell and swirl. As it survives, *The Ruin* requires readers to place themselves in the meaning-making process. It requires unriddling; it prompts responsiveness.[46] But it is clear that, as Patricia Dailey and Renée Trilling have both suggested, the poem ends on a remarkably upbeat note.[47] There is hope amidst the ruins. *The Ruin* is about making time, making memory and the futures this makes possible. Bruno Latour suggests that, 'What makes other people's "past" empty, frozen, nontemporal, is the supposition that the past is out-of-date.'[48] *The Ruin* insists that the past is present: a rich source of cultural potential and hope for the future.

Medieval ruins and the ruin of the medieval

The power of *The Ruin*, the affective charge to which Conybeare, Thorpe and so many others have responded, relies in part on the manner in which ruins can appear to collapse temporal boundaries. As Dylan Trigg suggests, ruins are 'both polymorphous and temporally dynamic'.[49] This is one reason why the image of the ruin is such a powerful vehicle of cultural memory: ruins seem to quite literally speak of the past in the present and bring distinct temporal moments and histories into presence.[50] Ruins have been at the

centre of the medievalist imagination since John Leland began his
survey of Britain in 1533. Leland described his project to his patron
Henry VIII as being 'to peruse and dylygentlye to searche all the
lybraryes of monasteryes and collegies of thys your noble realme
to the intente that the monumentes of auncient writers as well as
other nations, as of this yowr owne province might be brought
owte of the deadly darkeness to lyvely lighte'.[51] He trawled across
Britain collecting material of cultural, literary and historical inter-
est for the King's delectation. For James Simpson, Leland stands
at the beginning of English literary history, but he also formed part
of the programmes of iconoclasm of 1536 to 1550 which sought,
in Simpson's words, 'to distance the past from the present as rap-
idly and decisively as possible'. As Simpson explains, one legacy
of this work was the creation of 'the very concept of the medieval
as a site of ruin'.[52] While *The Ruin* meditates on how social identi-
ties of the past might survive into the present, Leland's work was
predicated on an idea of rupture and disintegration. He, along-
side other Protestant historians such as John Bale, sought 'to pre-
serve a past that their present *must*, in some ways, destroy'.[53] But as
Leland's struggles demonstrate, the past is sometimes never quite
destroyed – forms of personal, institutional and cultural memory
persist and its archives, materials and meanings continue to shift
according to perspective and historical context. As the Old English
Ruin makes clear, the image of the ruin suggests this dynamism,
as the ruin is always caught in a moment of stilled motion. Ruins
illustrate the territory between preservation and oblivion.

Leland's ruinology has significant medieval antecedents. The
history of medieval British ruin-thinking begins with Gildas, writ-
ing sometime in the fifth to sixth centuries to lament the conquest
of the Britons at the hands of the invading Saxons in his *De excidio
et conquestu Britanniae* (On the Ruin and Conquest of Britain).
Gildas' philosophy of history is eschatological and prophetic and
he sees little chance of survival among the ruins, lamenting that, 'Se
ne nunc quidem, ut antea, civitates patriae inhabitantur; sed deser-
tae dirutaeque hactenus squalent' (But the cities of our land are not
populated even now as they once were; right to the present they are
deserted, in ruins and unkempt).[54] He writes as a voice of a sub-
jugated people nervously contemplating a future of Anglo-Saxon
dominance, with only little hope of renewal. A later Welsh work,
Yr aelwyd hon, written perhaps in the late ninth century, similarly
meditates on the lost glories of British kingdoms and reflects upon a
hearth which has outlasted Urien, Prince of Rheged's, rule.[55]

Evidence of the dominance Gildas feared is visible in Anglo-Saxon texts such as the anonymous Life of St Cuthbert, written between 699 and 705. For instance, the story the Life tells of the saint's visit to Carlisle, thought to have taken place in May 685, insists on a powerful connection between the saint and the cultural memory of Roman rule:

> Eo tempore quo Ecgfridus rex Pictorum regionem depopulans, postremo tamen secundum praedestinatum iudicium Dei superandus et occidendus uastabat, sanctus episcopus noster ad ciuitatem Luel pergens, uisitauit reginam illic rei effectum exspectantem. Sabbato ergo die, sicut presbiteri et diaconi ex quibus multi adhuc supersunt adfirmauerunt, hora nona considerantibus illis murum ciuitatis, et fontem in ea a Romanis mire olim constructum, secundum id quod Waga ciuitatis praepositus ducens eos reuelauit. Stans episcopus iuxta baculum sustentationis, inclinato capite ad terram deorsum, et iterum eleuatis oculis ad celum suspirans ait, O O O, existimo enim perpetratum esse bellum, iudicatumque est iudicium de populis nostris bellantibus aduersum. Tunc iam diligenter sciscitantibus illis quid factum esset, scire uolentibus occultans respondit, O filioli mei considerate, quam admirabilis sit aer, et recolite quam inscrutabilia sunt iudicia Dei, et reliqua.[56]

> (At the time when King Ecgfrith was ravaging and laying waste the kingdom of the Picts, though finally in accordance with the predestined judgement of God he was to be overcome and slain, our holy bishop went to the city of Carlisle to visit the queen, who was awaiting there the issue of events. On the Saturday, as the priests and deacons declare of whom many still survive, at the ninth hour they were looking at the city wall and the well formerly built in a wonderful manner by the Romans, as Waga the reeve of the city, who was conducting them, explained. The bishop meanwhile stood leaning on his supporting staff, with his head inclined towards the ground and then he lifted up his eyes heavenwards again with a sigh and said: 'Oh! Oh! Oh! I think that the war is over and that judgement has been given against our people in the battle.' Then when they urgently asked him what had happened and desired to know, he said evasively: 'Oh, my sons, look at the sky, consider how wonderful it is, and think how inscrutable are the judgements of God.')

Although it is unclear which buildings Cuthbert was shown, his tour of Carlisle's Roman remains, conducted by Waga, the city's reeve, suggest that they were a source of local pride. As Luguvalium, the town was a key stronghold on the Roman frontier, capital of the province of Valentia, and Fred Orton writes that the tour suggests that 'Carlisle in the seventh century must have been a pretty impressive Roman place'.[57] One indicator of the importance of the town's Roman associations is the fact that while the anonymous Life refers to the town as 'Luel', in his version of Cuthbert's Life, Bede refers to it by its full Roman name, 'Lugubaliam', and notes that the English people corruptly call it 'Luel' ('populis Anglorum corrupte Luel uocatur').[58] The cultural esteem in which the town and its buildings were held is also suggested by the language of wonder used to describe them, which recalls the 'wrætlic weallstan' of *The Ruin*. The anonymous author describes the 'fontem' as 'Romanis mire olim constructum' (formerly built in a wonderful manner by the Romans), and Bede echoes this when he writes of a 'fontemque in ea miro quondam Romanorum opere extructum' (marvellously constructed fountain of Roman workmanship).[59]

But in this story Cuthbert has other things on his mind. As Waga explains Carlisle's rich heritage, Cuthbert turns away and reveals the king's failure in battle. While Waga deployed the cultural memory of Roman rule to illustrate the importance of his city, Cuthbert uses it as a vehicle to legitimise and celebrate Christian knowledge. He displaces the wonder generated by the buildings and appropriates it for his own spiritual powers. He measures the wonder of his own spiritual foresight against the 'mire' buildings. He is more interested in what the ruins might mean in the present and the future than their pre-Anglo-Saxon heritage. The meanings of the Roman wall and well are transformed by Cuthbert's vision. As he is moved to revelation by the buildings, new narratives are generated and new ways of understanding the past are produced. Cuthbert uses the ruins to narrate time and tell a story of linear progression from Roman occupation to the dominance of Anglo-Saxon Christian culture.

As Gildas would have well understood, the ways of knowing the past Cuthbert and his Life offer are framed by precise structures of authority. Indeed, the opening sentence of the passage captures a clear ideology of social agency. As King Ecgfrith's exploits in the north are reported, the author explains that his success is always subject to 'iudicium Dei' (the judgement of God), while the unnamed queen's role is limited to 'exspectantem' (waiting, expecting, hoping). In this vision of human life then, God plans, men do and women wait. Similarly, access to the past, as represented by the buildings, is bound up with hierarchies of knowledge, privilege and power, both secular and spiritual, while access to the written record of history the Life produces is determined by language (the Life is written in Latin) and gender (Eormenburg, the queen Cuthbert visits, is left unnamed).[60] This engagement with the past serves to mark the contours of a peculiarly Anglo-Saxon Christian identity, an identity which, as in *The Ruin*, gains status through its association with, and appropriation of, the cultural memory of the Roman past.

Another account of an encounter with the Roman past offers an alternative perspective on the potency of imperial remains and how gender intersects with narratives of the past. In his *Ecclesiastical History*, Bede tells us that when King Æthelberht agreed that Augustine and his missionaries could remain in Kent to attempt to convert his people, he allowed them to work from a church near Canterbury used by his wife Bertha. Bede explains:

> Erat autem prope ipsam ciuitatem ad orientam ecclesia in honorem sancti Martini antiquitus facta, dum adhuc Romani Brittaniam incolerent, in qua regina, quam Christianam fuisse praediximus, orare consuerat. In hac ergo et ipsi primo conuenire psallere orare missas facere praedicare et baptizare coeperunt, donec rege ad fidem conuerso maiorem praedicandi per omnia et ecclesias fabricandi uel restaurandi licentiam acciperent.[61]

> (There was nearby, on the east of the city, a church built in ancient times in honour of St Martin, while the Romans were still in Britain, in which the queen, who, as has been said, was a Christian, used to pray. In this church they first began to meet to chant the psalms, to pray, to say mass, to preach, and to baptise, until, when the king had been converted to the faith, they received greater liberty to preach everywhere and to build or restore churches.)

When Bertha married Æthelberht in the mid-570s, the ceremony took place on the condition that she was able to continue practising her Christian faith and bring her abbot, Liudhard, with her from Francia to Kent. St Martin's Church is the place where Bertha, Liudhard and unknown others practised Christianity in the years between the marriage and Augustine's arrival. While the site might have been celebrated for its long history of Christian worship, for Bede, St Martin's Anglo-Saxon future was more important than its Roman past. He uses the church to tell a story about restoration rather than renewal. The arrival of Augustine and his missionaries mattered more to him than the earlier presence of the Frankish Bertha and Bishop Liudhard. Like Leland and Bale, in this instance Bede's historical narrative is more interested in new beginnings than old continuities.

Bede's account of St Æthelthryth further clarifies how gender narratives of the past encode ideas about gender. After marrying

Ecgfrith (the king at war with the Picts during Cuthbert's visit to
Carlisle) in 660, Æthelthryth left him and was consecrated a nun
in 672 before establishing the abbey at Ely in 673. She died in 679,
and in 695 her sister, Seaxburh, also an abbess at Ely, arranged
for her body to be translated from the humble plot Æthelthryth
desired to a more fitting location. As part of the process of transla-
tion, a new tomb was required and Bede reports that a group of
monks left Ely to find one:

> Qui ascensa naui (ipsa enim regio Elge undique est aquis ac palu-
> dibus circumdata, neque lapides maiores habet) uenerunt ad ciui-
> tatulam quan/dam desolatam non procul inde sitam, quae lingua
> Anglorum Grantacaestir uocatur, et mox inuenerunt iuxta muros
> ciuitatis locellum de marmore albo pulcherrime factum, oper-
> culo quoque similis lapidis aptissime tectum. Vnde intellegentes a
> Domino suum iter esse prosperatum, gratias agentes rettulerunt ad
> monasterium.[62]

> (So they got into a boat (for the district of Ely is surrounded on all
> sides by water and marshes and has no large stones) and came to
> a small deserted fortress not far away which is called *Grantacæstir*
> (Cambridge) in English, and near the walls of the fortress they soon
> found a coffin beautifully made of white marble, with a close-fitting
> lid of the same stone. Realising that the Lord had prospered their
> journey, they brought it back to the monastery.)

Once they returned to the monastery with the tomb it was revealed
to fit Æthelthryth's body perfectly. Again, then, the material
remains and cultural memory of Roman rule is invoked to enhance
the status of Bede's subject. And, again, this episode uses the
material remains of the Roman past to outline subject positions in
the Anglo-Saxon present. Form is given to Æthelthyth's memory
through the association of Christian faith and Britain's admirable
past and she, or at least Bede's account of her life and her dead
body, is marked as suitable for admiration.

Bede's telling of the story of Æthelthryth's tomb is, like the
story of Cuthbert in Carlisle and *The Ruin*, a strategic deployment
of wonder.[63] Unlike Cuthbert, however, in this story Æthelthryth
is passive. While Cuthbert's association with the Roman remains
appropriates their cultural esteem and contrasts his vitality and
vision with their stillness, Æthelthryth and the Roman tomb are
both still, lifeless and dead. While Cuthbert speaks, interprets and
actively shapes the social world, Æthelthryth is silent and is shaped
by it. As Catherine Karkov writes, 'In the case of Æthelthryth we

are left not with the woman, her voice, or her actions, but with what she stood for to a series of male voices and their various agenda.'[64] The deployment of wonder mythicises the historical processes which condition the establishment of this agenda. These stories determine how, to use Stuart Hall's language, identities 'are positioned within the narratives of the past'.[65] Some, like Cuthbert, are allowed intimate contact with the signifiers of the past while others, such as Bertha and Eormenburg, are not.

As these stories suggest, the material remains of the imperial past were a common part of Anglo-Saxon life. In other texts, too, the physical legacies of Roman culture are appropriated, celebrated and meditated upon. In his long poem in praise of his home town of York, written in the late eighth century, Alcuin writes that its high walls and lofty towers were built by 'Romana manus' (Roman hands)[66] and in his late tenth-century *Chronicle* Æthelweard records that the Romans 'urbes etiam atque castellam nec non pontes plateasque mirabilis ingenio condiderunt, quæ usque in hodiernam diem videntur' (made cities, forts, bridges and streets with wonderful skill, and these are to be seen to this day).[67] As in the Lives of St Cuthbert, Roman remains are a source of civic pride and their origins are acknowledged and celebrated, even if they are not interrogated in any detail. For all the authors, the significance of these buildings' histories lies in how they can inform social identities in the present. The texts work hard to position their subjects – and audiences – within the narratives of the past. While Michael Hunter influentially suggested that Anglo-Saxon authors' use of 'mirabilis' to refer to Roman buildings 'expressed their awareness that they were unequal to such works', these examples suggest that the language of wonder is put to constructive cultural work to mark discursive boundaries and disguise human agency.[68] By describing a relic of the past as 'mira' or 'wrætlic', authors turn attention away from the political processes which define it. The past is presented as over in these accounts: it functions only on the terms of the present. Yet, to use Jonathan Gil Harris' language, the past continues to form a vital part of 'the polychronic assemblage that is the present'.[69] So the question these texts pose is why can some bodies, such as Cuthbert, the 'beorn' of *The Ruin* and Æthelthryth but apparently not Bertha, navigate between temporal moments more freely than others? What do these navigations enable and what conditions do they depend upon? What is at stake – politically and culturally – in these encounters? How do encounters with the past open up possible futures?

In a more explicit but not more powerful manner than the Lives
of Cuthbert or Bede's story of Æthelthryth, Alcuin's poem on the
raid of Lindisfarne of 8 June 793, *De clade Lindisfarnensis monas-
terii* (On the Destruction of the Monastery at Lindisfarne), uses
the language of ruin to imagine a glorious Anglo-Saxon future.
Alcuin describes Lindisfarne as a great and holy place and reads
its destruction as a mark of the imperfection of the material
world that stands in stark contrast to the eternal joys of heaven.[70]
Lindisfarne's fate is first of all presented by Alcuin through the
perspective of the Christian faith and then located within the map
of the Christian world, as he finds a comparison for the monas-
tery's destruction in the falls of the cities of Babylon, Jerusalem
and Rome:

> Roma, caput mundi, mundi decus, aurea Roma,
>   Nunc remanet tantum saeva ruina tibi[71]

> (Rome, head of the world, the world's glory, golden Rome, nothing
> is left of you now but dire ruins!)[72]

As he locates Lindisfarne on the map of European Christendom,
Alcuin creates a vision in which the monastery might transcend
contemporary historical struggles: through the attention he pays
to the past, Alcuin suggests a future in which Lindisfarne might
occupy a place among the other great cities of the Christian world.
For Alcuin, as for the Old English *Ruin*, there is reason for opti-
mism and this optimism is a result of cultural hegemony.

The Old English poem known as *The Wanderer* offers a com-
parable meditation on the transitory nature of human life and
suggests that:

> Ongietan sceal gleaw hæle   hu gæstlic bið
> þonne ealre þisse worulde wela   weste stondeð,
> swa nu missenlice   geond þisne middangeard
> winde biwaune   weallas stondað,
> hrime bihrorene,   hryðge þa ederas.
> Woniað þa winsalo;   waldend licgað
> dreame bidrorene,   duguþ eal gecrong,
> wlonc bi wealle.[73]

> (The wise man must realise how ghostly it will be when all the world's
> wealth stands waste, as now here and there across this middle-earth
> walls stand blasted by wind, beaten by frost, the buildings open to
> the elements. The wine halls teeter, the rulers lie deprived of light,
> the troops all fell proud by the walls.)

Unlike *The Ruin, The Wanderer* offers a personal meditation on loss that is resolved by the 'fæstnung' (115, stability) of heaven. Some critics have read *The Wanderer* alongside other Anglo-Saxon texts including *The Ruin, The Seafarer* and *Beowulf* as expressions of what Roy Liuzza describes as 'the nostalgia that accompanies any great cultural shift'.[74] But such readings overlook essential differences among the texts and the range of meanings they attribute to the ruins. There is no single 'Anglo-Saxon' understanding of ruins.[75] It is clear that some Anglo-Saxon authors were fascinated by the temporal and affective possibilities of historical relics, but it is also clear that these objects signified differently according to context and access to the past was bound up in ideas of social status, particularly regarding gender and class. Indeed the value *The Wanderer* places on these cultural signifiers perhaps indicates and confirms the cultural esteem in which they – and the socially elevated masculine ideals they represented – were held by the poem and its audiences, rather than an anxiety about their status and survival.

There is certainly plenty of anxiety present in Wulfstan's tub-thumping 'Sermo Lupi', however, when he refers directly to Gildas and uses the example of the ruin of the Britons as a warning to his early eleventh-century Anglo-Saxon audience. For Wulfstan, like Gildas, ruin was a moral matter and part of the cultural memory of the Anglo-Saxons.[76] Writing in the twelfth century, William of Malmesbury includes a long description of the 'parietum ruinis' (ruined buildings) of Carlisle in his *Gesta pontificum anglorum*. Despite the damage, William suggests that the 'mira Romanorum artifitia' (remarkable Roman work) is still evident.[77] There is a sense of cultural decay in William's description of the buildings which is compounded by his comment that 'Sane tota lingua Nordanhimbrorum, et maxime in Eboraco, ita inconditum stridet ut nichil nos australes intelligere possimus' (Of course, the whole language of the Northumbrians, particularly in York, is so inharmonious and uncouth that we southerners can make nothing of it).[78] Carlisle's Roman ruins represent the heights from which the contemporary cultures of the north have fallen and William's reading of them confirms his own superiority.

What emerges from this brief and partial survey is a sense of the multivalence of the ruin. Depending on perspective, context and rhetorical purpose, ruins might signify imminent doom and destruction (as in Gildas, William and Wulfstan) or future glory and continuity (as in Alcuin). What unites these disparate accounts is how their readings of ruins determine social identities. These social identities are always bound up with ideas of periodisation, which is evident in modern discourses of ruin, too. Although Rose Macaulay's *Pleasure of Ruins*, perhaps the most influential work of twentieth-century ruinology, begins with a broad survey of Classical and medieval texts, including Alcuin's *De clade Lindisfarnensis monasterii*, *The Ruin*, *The Wanderer* and *Beowulf*, the majority of modern studies of ruins and ruin-imagery occlude the medieval from their gaze.[79] In the introduction to their collection *Ruins of Modernity*, for instance, Julia Hell and Andreas Schönle suggest that, 'What we now call ruins began to be perceived and preserved as such during the Renaissance, when the awareness of historical discontinuities and the demise of ancient civilizations raised the status of traces from their past.'[80] In a text published to coincide with *Ruin Lust*, Tate Britain's 2014 survey of artistic representations of ruins, the co-curator Brian Dillon suggests that 'the taste for ruins' is specifically 'post-medieval'.[81] What is fascinating about this discourse is how the cultural memory of the Middle Ages at once defines and is denied by modern discourses of ruin. As in the medieval texts, the multivalence of the ruin, which the medieval sources demonstrate so well, is limited by the epochal imagination of the modern critics. An image which speaks of both continuity and discontinuity through time is reinvented to conform to a linear model of historical change. This exclusion enables the identification of a coherent category named 'modernity' and dependent identities. The ruin of the medieval – the systematic disregard or simplification of its cultures – enables the cultural dominance of modernity. But as the history of *The Ruin* demonstrates, the modern is marked by the continuing return of medieval signifiers.

Translation, transformation and intimacy

How many nows might a medieval text possess? When, or which, is the now of *The Ruin*? Along with Thorpe's various volumes, John Josias Conybeare's *Illustrations of Anglo-Saxon Poetry* marks a transformative moment in Anglo-Saxon Studies.[82] Conybeare was Professor of Anglo-Saxon at Oxford between 1808 and 1812 and Professor of Poetry from 1812 to 1821. Following his sudden death in 1824, the Society of Antiquaries encouraged the publication of Conybeare's work on Old English, and John's brother William

Daniel Conybeare, a geologist, assumed what he called the 'melancholy but yet gratifying task of editing these remains'.[83] The edited *Illustrations*, published posthumously in 1826, is divided into four parts. It begins with an essay John delivered to the Society of Antiquaries that introduces the styles and metrical rules of Old English poetry; part two is a catalogue of Old English poetry subdivided by genre; the third section is the only part which John had fully completed and prepared for publication and contains a translation and discussion of Cædmon's *Hymn*, *Widsith* (which the Conybeares titled 'The Song of the Traveller') and *Beowulf*. The final section of the book serves as an appendix and consists of transcriptions and translations from the Exeter Anthology, the Alfredian Boethius and the Junius Manuscript which were left unfinished at the time of John Conybeare's death. The Conybeares' translation of *The Ruin*, the first published translation of the poem into Modern English, entitled 'The Ruin'd Wall-stone', is included in this section.

It appears that this text particularly caught the editor's imagination. As part of his description of the Exeter Book, William writes,

> from the 122nd page on, the MS. is much mutilated to the end: the subjects appear to be principally ænigmatical; but their obscurity is rendered hopeless, from the imperfect state in which they occur. One of these fragments, however, is of a descriptive nature, the subject being a ruined city. As it possesses more than ordinary merit, it has been selected for publication among the following specimens.[84]

Turning to 'The Ruin'd Wall-stone' in particular, William explains that, 'This specimen was left by the late Author of these translations in a very imperfect state of preparation ... The Editor was unwilling, however, to suppress a fragment of so much interest, and so superior, both in picturesque description and in the tone of moral feeling which pervades it, to the great mass of Saxon poetry.'[85] William therefore decided to complete the translation himself, even though he was 'unpractised in poetical composition', and distinguished his additions by printing them in italics.[86]

As was common practice at the time, the Conybeares presented translations of the Old English into both Latin and Modern English. To gain a sense of the collaborative nature of this work it is worth quoting the whole of the first half of their English translation (William Conybeare was responsible for the entire second half):

> Rear'd and wrought full workmanly
> By earth's old giant progeny
> The wall-stone proudly stood. It fell
> When bower, and hall, and citadel
> And lofty roof, and barrier gate,
> And tower and turret bow'd to fate,
> And wrapt in flame and drench'd in gore
> The lofty burgh might stand no more.
> Beneath the Jutes' long vanish'd reign.
> Her masters ruled the subject plain;
> *But they have moulder'd side by side –*
> *The vassal crowd, the chieftain's pride;*
> *And hard the grasp of earth's embrace,*
> *That shrouds for ever all the race.*
> So fade they, countless and unknown
> The generations that are gone.[87]

It is easy to spot inaccuracies in the Conybeares' rendering: John Conybeare's 'workmanly' fails to capture the sense of wonder and mystery generated by 'wrætlic'; in line eleven, 'undereotone' (under-eaten) is mistranslated as 'Beneath the Jutes';[88] William Conybeare's 'hard grasp of earth's embrace' does convey the sense of 'heard gripe hrusan', but the brothers miss the 'hund cnea' (8, hundred generations) which provide a time frame for the events imagined.

Stylistically, 'The Ruin'd Wall-stone' is closer to nineteenth-century Romantic poetry than Old English verse. By way of an introduction to the text, William compared the poem to John Dyer's 'Grongar Hill' (1726), which he described as a 'more elaborate delineation ... of the contrast between past grandeur and actual desolation'.[89] Clearly, while he attempted to provide insight into the Old English text's meanings, William was aware of its contemporary resonance. Writing of John Conybeare's translation of *Beowulf*, Roy Liuzza suggests that he attempted to present it in 'a form his readers would recognize as natural, attractive, and heroic' and that 'he sought equivalence rather than imitation, a re-creation of the effect of the poem rather than a restoration of its original sound'.[90] Thus 'The Ruin'd Wall-stone' recalls Byron's 1816 poem 'The Siege of Corinth' more than *The Ruin* or any other early medieval text:

> The vaults beneath the mosaic stone
> Contain'd the dead of ages gone;

Their names were on the graven floor
But now illegible with gore.[91]

The Conybeares' translation provides a good example of what Lawrence Venuti has called the 'domestication' of a foreign text. As Venuti writes, some works of translation seek to 'bring back a cultural other as the same, the recognizable, even the familiar'. There is more in play than language or metre as, in Venuti's terms, 'domesticized' texts are reconstructed 'in accordance with values, beliefs and representations that pre-exist in the target language, always configured in hierarchies of dominance and marginality, always determining the production, circulation, and reception of texts'.[92] In the Conybeares' translation the alterity of Old English poetry – its metre and style as well as its language and imagery – is comprehensively reinvented according to contemporary cultural ideals, ideals which are already appropriating an invented past. This means that Anglo-Saxon verse is able to enter their present without disrupting it. Indeed, it enters their present on the condition that is does not disrupt it. This is translation as a form of cultural memory: images of the past are recreated according to the desires of the present. While this might be seen as cause for criticism, it is also cause for thinking through what their translation shares with *The Ruin*. Just as the Old English text places its Anglo-Saxon contemporaries among impressive Roman architecture, so nineteenth-century tastes are threaded through the Conybeares' visions of the Anglo-Saxon past. Rather than lamenting the lack of historical accuracy, it is more in keeping with *The Ruin*'s own philosophy of history to interrogate the manner in which the Conybeares' text straddles multiple contexts and traditions and speaks in and across time. Both *The Ruin* and 'The Ruin'd Wall-stone' express the hope of intersubjective contact across time.

A comparison with Thorpe's sober translation of *The Ruin*, from his *Codex Exoniensis* of 1842, the second published Modern English translation of the poem, further illustrates the remarkable nature of the Conybeares' work. Of his translations, Thorpe stated that 'From first to last it has been my endeavour to make it literal, and, at the same time, readable',[93] and on his own terms his work succeeds. The translation begins, 'Wondrous is this wall-stone, / the fates have broken it, / have burst the burgh-place' and maintains greater accuracy than the Conybeares, at the expense of poetic flourish, throughout.[94] Other pieces in the *Illustrations* come close to matching Thorpe's measured style. The Conybeares' version

of Cædmon's *Hymn* is restrained and sombre, for instance, while
their 'Song of the Traveller' is a ballad but without any of the
drama or verve of 'The Ruin'd Wall-stone'.[95] Indeed it is only the
selections from *Beowulf* which reach the melodramatic heights of
'The Ruin'd Wall-stone'.

Writing on her own work as a translator, Gayatri Chakravorty
Spivak comments that 'Translation is the most intimate act of
reading.' She writes that she 'surrenders' to the text when she
translates and that 'The translator earns permission to transgress
from the trace of the other – before memory – in the closest
places of the self.' Spivak might indeed be writing of the comfort
William Conybeare appears to have found in *The Ruin*. One of
the nows of the Conybeares' *Ruin* is the now of William's grief
at his brother's early death. Unlike Thorpe, William Conybeare
appears not to have worried about the relevance or accessibility
of Old English. Instead he relished literature's ability to speak
across as well as in time. The italic font which distinguishes
William Conybeare's work from his brother's is a striking rep-
resentation of a meeting point between past and present and
self and other. This is all the more affecting because, if he had
wished, the editor could have invisibly completed the text and
offered a finished, whole, poem, or simply left what material his
brother had finished incomplete. But instead, and it is worth
noting that he didn't do this for any other text in the *Illustrations*,
William not only filled in the gaps in his brother's translation,
but made his insertions clearly visible. The Conybeare broth-
ers' translation offers the reader a dialogue between presence
and absence. In Spivak's words, it speaks of 'contingency, beside
language, around language'.[96] The collaborative translation
reveals as much of brotherly grief as it does of the Old English
Ruin. This is translation as a hopeful practice. The Conybeares'
work is located at the centre of the network of affect that brings
contemporary trauma into contact with a nostalgic sense of the
early medieval past. Personal and cultural memory intertwine
to produce a text which speaks with as well as through the Old
English *Ruin*.

Spivak's thinking on translation complements Aranye
Fradenburg's work on what she describes as medieval literature's
ability to 'live on'. For Fradenburg, literary texts exist in a kind
of continually unfolding present as part of 'signifying networks
wherein relationships among writers and readers are ... somatic
and affective as well as cognitive'.[97] Again, the Conybeares' work

provides a fine example of the relations literary texts can form and sustain. Their translation does not write over *The Ruin*, but writes with it, alongside it. Thinking through the work historical texts achieve in the present, Fradenburg concludes that, 'The signifiers of the past are in us, whether we understand them "rightly" or not; we will never be certain what they mean, but we will certainly have been possessed by them. And our possession by (and of) past signifiers further transforms their range of meanings.'[98] These words speak equally to William Conybeare's project and the Old English *Ruin* itself, texts both possessive of and possessed by the signifiers of the past. Together, Fradenburg and Spivak encourage an approach to translation and reception that moves beyond questions of accuracy to privilege moments of encounter and transformation – of text, temporality and self. Such moments of contingency as Spivak describes, moments of porosity where the boundaries of the temporally situated self are momentarily breached, where past is brought into contact with present not as static history but as living memory, are rich resources for communities and individuals committed to conjuring new ways of knowing past and present. In the final sections of this chapter, I will outline some of the ways in which *The Ruin* has been reimagined in the twentieth and twenty-first centuries to demonstrate the transformative potential of such encounters.

Translating *The Ruin* in the twentieth century

The Conybeares' translation of *The Ruin* found an afterlife of its own when it was published in Henry Wadsworth Longfellow's influential 1845 collection *Poets and Poetry of Europe*.[99] As Chris Jones has demonstrated, however, the greatest influence on twentieth-century poetic translations from Old English was exerted not by the Conybeares or Longfellow, but by Ezra Pound, whose archaic translation of *The Seafarer* was first published in 1911 and offered, in Latour's terms, a 'bifurcation' in the textual networks of early medieval translation.[100] The creative archive of *The Ruin* – its poetic and artistic translation and appropriation – is defined by Pound's *Seafarer*. Pound's strident work privileged sound over sense and moved between literal and figurative translations, rendering, to take just a few examples, 'siþas secgan' (2, tell of journeys) as 'journey's jargon', 'bitre breostceare' (4, bitter heart-care) as 'bitter breastcare', 'burgum' (28, cities) as 'burghers'.[101] While

Pound's work has been criticised for the liberties it takes with the Old English text, it is instructive to consider how much his philosophy of translation shares with the Conybeares'. Both transform the text, and while Pound maintains the 'strangeness' and the Conybeares 'domesticise', each submits the poem to their own poetic and cultural agenda. It is also important to recognise that the greatest liberty Pound took with the text – translating only the first ninety-nine lines – followed a scholarly tradition that survived until the mid-twentieth century.[102] To rework Homi Bhabha's language, translations, like scholarly study, remake *The Ruin* and in each case the Old English text emerges 'in-between the claims of the past and the needs of the present'.[103] There is no grand progression by which the true, singular meaning of the text is slowly uncovered, rather these works create networks of influence, affect and memory which chart some of the ways in which the past is threaded through the present.

The version of *The Ruin* produced by the Scottish poet Edwin Morgan in the early 1950s shares Pound's philosophy of translation as transformation. As with the Conybeares' translation – although unlike Pound's 'Seafarer' – it would be difficult to guess the provenance of Morgan's poem, as the stresses are heavy but inconsistent and the alliterative patterns come and go. Like the original, however, many of the verbs are past participles and the heavy stresses, dissonance and flexible metre make this a very difficult poem to read quickly:

> Wonder holds these walls. Under destiny destruction
> Splits castles apart. Gigantic battlements are crumbling,
> Roofs sunk in ruin, riven towers fallen,
> Gates and turrets lost, hoarfrost for mortar,
> Rain-bastions beaten, cleft, pierced, perished,
> Eaten away by time. Earth's fist and grasp
> Holds mason and man, all decayed, departed.[104]

The very wholeness of Morgan's 'Ruin' is striking: there are no gaps, only two ellipses indicate the state of the manuscript. Morgan's translation is concerned not with the physicality of *The Ruin*, but its textuality. Linguistically, too, Morgan is unafraid to stray from the source text: 'riven' entered English usage in the fourteenth century, 'bastion' is a loan word from French first used in English in the sixteenth century and 'tempests' is of similar origin. As in *The Ruin*, these linguistic choices create a rich, textured sense of time.[105] This speaks eloquently to the philosophy of history presented in *The Ruin*, a philosophy that privileges connections over rupture and seeks to reveal how the cultural forms of the past can transform (and be transformed) in the present. But Morgan's text is imbued with a sense of nostalgia absent from the Old English. While what remains of *The Ruin* speaks in the present tense of a 'cynelic þing', Morgan's poem ends, 'The stone courts stood then ... and where the baths lay / Hot at the heart of the place, that was the best of all ...' There is the suggestion that, despite the survival of the poem and Morgan's own translation of it, the past is irrecoverable and the present a pale imitation of it.

The influence of Pound is plain to see in the English poet Peter Russell's *Visions and Ruins* of 1964. Russell was a friend and protégé of Pound's, and *Visions and Ruins* is a long autobiographical poem that meditates on science, memory, temporality and the imagination. It was published with a foreword by the poet, critic and scholar Kathleen Raine, who claimed that, 'It is perhaps impossible to write significant poetry without command of the image of the universe which science has created.'[106] This is a key insight into Russell's subject matter, as he writes of the struggle to comprehend the scale of deep time and what he called 'the same stretched-out sheet of nothingness that is the stars / Colloidal and impermanent in time as wisps of speech' (7).

In *Visions and Ruins* it is culture that provides the 'colloid' that joins human beings together. Against the stark background of a godless universe, the art humans create retains its meaning. Russell draws on *The Ruin* in the ninth section of the poem, which is titled 'Ruin' and consists of rearrangements of translated passages from *The Ruin* that are supplemented by original material. Before we turn to those lines in detail, it is worth considering the lines which preface them:

> Despair is a ruin of the mind, the brain-cells crumbling
> That once enjoyed Mozart, Picasso or cricket.
> Is putrid Despair a war in the mind leaving ruins and only ruins
> Where once were bright castles and palaces built for delight,
> Labyrinths where young Cretan girls gazed in their mirrors
> And delighted the world with their fashions –
> Palace of Minos, Troy, Mada'in, Aquae Sulis –
>
> All is a ruin now ... (16)

Here cricket takes a place beside the work of Mozart and Picasso and the architecture of ancient civilisations as a sign of the richness of human life and the value of human community. The continuous present tense of art, like the nonhuman temporalities of science, provides a keen contrast to the limits of human life. Russell treats *The Ruin* as a source of affective consolation, in a manner that recalls the work of the Conybeares. The meanings of the text reside in what the text might become, the work it might be put to in the present, but this does not mean its Anglo-Saxon contexts hold no value. Rather, for Russell, it is precisely the text's movement between temporal moments that defines its power.

Russell's reference to Aquae Sulis points to another aspect of *The Ruin*'s history, as one of the most significant strands of its critical reception is the tradition of attempting to locate the actual site it describes and the most common view, first suggested by Heinrich Leo in 1865, is that the ruins described by the poem are the ruins of the Roman city of Bath.[107] Russell's invocation brings to attention how scholarship informs the reception and interpretation of Anglo-Saxon texts but, in *Visions and Ruins*, *The Ruin* is transformed to become an emblem of all past times and of the historical imagination itself. Like Pound's 'Seafarer', *Visions and Ruins* is an archaic, didactic, esoteric and personal meditation on the relics of the past and their relation to the present and future. His appropriation of *The Ruin* allows Russell to gesture towards the histories that remain unseen to human beings. Like the science of atoms and particles, the language of these lines reveal, to the reader familiar with *The Ruin*, the temporal possibilities of art, the potential for affective relations across broad temporal periods and the vast spans of time which inhere in language. *The Ruin* also allows Russell to write of his own life from a distance and permits an ironic reflection on the unheroic travails of human existence:

> Stone courts stood here, the sulphurous healing stream
> Like a severed artery gushed out in this place
> Where I was born just forty years ago. It was warm –
> The chalybeate spring that broke from the chthonic depth.
> Dark is the first memory dark as the earth
> Much was to come and much to go
> Wonderful still are the walls but the rooves have fallen
> Castles and towers have tottered tiles have crashed to the ground
> Frost has loosened the mortar the north wind flaked the stone
> The builders are dead their daughters no longer for sale
> Stout earth that clasped the foundations
> Binds their cold bones Councils and kingdoms have come
> Leisure prosperity government – gone … (17)

The section finishes with the bleak lines, 'Bright buildings crumble in time / And we too tumble' (17), but Russell retains the possibility of hope when he suggests that 'the mass seems aimless but the pattern emerges' (20) and ends with the suggestion that 'Death is a new beginning …' (27).

Michael Alexander's translation of *The Ruin* was included in his volume of poetic translations of Old English verse, *The Earliest English Poems*, first published in 1966. Alexander has recalled that it 'was Ezra Pound's translation of *The Seafarer* which prompted me to translate other Old English poems into verse' and *The Earliest English Poems* was dedicated to Pound. His influence on Alexander is clear.[108] Alexander's 'Ruin' exerts considerable pressure on Modern English as it attempts to accommodate the alterity of Old English and is littered with archaisms:

> Well-wrought this wall; Wierds broke it.
> The stronghold burst …
>
> Snapped rooftrees, towers fallen,
> the work of Giants, the stonesmiths,
> mouldereth.
>   Rime scoureth gatetowers
>   rime on mortar.[109]

In the first line the alliterative pattern of the Old English is cemented by the archaic 'Wierds', a form uncommon in Modern English which heavily echoes *The Ruin*'s 'wyrde' (1, events). Like Alexander's use of the archaic forms 'mouldereth' and 'scoureth', in Venuti's terms, 'wierds' disrupts 'the cultural codes that prevail in the target language'.[110] Most translators prefer the politely otherworldly 'fate' or 'fates'.[111] It is telling that the latest citation the *Oxford English Dictionary* provides for the use of 'weird' to signify 'fate', which is the form from which Alexander's usage of 'wierds' stems, is taken from William Morris and A. J. Wyatt's hyper-archaising 1895 translation of *Beowulf*.[112] As with Russell's reference to Bath, the history of Anglo-Saxon Studies is woven through this work. By employing archaic forms, Alexander, like Morris and Wyatt, posits the possibility of a return or rediscovery of the linguistic forms (and, by implication, the cultures) of the past.[113] But if his language is not quite of the present day, it is also not quite of the past. As in the Conybeares' work, the past is suggested to be stable and recoverable, but both past and present are transformed as they are brought into contact. Unlike Russell and

Morgan, Alexander finds the agents of this transformation in the linguistic and cultural forms of the past and, unlike Venuti's sense of 'domesticising' translations, Alexander's language disrupts the forms and styles of his target language. He attempts to speak with the past, against the contemporary. In Alexander's translation language offers a way of thinking about time, history and memory that is neither linear nor teleological. Like the material remains at the centre of the Old English *Ruin*, Alexander's language is untimely – not without time but suffused with it, looking to the past and future.

While Alexander's work may be defined as a critical rather than a creative translation and certainly takes fewer liberties with the sense and sound of the Old English than the other translations I consider here, his work illustrates the blurred boundaries between the categories. A useful comparison is Harold W. Massingham's reworking of *The Ruin* which was published in the *Times Literary Supplement* the same year Alexander's collection appeared. Massingham's piece opens with the bravura lines: 'This wall-stone's well worth seeing: such / crumbling masonry, the cracking architecture of castles'. The mundane and colloquial 'well worth seeing' speaks of heritage tourism rather than philological study and the pun 'cracking', which describes the condition of the fabric of the castle but also carries the slang sense of praise, generates an ironic and playful tone that contrasts with all other published translations of the poem. As the text progresses, however, a sense of seriousness develops:

> The builders,
> The hard committed hands, are locked in clay:
> Like hundreds more, stoned-in, stoned-under.
> They are their own debris.

Massingham's work is a further example of 'domestication' but it generates a sense of untimeliness by the manner in which it associates the human and nonhuman elements of its vision. In the verse quoted above, the builders seem to have become one with their work: 'They are their own debris.' Later, Massingham writes that 'Tiles are brushed off, like scales from a scalp', while the poem finishes with an image of 'wide-armed, welcoming walls'.[114] Unlike the source text, Massingham's 'Ruin' imagines a single community occupying the site. There is an egalitarian aspect to his vision, which is confirmed by its clear and direct language. While

Alexander's site is perhaps culturally elevated by the appearance of an 'acropolis' at line 28, Massingham's survey is resolutely domestic. But both transform the source text's range of meanings and also share an unmistakable note of nostalgia.

One signal of the influence of Alexander's work is the fact that Peter Reading's knowledge of Old English 'came primarily' from *The Earliest English Poems*.[115] Reading first published poems influenced by Old English in his 1992 collection *Evagotory* and published a version of *The Ruin* as 'Fragmentary', a piece composed of a mixture of accurate and loose translations from the Old English text as well as original compositions, in his 1994 collection *Last Poems*. 'Fragmentary' has none of the redemption of *The Ruin* or the grim optimism of Russell's version: Reading's ruin is a symbol of total destruction. What Reading shares with *The Ruin* is the conviction that destruction is not without meaning. Silence, like absence, can speak. It is generative, creative. *Last Poems* purports to be Reading's final pieces of writing, found after his death, as the foreword claims, 'contained in an envelope bearing the superscription, in the author's hand, "Last Poems"'.[116] As this suggests, *Last Poems* is concerned with endings – personal, political and literary.[117]

The poem begins with these abrupt lines:

felled by Fate, this fine-wrought wall.
… castle is crumbled, constructed by giants.
Rooftrees are wrecked, ruined towers
fester and fall. Fate fells all.
What of the craftsmen? Clasped in earth.[118]

The lower-case 'f' which opens the poem, as well as the ellipsis in line two, suggest that this text is itself a ruin. In the course of the poem there are four ellipses and a postscript enclosed in square brackets which give the impression of editorial interference. This is all of course Reading's invention and gestures towards a lack, a loss, an array of missing fragments that will explain the remains the reader must contemplate. As with *The Ruin*, the obscurity of 'Fragmentary' is a significant aspect of its potential meanings. The reader is forced to question what is missing and evaluate how the absent material might inform their understanding of the text. But the reader also has to accept that the apparently missing elements perhaps never existed. Like *The Ruin*, Reading is interested in ambiguity and obscurity, the struggle to make meaning and the temporal complexities of the meaning-making process. As the reader is encouraged to self-consciously reflect upon how meaning might be generated, the absences Reading uses to frame his text become imbued with meaning. As with *The Ruin*, absences determine the experience of reading, or attempting to read, the text. They exert an agency which marks out the meanings that may, or may not, be available to the reader. Like Russell and the Old English *Ruin*, Reading places the reader in ruin. There is no spectacular visage to regard, only fragments to piece together.

As the complex metatextual narratives Reading created suggest, *Last Poems* is autobiographical, even in its obscurity. It is an attempt to write a life, despite how much Reading invests in the idea that life is ultimately unwritable. Reading's response to *The Ruin* is elucidated by Jacques Derrida's work on self-portraiture. For Derrida there is an element of ruination in all representations. 'The ruin does not supervene like an accident upon a monument that was intact only yesterday', he writes. Rather, 'In the beginning there is ruin. Ruin is that which happens to the image from the moment of the first gaze.'[119] For Derrida the ruin is a sign of the impossibility of accurate representation, in particular it signifies the inevitability of the mediation of memory in the process of drawing or writing; it confirms the heterogeneity and hybridity of all moments of time, all presents and all presences, all subjects. Working with *The Ruin* allows Reading, like the other translators whose work I have explored in this chapter, to create a poetic voice that recognises the difference at the centre of subjectivity. If, as Mladen Dolar argues, the voice 'is the element which ties the subject and the Other together', then medievalist cultural memory is the point where modernity and its Other meet.[120] This is as true on the micro level of the poet and translator as it is at the macro level of culture. And it is this that connects the discourses of ruinology outlined above with the disparate translations of the poem – what unites the examples is not their similarity but their diversity and the manner in which context determines their meaning. Reading's 'Fragmentary' also reminds us that it is impossible to read to the Old English *Ruin* without ruining it, without bringing it into contact with our own historical moment, our own ruined identity. Its historicity is not simply defined by its Anglo-Saxon pasts, but its multiple presents. And this ruination does not necessarily involve what Bede would call a loss of 'decoris ac dignitatis'. Rather, it enriches the manner in which these texts speak of human experience and enriches the meanings the early medieval *Ruin* generates.

Futures past

The mediation of memory is the one of the subjects of two twenty-first-century versions of *The Ruin*. Chris Jones' *Ruin* was published in 2007 and seeks to rewrite the text in light of the conflicts of the early 2000s rather than offer a transparent translation of the Old English. 'Beorht wæron burgræced' (21, bright were the city-dwellings) becomes 'City-blocks gleamed' and 'Crungon walo wide, cwoman woldagas' (25, The slain fell all around, days of pestilence came) becomes 'Tall towers flat-lined zero hour came' to bring the events of 11 September 2001 to mind. This association is clarified and developed as the poem continues:

> The target collapsed into ruin
> Reduced to rubble where crowds
> once sparkled with jewellery and gadgetry
> prosperous successful trading greetings and goods
> contemplating profit and investment
> second cars holiday homes
> and luxury condos in high-rise blocks.[121]

The military overtones of 'target' and the modernity of 'gadgetry', 'profit and investment' and 'luxury cars' combine to associate the Old English source text with the cultural memory of early twenty-first-century warfare.

In 2011 Imogen Cloët and Jacob Polley staged *Bathtime*, an immersive art installation in a bathhouse at Segedunum Roman Fort, Baths and Museum near Wallsend in the northeast of England. The work was a complex interplay between text, site, sound, image and performance, and Polley's version of *The Ruin* was the thread that tied these elements together.[122] Polley's text, like Jones' earlier work, reimagined *The Ruin* through the lens of contemporary cultural memory. Polley's version brought Segedunum's Roman past into contact with Wallsend's late twentieth-century history of industrial decline. The earlier generations of builders are not 'heard gripe hrusan, oþ hund cnea / werþeoda gewitan' (8–9, held in the grip of the ground until a hundred generations of people have passed away), but rather are 'A long time laid off, fast in the earth, / while their sons passed, and the sons of their sons / knew no like work.'[123] Polley's version shares with Jones' a pessimistic ending which stands in contrast to the Old English text. Disregarding the material condition of the manuscript, Polley writes,

> Houses were here.
> Hot water sprang from wells and the walls held
> vaults of steam and banked beds of embers, like precious stones.
> Frost could get no grip. But all such days are gone.[124]

Jones' final lines are closer to the Old English, but even bleaker:

> ...l the boiling cauldron
>   where the tanks were
> Then ... is ...
>   ...re. It's barbaric
> how ... the ...   city ...

Yusef Komunyakaa's restrained translation of *The Ruin*, published in 2012, offers a useful contrast to Jones' and Polley's work. As Jones and Polley seek to bring *The Ruin* into contact with a precise historical context, Komunyakaa holds his scene beyond an identifiable moment of culture. While Jones transforms the 'meodoheall monig dreama full' (mead-hall full of many pleasures) into 'cafés and bars crammed with human desire' and Polley offers an unsettling vision of 'great halls' gleaming 'with muscle girls and monster fish', Komunyakaa restricts his scene to 'many mead halls filled with revelry'. His close translation is positively low-key, and clearly working with different goals than Jones and Polley, achieving its power through a final line that insists that the destruction – and, presumably, the poem – 'is still a fitting thing for this city'.[125]

To return to Fradenburg's language, the translation history of *The Ruin* recounted here – which runs parallel to the poem's critical history – reveals how the poem has possessed and been possessed by readers and writers and how its meanings have been transformed through those relations. It has provided a source of energy and inspiration for poets and translators working across the spectrum of literary practice. This poetic history demonstrates and is determined by the dialectal relationship between memory and history. According to shifts in the cultural memories of Anglo-Saxon England, the commitments of the author and the needs of the present, the text is recreated as heroic, nostalgic, strange, familiar or fragile. As this chapter has demonstrated, it is possible to locate the Old English *Ruin* at the centre of a network of memory and influence. That male translators and critics dominate this network should give us pause. As with the stories of Cuthbert, Bertha and Æthelthryth recounted in this chapter, it is clear that gender, race, class and ethnicity continue to determine access to and engagement with the past.

To close this chapter I would like to turn to one final use of *The Ruin*, by the filmmaker Julien Temple. Temple's 2010 documentary *Requiem for Detroit?* studies the industrial growth and decay of Detroit, from the capitalist and cultural promise of Ford and Motown to the economic downturn and urban disintegration of the late twentieth century.[126] In the final minutes of the film, Temple interviews residents of Detroit, who are invited to speculate on the relationship between the city's past and future. One group outlines their plans for an experiment in urban agriculture, another reflects on the various corporations and civic authorities that bear responsibility for Detroit's collapse, and then the camera cuts to the Detroit People Mover. The viewer is placed at the front of an automated monorail train, a technological innovation that dates to Detroit's years of cultural and economic success in the late 1960s, and as the camera moves slowly through the downtown area of the city, surveying wrecked and ruined buildings, a translation of *The Ruin* is spoken in voiceover, beginning: 'Wondrous is this wall stead / wierd made it, fate broke it / battlements broken, giants' work shattered / roofs are in ruin towers destroyed / broken the barred gate, frost on the concrete'.

The poem is not credited but the translation Temple uses appears to be adapted from the work of Siân Echard, Professor of English at the University of British Columbia, again illustrating the interdependence of creative and critical approaches to the text.[127] This is a rich and suggestive use of *The Ruin*. In the spirit of the Old English text, it is ambiguous yet affecting. What, indeed, does the modern, largely black city of Detroit have in common with *The Ruin*? This appropriation is another example of how *The Ruin* is located, and locates itself, in multiple networks of affect that signify in and through time, but it is also a reminder that ruins are produced and preserved through political action. Ruination is not distributed equally and not all ruins are held in equal cultural esteem. The ruination of some bodies and some cultures is allowed and, as the interviewees in the documentary note, even encouraged. Other bodies, other cultures, are able to flourish across time and remake the past and make the future in their own image. As in the case of Detroit, ruination can be the result of political will, and the contemplation of ruins, of the twenty-first century city or the early medieval poem, can mitigate as well as express, as Derrida would have it, the ruins of one's own self. So the poem provides a shock of historical depth to Temple's images, a historical depth that emphasises common humanity rather than race, class or precise historical context. The sense of untimeliness jolts the viewer and draws attention to the possibility of shared experience across time. It opens up the potential of community formation beyond the boundaries of nation, race, class, gender or even time. In his study of the aesthetics of ruins, Christopher Woodward writes that, 'When we contemplate ruins, we contemplate our own future',[128] and Temple's appropriation of *The Ruin* is explicitly future-oriented. It refashions the cultural memory of twentieth-century Detroit by associating it with more privileged narratives of historical time in order to open up a future for the city beyond the possibilities of the present. In turn, and this surely is a lesser point, it opens up alternative futures for the poem, beyond the history of translation recounted in this chapter. It reminds us that the medieval is open, relational and always already ruined although not without 'decoris ac dignitatis'. But it also directs us to the structures in which medievalist cultural memory might flourish and how it forms collective as well as personal identities, one topic that will be investigated further in the next chapter.

Notes

1 Jacques Derrida, *Memoirs of the Blind: The Self-Portrait and Other Ruins*, trans. Pascale-Anne Brault and Michael Naas (London: University of Chicago Press, 1993), p. 68.
2 Benjamin Thorpe, 'Translator's preface', *Cædmon's Metrical Paraphrase of Parts of the Holy Scriptures, in Anglo-Saxon* (London: Society of Antiquaries of London, 1832), p. v ('the Father of English Song') and p. viii (on attribution). On the 'fatherhood' of English poetry see Clare A. Lees and Gillian R. Overing, *Double Agents: Women and Clerical Culture in Anglo-Saxon England*, 2nd edn (Cardiff: University of Wales Press, 2009), pp. 19–55.
3 Thorpe, 'Translator's preface', p. xvi.
4 Bede, *Ecclesiastical History of the English People*, ed. and trans. Bertram Colgrave and R. A. B. Mynors (Oxford: Clarendon Press, 1969), Book IV, ch. 24, pp. 416–17.

5 See Andy Orchard, 'Poetic inspiration and prosaic translation: The making of Cædmon's *Hymn*', in M. J. Toswell and E. M. Tyler (eds), *'Doubt Wisely': Papers in Honour of E. G. Stanley* (London: Routledge, 1996), pp. 402–22 and Kevin Kiernan, 'Reading Cædmon's *Hymn* with someone else's glosses', *Representations* 32 (1990), 157–74.

6 See Ann Hawkshaw, 'Cædmon the Anglo-Saxon poet', *Sonnets on Anglo-Saxon History* (London: John Chapman, 1854), p. 39; Christopher Fry, *One More Thing, Or, Caedmon Construed* (London: King's College London, 1986); Paul Muldoon, 'Cædmon's *Hymn*', *Moy Sand and Gravel* (London: Faber, 2002), p. 23; U.A. Fanthorpe, 'Caedmon's song', *Queueing for the Sun* (Calstock, Cornwall: Peterloo Poets, 2003), p. 28; and Maureen Duffy, 'Cenewyf', *Environmental Studies* (London: Enitharmon, 2013), pp. 56–7.

7 Denise Levertov, 'Caedmon', *Breathing the Water* (Newcastle: Bloodaxe Books, 1988), p. 60.

8 Seamus Heaney, 'Whitby-sur-Moyola', *The Spirit Level* (London: Faber and Faber, 1996), p. 41. Thanks to Clare Lees for tracking down modern Cædmons.

9 Allen Frantzen makes a similar point in *Desire for Origins: New Language, Old English, and Teaching the Tradition* (New Brunswick: Rutgers University Press, 1990), p. 125.

10 Tom Boellstoff, 'When marriage falls: Queer coincidences in straight time', *GLQ: A Journal of Lesbian and Gay Studies* 13 (2007), 227–48, p. 232. See also Bettina Bildhauer, *Filming the Middle Ages* (London: Reaktion, 2011), pp. 94–6.

11 Rita Felski, *The Limits of Critique* (Chicago: University of Chicago Press, 2015), p. 157.

12 Felski, *Limits*, pp. 157, 161.

13 Bruno Latour, *Reassembling the Social: An Introduction to Actor-Network-Theory* (Oxford: Oxford University Press, 2007), p. 128.

14 'The Ruin', lines 1 and 31–2, in Bernard J. Muir (ed.), *The Exeter Anthology of Old English Poetry: An Edition of Exeter Dean and Chapter MS 3501*, 2 vols (Exeter: University of Exeter Press, 2000), vol. 1, pp. 357–8. Hereafter cited by line number. All translations my own unless otherwise stated.

15 Chris Abram, 'In search of lost time: Aldhelm and the *Ruin*', *Quaestio* 1 (2000), 23–44, p. 23.

16 Michael Swanton, *English Poetry before Chaucer* (Exeter: Exeter University Press, 2002), pp. 132–3.

17 See further Emily V. Thornbury, 'Admiring the ruined text: The picturesque in editions of Old English verse', *New Medieval Literatures* 8 (2006), 215–47.

18 Benjamin Thorpe, *Codex Exoniensis: A Collection of Anglo-Saxon Poetry* (London: Society of Antiquaries of London, 1842), p. x.

19 John Josias Conybeare, *Illustrations of Anglo-Saxon Poetry*, ed. William
    Daniel Conybeare (London: Harper and Lepard, 1826), pp. 249–50.
20 Helena Znojemská, 'The Ruin: A reading of the Old English
    poem', *Litteraria Pragensia* 8 (1998), 15–33. See also, for example,
    Stanley Greenfield, *Hero and Exile: The Art of Old English Poetry*
    (London: Hambledon Press, 1989), pp. 95–5 and Lawrence Beaston,
    'The Ruin and the brevity of human life', *Neophilologus* 95 (2011),
    477–89.
21 Nicholas Howe, *Writing the Map of Anglo-Saxon England: Essays in
    Cultural Geography* (New Haven: Yale University Press, 2008), p. 86.
    On 'the temptation of nostalgia' see p. 89.
22 James F. Doubleday, 'The Ruin: Structure and theme', *JEGP* 71
    (1972), 369–81, p. 370.
23 See, for instance, Richard Marsden, *The Cambridge Old English Reader*
    (Cambridge: Cambridge University Press, 2004), who writes that, 'the
    city itself has been identified convincingly as Bath in Somerset, the
    Roman city of Aquae Sulis' (p. 322). Andy Orchard provides a sum-
    mary of the scholarship on this poem in 'Reconstructing *The Ruin*', in
    Virginia Blanton and Helene Scheck (eds), *Intertexts: Studies in Anglo-
    Saxon Culture Presented to Paul Szarmach* (Tempe, AZ: ACMRS and
    Brepols, 2008), pp. 45–69, p. 46.
24 Paul Strohm, 'Historicity without historicism?', *Postmedieval: A
    Journal of Medieval Cultural Studies* 1 (2010), 380–91, p. 386.
25 John Frow, 'On midlevel concepts', *New Literary History* 31 (2010),
    237–52, p. 221.
26 Muir (ed.), *Exeter Anthology*, vol. 1, pp. 2–3.
27 Muir (ed.), *Exeter Anthology*, vol. 1, p. 2.
28 On Grundtvig, see further Chapter 3.
29 See R. W. Chambers, Max Förster and Robin Flower, *The Exeter Book
    of Old English Poetry* (London: P. Lund, Humphries & Co., 1933).
30 George P. Krapp and Elliott van Kirk Dobbie, *The Exeter Book*, The
    Anglo-Saxon Poetic Records 3 (New York: Columbia University
    Press, 1936).
31 See Muir (ed.), *Exeter Anthology*, vol. 1, pp. 3–7. For a cultural his-
    tory of the manuscript see Patrick W. Conner, *Anglo-Saxon Exeter: A
    Tenth-Century Cultural History* (Woodbridge: Boydell Press, 1993).
32 For a reading of *The Ruin* that privileges its description of archi-
    tecture see Lori Ann Garner, *Structuring Spaces: Oral Poetics and
    Architecture in Early Medieval England* (Notre Dame, IN: University
    of Notre Dame Press, 2011), pp. 155–62. On the use of Roman archi-
    tecture in Anglo-Saxon England see Tim Eaton, *Plundering the Past*
    (Stroud: Tempus, 2000).
33 On the use of rhyme in Old English poetry see E. G. Stanley, 'Rhymes
    in medieval English verse: From Old English to Middle English', in
    Edward Donald Kennedy, Ronald Waldron and Joseph S. Wittig (eds),

Medieval English Studies Presented to George Kane (Cambridge: D. S. Brewer, 1988), pp. 19–54.

34 Howell Chickering, 'Lyric time in *Beowulf*', *JEGP* 91 (2004), 489–509, p. 493.

35 Alain Renoir, 'The Old English *Ruin*: Contrastive structure and affective impact', in Martin Green (ed.), *The Old English Elegies* (Cranberry, NJ: Associated University Presses, 1983), pp. 148–74, p. 150.

36 Renée R. Trilling makes a similar point in *The Aesthetics of Nostalgia: Historical Representation in Old English Verse* (Toronto: University of Toronto Press, 2009), p. 52.

37 See Jonathan Gil Harris, *Untimely Matter in the Time of Shakespeare* (Philadelphia: University of Pennsylvania Press, 2009). See also Jonathan Gil Harris, 'Four exoskeletons and no funeral', *New Literary History* 42 (2011), 615–39.

38 'Wer', in Joseph Bosworth, *An Anglo-Saxon Dictionary*, ed. Thomas Northcote Toller (Oxford: Clarendon Press, 1972), p. 1205.

39 See *The Toronto Dictionary of Old English, A–H online*, http://tapor. library.utoronto.ca/doe/, accessed 24 October 2017.

40 Bosworth–Toller, *An Anglo-Saxon Dictionary*, p. 86.

41 'The Gifts of Men', lines 39–40, in Muir (ed.), *Exeter Anthology*, vol. 1, p. 221, where it is titled 'God's Gifts to Humankind'.

42 'The Dream of the Rood', in Michael Swanton (ed.), *The Dream of the Rood* (Exeter: University of Exeter Press, 2000), line 42, p. 95.

43 All information on usages is derived from the University of Toronto's Dictionary of Old English Corpus. See *The Toronto Dictionary of Old English Web Corpus*, http://tapor.library.utoronto.ca/doecorpus/, accessed 24 October 2017.

44 See, for example, Michael Hunter, 'Germanic and Roman antiquity and the sense of the past in Anglo-Saxon England', *Anglo-Saxon England* 3 (1974), 29–50, p. 46, and Trilling, *Aesthetics of Nostalgia*, p. 56.

45 In this passage of translation I have maintained the modern editorial structure of the poem in order to represent the impact of the damage done to the manuscript and text.

46 On 'responsiveness' and Old English poetry see Patricia Dailey, 'Riddles, wonder, and responsiveness in Anglo-Saxon literature', in Clare A. Lees (ed.), *The Cambridge History of Early Medieval English Literature* (Cambridge: Cambridge University Press, 2013), pp. 451–72.

47 See Patricia Dailey, 'Questions of dwelling in Anglo-Saxon poetry and medieval mysticism: Inhabiting landscape, body, and mind', *New Medieval Literatures* 8 (2006), 175–214, p. 208, and Trilling, *Aesthetics*, p. 29.

48 Michel Serres with Bruno Latour, *Conversations on Science, Culture, and Time*, trans. Roxanne Lapidus (Ann Arbor: University of Michigan Press, 1995), p. 48.

49 Dylan Trigg, 'The place of trauma: Memory, trauma, and the tempo-
    rality of ruins', *Memory Studies* 2 (2009), 87–101, p. 95.
50 On the image of the ruin and the medieval past see Sarah Beckwith,
    'Preserving, conserving, deserving the past: A meditation on ruin in
    postwar Britain in five fragments', in Clare A. Lees and Gillian R.
    Overing (eds), *A Place to Believe In: Locating Medieval Landscapes*
    (University Park, PA: Penn State University Press, 2006), pp. 191–210.
51 John Leland, 'The laboriouse journey and serche of Johan
    Leylande for Englandes antiquities…', in Lucy Toulmin Smith
    (ed.), *The Itinerary of John Leland, in or about the Years 1535–1543,
    Parts I–III*, vol. 1 (London: George Bell and Sons, 1907), pp. xxxvii–
    xliii, pp. xxxvii–xxxviii.
52 James Simpson, 'The rule of medieval imagination', in Jeremy
    Dimmick, James Simpson and Nicolette Zeeman (eds), *Images,
    Idolatry and Iconoclasm in Late Medieval England* (Oxford: Oxford
    University Press, 2002), pp. 4–24, p. 11. See also James Simpson,
    'Ageism: Leland, Bale and the laborious start of English literary his-
    tory, 1350–1550', *New Medieval Literatures* 1 (1997), 213–35.
53 James Simpson, *Reform and Cultural Revolution, 1350–1547* (Oxford:
    Oxford University Press, 2002), pp. 29–30.
54 Gildas, 'The ruin of Britain', in Michael Winterbottom (ed. and
    trans.), *The Ruin of Britain and Other Works* (London: Phillimore,
    1978), p. 98 (Latin) and p. 28 (translation).
55 See Anne Klinck, *The Old English Elegies* (London: McGill-Queen's
    University Press, 1992), pp. 276–9 for text and translation.
56 'Vita Sancti Cuthberti auctore anonymo', in Bertram Colgrave (ed.
    and trans.), *Two Lives of Saint Cuthbert* (Cambridge: Cambridge
    University Press, 1985), pp. 60–139, Book IV, ch. 8, pp. 122–3.
    See also 'Vita Sancti Cuthberti auctore Beda', *ibid.*, pp. 142–307,
    pp. 242–5.
57 Fred Orton, 'At the Bewcastle Monument, in place', in Lees and Overing
    (eds), *A Place to Believe In*, pp. 29–66, p. 59. See also Mike McCarthy,
    Roman Carlisle and the Lands of the Solway (Stroud: Tempus, 2002).
58 'Vita Sancti Cuthberti auctore Beda', in *Two Lives*, pp. 242–3.
59 'Vita Sancti Cuthberti auctore Beda', in *Two Lives*, pp. 242–5.
60 See 'Eormenburg', in Prosopography of Anglo-Saxon England, www.
    pase.ac.uk, accessed 24 October 2017.
61 Bede, *Ecclesiastical History*, Book I, ch. 26, pp. 76–77 for text and
    translation.
62 Bede, *Ecclesiastical History*, pp. 394–5.
63 On medieval meanings of wonder see Caroline Walker Bynum,
    Metamorphosis and Identity (New York: Zone Books, 2001) and
    Patricia Clare Ingham, '"In contrayez straunge": Colonial relations,
    British identity, and *Sir Gawain and the Green Knight*', *New Medieval
    Literatures* 4 (2001), 61–93, esp. pp. 67–9.

64 Catherine E. Karkov, 'The body of Saint Æthelthryth: Desire, conversion and reform in Anglo-Saxon England', in Martin Carver (ed.), *The Cross Goes North: Processes of Conversion in Northern Europe, AD 300–1300* (Woodbridge: Boydell Press, 2005), pp. 397–411, p. 399.

65 Stuart Hall, 'Cultural identity and diaspora', in Jonathan Rutherford (ed.), *Identity: Community, Culture, Difference* (London: Lawrence and Wishart, 1990), pp. 222–37, p. 225.

66 Alcuin, 'The bishops, saints and kings of York', in Peter Godman (ed. and trans.), *The Bishops, Saints and Kings of York* (Oxford: Clarendon Press, 1982), pp. 4–5, lines 19–20.

67 *The Chronicle of Æthelweard*, ed. and trans. A. Campbell (London: Thomas Nelson and Sons, 1962), pp. 5–6.

68 Hunter, 'Sense of the past in Anglo-Saxon England', pp. 35–36. For one signal of the influence of this essay see David Lowenthal, *The Past is a Foreign Country* (Cambridge: Cambridge University Press, 1985), p. 390.

69 Harris, 'Four exoskeletons', p. 618.

70 On the relationship between Alcuin's poem and the Old English poetic tradition see Christine Fell, 'Perceptions of transience', in Malcolm Godden and Michael Lapidge (eds), *The Cambridge Companion to Old English Literature* (Cambridge: Cambridge University Press, 1991), pp. 172–90.

71 Alcuin, 'De clade Lindisfarnensis monasterii', in E. Duemmler (ed.), *Poetae latini aevi Carolini*, MGH, Poetarum latinorum medii aevi 1 (Berlin: Weidmann, 1881), pp. 229–35, lines 37–8, p. 230.

72 Alcuin, '*On the Sack of the Monastery of Lindisfarne*', trans. Michael J. B. Allen and Daniel G. Calder, in Michael J. B. Allen and Daniel G. Calder (eds), *Sources and Analogues of Old English Poetry: The Major Latin Texts in Translation* (Totowa, NJ: Rowman and Littlefield; Cambridge: D. S. Brewer, 1976), pp. 141–6.

73 'The Wanderer', in Muir (ed.), *Exeter Anthology*, vol. 1, pp. 215–19, lines 73–80a, p. 217.

74 R. M. Liuzza, 'The Tower of Babel: *The Wanderer* and the ruins of history', *Studies in the Literary Imagination* 36 (2003), 1–35, p. 14. See also Kathleen Davis, 'Old English lyrics: A poetics of experience', in Lees (ed.), *Cambridge History of Early Medieval English Literature*, pp. 332–56.

75 See Kathryn Hume, 'The ruin motif in Old English poetry', *Anglia* 94 (1976), 339–60. Kathleen Davis similarly states that there is 'no single "medieval" category of time and history' in *Periodization and Sovereignty: How Ideas of Feudalism and Secularization Govern the Politics of Time* (Philadelphia: University of Pennsylvania Press, 2008), p. 104.

76 Wulfstan, 'Sermo Lupi ad Anglos', in Dorothy Whitelock (ed.), *Sermo Lupi ad Anglos* (Exeter: University of Exeter, 1976), pp. 65–6.

77 William of Malmesbury, *Gesta pontificum anglorum: The History of the English Bishops*, vol. 1: *Text and Translation*, ed. and trans. Michael Winterbottom, with the assistance of R. M. Thomson (Oxford: Clarendon Press, 2007), pp. 324–5.

78 William of Malmesbury, pp. 325–6. See further William Kynan-Wilson, 'Mira Romanorum artifitia: William of Malmesbury and the Romano-British remains at Carlisle', *Essays in Medieval Studies* 28 (2012), 35–49.

79 See Rose Macaulay, *Pleasure of Ruins* (London: Thames and Hudson, 1953), pp. 1–39.

80 Julia Hell and Andreas Schönle, 'Introduction', in Julia Hell and Andreas Schönle (eds), *The Ruins of Modernity* (Durham, NC: Duke University Press, 2010), pp. 1–14, p. 5.

81 Brian Dillon, *Ruin Lust: Artists' Fascination with Ruins from Turner to the Present Day* (London: Tate, 2014), p. 5. On the exhibition see www.tate.org.uk/whats-on/tate-britain/exhibition/ruin-lust, accessed 24 October 2017. Dillon's claim is all the more remarkable given the fact that the publicity material for the exhibition featured an extract from Michael Alexander's translation of the Old English *Ruin*. On Alexander's *Ruin* see below.

82 On Conybeare's work see Richard C. Payne, 'The rediscovery of Old English poetry in the English literary tradition', in Carl T. Berkhout and Milton McCormick Gatch (eds), *Anglo-Saxon Scholarship: The First Three Centuries* (Boston, MA: G. K. Hall and Co., 1982), pp. 149–66 and Haruko Momma, *From Philology to English Studies: Language and Culture in the Nineteenth Century* (Cambridge: Cambridge University Press, 2013), pp. 84–90.

83 Conybeare, *Illustrations*, p. 171.

84 Conybeare, *Illustrations*, p. 214.

85 Conybeare, *Illustrations*, pp. 249–50.

86 Conybeare, *Illustrations*, p. 250.

87 Conybeare, *Illustrations*, p. 252.

88 See María José Mora, 'The invention of the Old English elegy', *English Studies* 76 (1995), 129–39, p. 134. As Mora points out, Thorpe's *Codex Exoniensis* contains the same errors.

89 Conybeare, *Illustrations*, p. 250.

90 Roy Liuzza, 'Lost in translation: Some nineteenth-century versions of *Beowulf*', *English Studies* 83 (2002), 281–96, p. 286. On the early editing of the poem see Thornbury, 'Admiring the ruined text'. On the disciplinary history of Anglo-Saxon studies see Eric Stanley, *The Search for Anglo-Saxon Paganism* (Cambridge: D. S. Brewer, 1975) and Frantzen, *Desire for Origins*.

91 Lord Byron, 'The siege of Corinth', lines 920–24, in Susan J. Wolfson and Peter J. Manning (eds), *Selected Poems* (Harmondsworth: Penguin, 1996), pp. 359–90, p. 387.

92 Lawrence Venuti, 'Translation as cultural politics: Regimes of domestication in English', *Textual Practice* 7 (1993), 208–23, p. 209.

93 Thorpe, *Codex Exoniensis*, p. xi.

94 Thorpe, *Codex Exoniensis*, p. 476.

95 See Conybeare, *Illustrations*, p. 6 and pp. 22–7.

96 Gayatri Chakravorty Spivak, *Outside in the Teaching Machine* (New York: Routledge, 2009), pp. 201–2.

97 Aranye Fradenburg, 'Living Chaucer', *Studies in the Age of Chaucer* 33 (2011), 41–64, p. 44.

98 Fradenburg, 'Living Chaucer', p. 45.

99 Henry Wadsworth Longfellow, *The Poets and Poetry of Europe with Introductions and Biographical Notes* (Philadelphia: Porter and Coates, 1871), p. 29. The full text of 'The Ruined Wall-stone' is reproduced, but without the italics that distinguish William Conybeare's contributions.

100 Pound's 'Seafarer' was first published in *The New Age* 10 (1911), 107. I have taken the text of the poem from *The Norton Anthology of English Literature*, 5th edn, ed. Margaret Ferguson, Mary Jo Salter and Jon Stallworthy (New York: Norton, 2005), pp. 12–15. On Pound's translation see Chris Jones, *Strange Likeness: The Use of Old English in Twentieth-Century Poetry* (Oxford: Oxford University Press, 2006), 17–67 and Fred C. Robinson, '"The Might of the north": Pound's Anglo-Saxon studies and *The Seafarer*' and 'Ezra Pound and the Old English translation tradition', in *The Tomb of Beowulf and Other Essays*, pp. 259–74 and pp. 275–303.

101 Text from *The Seafarer* taken from Muir (ed.), *Exeter Anthology*, vol. 1, pp. 229–33.

102 See Jones, *Strange Likeness*, pp. 29–30.

103 Homi Bhabba, *The Location of Culture*, 2nd edn (London: Routledge, 1994), p. 313.

104 'The Ruin', lines 1–10, in Edwin Morgan, *Collected Poems, 1949–1987* (Manchester: Carcanet, 1990), p. 31. See Jones, *Strange Likeness*, pp. 122–81. Morgan's *Ruin*, along with translations of *The Wanderer*, *The Seafarer*, four Old English riddles and the Middle English poem *The Grave*, was composed for his collection *Dies Irae*, which was prepared for publication in 1952. Due to financial problems at the intended publishers, however, the collection did not appear in print until three decades later. See Hamish Whyte, 'Edwin Morgan: A checklist', in Robert Crawford and Hamish Whyte (eds), *About Edwin Morgan* (Edinburgh: Edinburgh University Press, 1990), pp. 140–256, p. 143. On the importance of Old English to Morgan see Chris Jones, 'While crowding memories came: Edwin Morgan, Old English and nostalgia', *Scottish Literary Review* 4 (2012), 123–44.

105 For Morgan's thoughts on translation see his 'Introduction', in Edwin Morgan, *Beowulf: A Verse Translation into Modern English* (Manchester: Carcanet, 2002), p. xiii.

106 Kathleen Raine, 'Foreword', in Peter Russell, *Visions and Ruins* (Aylesford, Kent: St Albert's Press, 1964), p. 5. *Visions and Ruins* is not the only work that demonstrates Russell's interest in the OE *Ruin*. The 1951 poem 'The Ruin' follows a similar theme to the OE text, although its relationship to *The Ruin* is more obscure. 'The Ruin' is published in Peter Russell, *All for the Wolves: Selected Poems 1947– 1975*, ed. Peter Jay (London: Anvil Press 1984), pp. 22–3. See also Stephen Wade, 'Touchstone and his dilemma: The poetry of Peter Russell', in James Hogg (ed.), *Vitalism and Celebration: Anthony Johnson, William Oxley, Peter Russell: Three European Poets* (Salzburg: Institut für Anglistik und Amerikanistik, Universität Salzburg, 1987), pp. 177–85. There are also oblique references to the OE poem *Deor* ('That passed away so may this') on p. 17 of *Visions and Ruins*. Further references to *Visions and Ruins* are given in the text by page number.

107 For the early arguments see Heinrich Leo, *Carmen anglosaxonicum in codice Exoniensi servatum quod vulgo inscribitur 'Ruinae'* (Halle, 1865), p. 5 and John Earle, 'An ancient Saxon poem of a city in ruins supposed to be Bath', *Proceedings of the Bath Natural History and Antiquarian Field Club* 2 (1870–73), 259–70. See also Cecilia Hotchner, *Wessex and Old English Poetry, with Special Consideration to The Ruin* (New York: Lancaster Press, 1939), pp. 1–8 and R. F. Leslie (ed.), *Three Old English Elegies* (Manchester: Manchester University Press, 1962), pp. 22–8. Other sites have been suggested. William Conybeare suggested that *The Ruin* 'probably relates to the same destruction' as the 'Fight at Finnsburgh', *Illustrations*, p. 174. For Hadrian's Wall see Stephen J. Herben, '*The Ruin*', *Modern Language Notes* 54 (1939), 37–9; for Chester see Gareth W. Dunleavy, 'A "De excidio" tradition in the Old English *Ruin*?', *Philological Quarterly* 38 (1959), 112–18; for Caerleon-on-Usk see Karl P. Wentersdorf, 'Observations on *The Ruin*', *Medium Ævum* 46 (1977), 171–80; in support of Babylon see Hugh T. Keenan, '*The Ruin* as Babylon', *Tennessee Studies in Literature* 2 (1966), 109–17. See also Anne Thompson Lee, '*The Ruin*: Bath or Babylon? A non-archaeological investigation', *NM* 74 (1973), 443–55. Andy Orchard provides a summary of the scholarship on this poem in 'Reconstructing *The Ruin*', p. 46.

108 Michael Alexander, 'Old English poetry into modern English verse', *Translation and Literature* 3 (1994), 69–75, p. 70.

109 Michael Alexander, 'The Ruin', lines 1–7, in *The Earliest English Poems* (Harmondsworth: Penguin, 1966), pp. 30–1, p. 30.

110 Venuti, 'Translation as cultural politics', p. 210.

111 See Thorpe, *Codex Exoniensis*, p. 476 for 'fates'. Kevin Crossley-Holland offers 'fate' in *The Anglo-Saxon World* (Oxford: Oxford University Press, 1982), p. 59, as does Burton Raffel in Burton Raffel and Alexandra H. Olsen (eds), *Poems and Prose from the Old English* (London: Yale University Press, 1998), p. 19; Richard Hamer, *A Choice of Anglo-Saxon Verse* (London: Faber, 1970), p. 27; and Yusef Komunyakaa in Greg Delanty and Michael Matto (eds), *The Word Exchange* (London: Norton, 2011), p. 299.

112 'weird, n.', *OED Online*, www.oed.com/view/Entry/226915?rskey=H22LfZ&result=1&isAdvanced=false, accessed 24 October 2017. See William Morris and A. J. Wyatt, *The Tale of Beowulf* (Hammersmith: Kelmscott Press, 1895), pp. 16–17.

113 See Chris Jones, 'The reception of William Morris' *Beowulf*', in David Latham (ed.), *Writing the Image: Reading William Morris* (London: University of Toronto Press, 2007), pp. 197–208.

114 Harold W. Massingham, 'The Ruin (after the Anglo-Saxon)', *Times Literary Supplement* 2264 (18 August 1966), p. 745.

115 Isabel Martin, *Reading Peter Reading* (Newcastle: Bloodaxe Books, 2000), p. 297.

116 Along with translations from Ovid's *Metamorphoses* and Homer's *Odyssey*, *Last Poems* included 'versions' (as the Foreword puts it), of the Old English poems *The Ruin*, *The Wife's Lament*, *The Fates of Men* and a short passage from *Beowulf*. See Rebecca Anne Barr, 'Resurrecting Saxon things: Peter Reading, "species decline", and Old English poetry', in David Clark and Nicholas Perkins (eds), *Anglo-Saxon and the Modern Imagination* (Cambridge: D. S. Brewer, 2010), pp. 255–78.

117 Despite this, *Last Poems* was not Reading's final work. He published a further twelve collections before his death.

118 Peter Reading, 'Fragmentary', *Last Poems* (London: Chatto & Windus, 1994), p. 35.

119 Derrida, *Memoirs of the Blind*, p. 68.

120 Mladen Dolar, *A Voice and Nothing More* (Cambridge, MA: MIT Press, 2006), p. 103.

121 Chris Jones, 'The Ruin (after the Anglo-Saxon)', *The Reader* 28 (2007), 46–7.

122 See http://bathtimesegedunum.wordpress.com/, accessed 24 October 2017.

123 Jacob Polley, 'The Ruin', in *The Havocs* (London: Picador, 2012), pp. 14–15, p. 14.

124 Polley, 'The Ruin', p. 15.

125 Yusef Komunyakaa, 'The Ruin', in Delanty and Matto (eds), *The Word Exchange*, p. 301.

126 *Requiem for Detroit?* Dir. Julien Temple (Films of Record, 2010), https://learningonscreen.ac.uk/ondemand/index.php/prog/ 014C1EA7, accessed 19 May 2017.

127 Echard's translation is archived online at http://faculty.arts.ubc.ca/ sechard/oeruin.htm, see also http://library-keeper.livejournal.com/ 9462.html, accessed 24 October 2017.

128 Christopher Woodward, *In Ruins* (London: Chatto & Windus, 2001), p. 2.

2

Queen Eleanor and her crosses: Trauma and memory, medieval and modern

Although he was one of the twentieth century's most celebrated ruinologists, Sigmund Freud gave medieval culture little attention in his writing. In the first of his 'Five lectures on psychoanalysis', however, Freud used a famous medieval monument to formulate his reflections on the dynamics of personal and collective identity:

> I should like to formulate what we have learned so far as follows: *our hysterical patients suffer from reminiscences.* Their symptoms are residues and mnemic symbols of particular (traumatic) experiences. We may perhaps obtain a deeper understanding of this kind of symbolism if we compare them with other mnemic symbols in other fields. The monuments and memorials with which large cities are adorned are also mnemic symbols. If you take a walk through the streets of London, you will find, in front of one of the great railway termini, a richly carved Gothic column – Charing Cross. One of the old Plantagenet kings of the thirteenth century ordered the body of his beloved Queen Eleanor to be carried to Westminster; and at every stage at which the coffin rested he erected a Gothic cross. Charing Cross is the last of the monuments that commemorate the funeral cortège. At another point in the same town, you will find a towering, and more modern, column which is simply known as 'The Monument'. It was designed as a memorial of the Great Fire, which broke out in that neighbourhood in 1666 and destroyed a large part of the city. These monuments, then, resemble hysterical symptoms in being mnemic symbols; up to that point the comparison seems justifiable. But what should we think of a Londoner who paused to-day in deep melancholy before the memorial of Queen Eleanor's funeral instead of going about his business …? Or again what should we think of a Londoner who shed tears before the Monument that commemorates the reduction of his beloved metropolis to ashes …? Every single hysteric and neurotic behaves like these two unpractical Londoners. Not only do they remember painful experiences of the remote past, but they still cling to them emotionally; they

cannot get free of the past and for its sake they neglect what is real and immediate.[1]

For Freud the memorials are simply a means of explaining the problems of his 'unpractical Londoners', but his description of the constructions is nevertheless very revealing. Charing Cross is 'a richly carved Gothic column', erected by 'One of the old Plantagenet kings of the thirteenth century'; the Monument is 'a towering, and more modern, column', erected as 'a memorial of the Great Fire'. While his description of Charing Cross is vague, Freud dates the Monument precisely and claims it to be 'more modern'. This is interesting as the monumental stone memorial that stands in the courtyard of Charing Cross Station was designed and built, just under 200 years after Christopher Wren and Robert Hooke designed and built the Monument, by E. M. Barry in 1865 (see Figure 2.1). Although it is a restoration of a cross commissioned by Edward I in the 1290s to commemorate his wife Eleanor of Castile, Freud mistakes the copy for the original.

As Freud insisted, mistakes are never without meaning.[2] What, then, does this mistake signify? Most straightforwardly, it betrays a lack of interest in the medieval past. The Cross was built by one or other of the Plantagenet kings (it matters little which) and its gothic design may be richly decorated but is decidedly less modern (and therefore less important) than the Monument's Roman Doric column. To use Margreta de Grazia's language, Freud's mistake reveals 'the exceptional force of that secular divide' between medieval and modern that 'determines nothing less than relevance'.[3] It reveals Freud's faith in this divide but also indicates the frequent difficulty of identifying the medieval. For medieval culture has been so variously reused, reappropriated and reimagined – in the architecture of the Gothic Revival, in visual and dramatic art, literature and cinema – that it can be very difficult to distinguish the real from the fake.[4] The connections between the medieval and the modern are so diverse, complex and numerous that the intermingling of the periods is inevitable, even as one is used to define the other.

A footnote added by Freud to the published text of the 'First lecture' corrects his misidentification of the cross but adds another: the present cross, Freud writes, 'is a modern copy of one of these monuments. As Dr Ernest Jones tells me, the name "Charing" is believed to be derived from the words "chère reine".'[5] Unlike Freud's misreading of Barry's cross for the original, Jones'

2.1 Charing Cross by E. M. Barry (1865)

error has a long history.[6] The place name in fact derives from the Old English noun 'cier' (turn) and refers to the bend in the Thames which occurs near the site.[7] Again, the mistake reveals cultural hierarchies. The folk etymology removes Anglo-Saxon and Old English from the historical record in favour of a sentimental image of royal love. The resilience of this onomastic error discloses a lack of interest in and knowledge of early medieval culture and history and a preference for romance, but it also voices an assumption that the past might be defined on the terms of the present, that the difference of the past might be easily resolved.

Freud's errors mark out the territory I will investigate in this chapter: the histories and legacies of the Eleanor Crosses. Famously, their origins apparently begin with the trauma of an early death and the grief of Edward I but, as I will explore, the crosses were deeply political and more committed to reimagining than remembering the past. They fashioned an idealised image of Eleanor that stands distinct from the historical record but defined cultural memories of her. Over time, however, what were once memorials to an individual woman came to signify a more general sense of loss, melancholy and nostalgia that spoke to particular times, places and experiences. Barry's Charing Cross is one of a number of nineteenth- and twentieth-century monuments that self-consciously repeated and reflected the medieval precedents of the Eleanor Crosses to create an idealised image of the medieval past, but which also worked through traumatic contemporary events and attempted to fashion visions of the future from the materials of the past.

In 'Remembering, repeating and working-through', a short text written in 1914, Freud suggests that repetition can sometimes be read as a substitute for understanding. He writes of a patient who 'does not *remember* anything of what he has forgotten and repressed, but *acts* it out. He reproduces it not as a memory but as an action; he *repeats* it, without, of course, knowing that he is repeating it.'[8] The traumatic event remains too close, too real, to be understood as history – it is of the past, but it remains present – and historical distance is key to being able to remember rather than repeat. Freud's work reveals the experience of time to be deeply subjective and decidedly non-linear – some pasts remain present. In his insightful reading, Adam Phillips suggests that 'one might see Freud's work as one site in which the constructing of historical distance – at the level of the individual – is being studied'.[9] While the reception history of *The Ruin* discussed in the previous chapter reveals individual negotiations with the languages and images of the past, the Eleanor Crosses and their nineteenth-century legacies reveal sites of the construction of historical distance at the level of the collective. Like Freud's conception of traumatic memory, both offer a nonlinear and discontinuous model of history. In their thirteenth-century context, one of the stories the Eleanor Crosses tell is of the proximity between a queen and her subjects, but at other moments other stories emerge. The postmedieval reiterations of the crosses tell part of the story of how the distance and proximity between modernity and the medieval has been constructed, maintained and visualised, but also speak to and of individual and collective ideals, losses and desires in precise local contexts. Why was this history charged at some moments and latent at others? What do the crosses reveal about the interaction of time, history and memory in the production of personal and collective identities? How did the meanings of the crosses alter according to historical context and what ideas of time and history do they participate in and generate? Unlike Freud, I will not draw a distinction between remembering and repeating, or between repetition and understanding, the reconstructions of medievalism and the work of medieval studies. Instead this chapter explores how and why people have turned to the Eleanor Crosses and traces some of the critical and cultural constellations that have formed around the crosses, how the crosses and their respondents have formed relations among specific times, events and people and imagined the past to be 'real and immediate'.

Eleanor as queen

The Eleanor Crosses project was as interested in forgetting as remembering. When Eleanor died in the winter of 1290, the chronicler of Dunstable Abbey recorded a pithy memorial: 'Hyspana genere', he wrote, 'quæ plura et optima maneria adquisivit' (A Spaniard by birth, she acquired many fine estates).[10] Following this brief obituary, he recorded that the queen's body stayed in the abbey for a night on its journey back to London and that Edward I later erected a cross in the marketplace to record his wife's final journey. The Dunstable cross was one of twelve erected to commemorate the queen. Eleanor died in Harby near Lincoln in November 1290 and the route of the journey by which her body returned to London took in stops at twelve sites of political, royal or religious significance (see Figure 2.2).[11] In the years following Eleanor's death, crosses were erected at public sites near each of these places – at junctions, squares and highways. Three crosses remain standing, in various states of disrepair, at Northampton, Geddington and Waltham. The final two stages of her funeral procession were marked by crosses on Cheapside and at what was then the village of Charing.

John Carmi Parsons describes the events and monuments that marked Eleanor's death as 'the first instance of an English royal funeral deliberately exploited to enhance monarchy'.[12] Edward executed an unprecedented project in the construction of cultural memory which, although often later read as a lesson in love

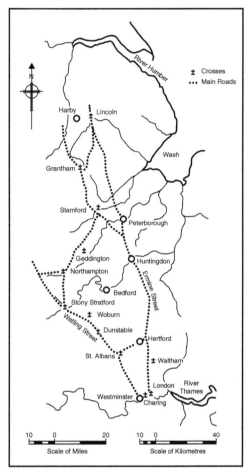

2.2 Route of Eleanor of Castile's funeral procession and the location of the Eleanor Crosses

and loss, was deeply political in purpose. As the brief note in the Dunstable Annals suggests, Eleanor's reputation was knottier than her memorials acknowledge. The crosses created an image of the queen that privileged the spiritual over the temporal and the institutional over the personal. Their design concealed and revealed in equal measure.

Louise O. Fradenburg reminds us that, 'the condition of many forms of queenship may be found not so much in the glamorised, special, suspended states associated with communitas as in the fact

of queens' being so often at the nodal points of cultural work, of
their working to enable the crossing-over of difference into iden-
tity, the unfamiliar into the familiar'.[13] The histories of the Eleanor
Crosses reveal a number of crossing-overs, from life to death,
from memory to history, and from medieval to modern, which rely
on the 'glamorised, special, suspended' states of Eleanor and the
Eleanor Crosses to negotiate the movement from, and the return
to, the unfamiliar and the familiar. In her life as Queen, moreover,
Eleanor had to negotiate the prosaic but politically sensitive differ-
ences – of culture and language most immediately – that existed
between her and her subjects.

When Henry III died on 16 November 1272, Edward and Eleanor
were in southern Italy, returning from crusade in Acre. Following
their arrival in England, they were crowned at Westminster on 19
August 1274. As Queen, Eleanor did not directly influence gov-
ernment policy but did embark on a programme of land acqui-
sition that, although condoned and supported by Edward, made
her deeply unpopular with the landed classes of England. This
project, which began shortly after her marriage, escalated in
urgency and ambition once she was crowned. As Parsons notes in
his magisterial study of Eleanor's life, 'the traditional sources of
an English Queen-consort's income were manifestly inadequate'
at this time, so her accumulation of land should not be seen solely
as a symptom of her acquisitiveness.[14] Eleanor's life at court was
privileged but precarious. Although her position was directly
related to the king, she conducted many of her affairs indepen-
dently. Similarly, while Edward's political dealings were largely
independent of Eleanor, they occasionally related directly to her
interests or reputation.

One of the most significant statutes of Edward's early reign, and
certainly the statute which had the greatest effect on Eleanor's life
and reputation, was the 1275 Statute of the Jewry. Since William
the Conqueror had encouraged Jews to settle in England in the
years following the Conquest, small communities had lived in
various towns and cities and Jews played an important role in the
economy of the country, facilitating the loans upon which busi-
ness relied. Jews were direct subjects of the King and enjoyed
his protection and support in the collection of their debts. In law
they were defined as the property of the crown and subsequently
could be taxed at will. As David Carpenter writes, 'Religion and
usury made the Jews deeply unpopular, but until their wealth was
destroyed in the second half of the thirteenth century they were a

vital lubricant to the economy and adjunct to the money supply.'[15] Jewish wealth was decimated by aggressive taxation between 1240 and 1260, and the 1275 statute further undermined their way of life, not only placing tight restrictions on the conduct, dress and occupation of Jews in England, but outlawing the practice of usury altogether.

Paul Brand describes the 1275 statute as 'the most wide-ranging, the most detailed and the most radical of all the legislation of the thirteenth century concerned with the Jewish community'.[16] This assault on the Jews, which was confirmed by their expulsion from England in 1290, shortly before Eleanor's death, only made political sense for Edward because their wealth had been so systematically savaged. Carpenter reports that while Jewish taxation raised just under £73,333 for the crown between 1241 and 1256, it raised only £9,300 between 1272 and 1290.[17] The statute did make provision for Jews to enter other professions, but the primary purpose of the legislation was to outlaw usury to satisfy the anti-Semitism of the English elite.

As Marc Morris writes, the expulsion 'cut the Gordian knot of England's Jewish problem'.[18] The intricacy of the problem is most clearly demonstrated by the close ties that existed between the royal family and members of the Jewish community. Amid the virulent anti-Semitism of the thirteenth century, Edward and Eleanor did have personal relationships with Jews. In May 1281, for instance, Eleanor petitioned for Cok Hagin, also known as Hagin son of (Deule) Cresse, to be appointed presbyter of the Jews. Hagin was one of a number of Jews who worked for Eleanor as financial agents. Even after the 1275 statute, Eleanor's finances were often bolstered through the acquisition of Jewish debts. But there is no evidence this familiarity informed her broader feelings towards Jews, which remained within the scope of contemporary anti-Semitism.[19] There was, however, a widespread perception that Eleanor relied too much on Jewish financiers and, even though Parsons' catalogue of Eleanor's lands reveals that most of her acquisitions did not involve Jews, her dealings with Jews threatened political trouble.[20]

In two letters, sent in 1283 and 1286, the Archbishop of Canterbury, John Pecham, warned Eleanor and her advisers that her behaviour was causing scandal. In the first letter, sent to the Queen herself, Pecham warned her that 'quant vus recevez terre ou manoir, encuru par usure de Juis, pernez vus garde ke usure est peche mortel a ceus qui funt la usure, e ceus qui les meintenent, e ceus qui part en unt' (when you receive land or manor acquired by usury of Jews, take heed that usury is a mortal sin to those who take the usury and support it, and those who have a share in it) and suggested she should make amends to those whose lands she had acquired through her dealings with Jews.[21] The second letter, sent to Geoffrey de Aspale, keeper of Eleanor's wardrobe, reported:

> Per regnum Angliæ clamor validus invalescit et scandalum inde plurimum generatur, super eo quod dicitur dominam reginam Angliæ illustrem, cui assistitis, plura maneria nobilium, terras et possessiones alias occupare, et in suum peculiam reduxisse, quæ Judæi a Christicolis extorserunt; et adhuc de die in diem dicitur prædicta domina nancisci prædia et possessiones alias per hunc modum; quibusdam etiam clericis de sorte Diaboli et non Christi, sibi, ut dicitur quod non credimus, ministrantibus in hac parte; et de hoc est in omni latere Angliæ publica vox et fama. Quia igitur lucrum tale est illicitum et damnatum, vos rogamus et vobis sicut clerico nostro firmiter et districte præcipiendo mandamus, quatenus cum opportunitatem videritis, velitis ex parte nostra prædicte dominæ nostræ humiliter supplicare, ut a prædictis suos jubeat penitus abstinere, et ablata restituat in hac forma, vel saltem satisfaciat Christicolis, usuraria nequitia spoliatis.[22]

> (A rumour is waxing strong through the kingdom of England, and much scandal is thereby generated, because it is said that the illustrious lady queen of England, whom you serve, is occupying many manors, lands and other possessions of nobles, and has made them her own property, lands which the Jews extorted with usury from Christians under the protection of the royal court. It is said that day by day the said lady continues to acquire plunder and the possessions of others by this means, with the assistance (though we ourselves do not believe it) of certain clerks who are of the tribes of the devil and not of Christ. There is public outcry and gossip about this in every part of England. Wherefore, as gain of this sort is illicit and damnable, we beg you, and firmly command and enjoin you as our clerk, that when you see an opportunity you will be pleased humbly to beseech the said lady on our behalf, that she bid her people entirely to abstain from the aforesaid practices, and restore what has been seized in this way, or at any rate make satisfaction to those Christians who have been wickedly robbed by usury.)

Pecham's direct language provides a vivid sense of the religious and political elite's perception of Eleanor's business dealings. There was of course resentment at the King's conduct, too, and Walter of Guisborough's chronicle, written in the first quarter of the fourteenth century, records a doggerel that aligned the queen's

greed with the king's and expresses the bitterness of some of their
subjects: 'Le roy cuuayte nos deneres, / e la rayne nos beau man-
ers' (The king would like to get our gold, / The queen, our manors
fair to hold).[23] But it is likely that the perceived murkiness of the
Queen's dealings was deepened by the very fact of Eleanor's own
foreignness. Her association with these other aliens surely qualified
and confirmed her status as an outsider within the English court.[24]

Eleanor's problematic reputation was also formed by the vig-
our with which her administrators pursued her business interests
and the key role she played in the governance of her estates. That
Eleanor took responsibility for the management of her interests
and the behaviour of her officials is demonstrated by the request
reportedly made on her deathbed that an inquest be set up to set-
tle any wrongs committed in her name. The inquest, held between
1291 and 1292, certainly did uncover questionable methods and
dubious deeds. Payments of compensation, made to those swin-
dled or badly treated by Eleanor and her employees, are recorded
in the royal accounts at the same time as the crosses were being
commissioned, designed and built.[25] Eleanor's suggestion of an
inquest suggests not only that she was aware of the conduct of her
employees, but can also be taken as an acknowledgement of her
unpopularity among the landed classes and as evidence that she
understood that this had become a political issue.

The Queen's crosses

Eleanor lived a life more complex than her memorials allowed.
As the three surviving crosses demonstrate, their design reduced
Eleanor to ritual (see Figures 2.3, 2.4, 2.5). While there are signif-
icant differences between each surviving work, their similarities
suggest they were executed according to an overarching scheme.
Within a tripartite structure, the lower sections of each surviving
monument are dominated by the arms of Castile, England, Leon
and Ponthieu. Multiple statues of Eleanor rise above the arms in
niches decorated with foliage, located between the arms below
and the architectural detailing and crosses above, meaning that
the queen is framed by images of sacred and secular authority.
In the statues, Eleanor's head is bowed and crowned, her hair
hangs loose and she holds a sceptre in her right hand. These stat-
ues draw on Marian imagery to present Eleanor as submissive
and graceful and share their visual language with the Queen's

2.3 Geddington Cross

tombs at Lincoln and Westminster.[26] Eleanor's power and identity in these representations is contingent on her ancestry and the performance history of the rituals embedded in the images. In their representation of the rituals of queenship, the crosses insist on the copresence of the two key moments in Eleanor's life: her crowning as queen and her death as consort. Perhaps counterintuitively, the multiple reiterations of the Queen's body and the focus on her familial ties produce a powerful sense that Eleanor was a unique individual.

This image of Eleanor pieced together from the rituals of state and church removes her life from the complexities of the temporal world. The personal is sublimated by the political, the image overshadows the reality. Paul Binski describes the crosses as 'like spiritualized versions of the geometry of fortress towers at Edward I's Caernarvon Castle, and in a way their role is no less authoritarian'. He goes on to suggest that:

> The strategy is twofold: the queen's gaze is rendered universal and panoptical, as a sign of her power and her territory; and her image is inescapable to the faculties of sight and memory of the onlookers,

2.4   Northampton Cross

but protected and elevated by height. The Eleanor Crosses are the finest symbols of the role of the procession, which was central to the funeral ritual, in establishing ideas of power (because of their elaborate display) and surveillance (images should be seen as active).[27]

To use Emmanuel Levinas' language, the crosses are 'the facade' which keeps Eleanor 'enclosed in its monumental essence and in its myth', in which she gleams like a splendour but does not deliver herself. The crosses captivate by their 'grace as by magic', but Eleanor herself is not revealed.[28]

The power the crosses exerted over cultural memory is demonstrated by the record of Eleanor's life made by a historian writing in 1308 at St Albans. Surely influenced by the Queen's lavish

2.5 Waltham Cross

monuments, he praised Eleanor as an ideal queen and suggested that she could be seen as a 'columna' (pillar) of the kingdom:

Anno ab Incarnatione Domini, millesimo ducentesimo nonagesimo, qui est annus regni Regis Edwardi Tertii decimus-nonus, Domina Alienora Secunda, Regina Angliæ, migravit de hoc sæculo, in villa de Herdebi, juxta Lincolnian; cujus animæ propitietur Deus. Quoniam de optimis moribus ejus pauca quædam lamentando descripsi, ob mortis ejus dolorem, et cordis mei amaritudinem, dignum enim duxi genealogian ejus breviter veraciterque subtexere; ut cum

diligens indagator progenitorum suorum probitates rimatur, qua-
lis in eis virtus enituerit, qualis pietas splenduerit, agnoscat quam
naturale sit abundare divitiis, florere virtutibus, victoriis illustrari,
et, quod hiis omnibus præstat, Christiana religione et justitiæ præ-
rogativa fulgere. Est enim ad optimos mores obtinendos maximum
incentivum, scire se ab optimis quibusque nobilitatem sanguinis
meruisse; cum ingenuum animum semper pudeat ingloriosa prog-
enie degenerem inveniri; et contra rerum sit naturam, de bona
radice fructus malos pullulare. Licet igitur regnum non amittens
sed mutans, temporale deserens et adipiscens æternum, tamen ejus
transmigrationem nonnulli lacrymabiliter pianxerunt. Erat enim
quasi columna totius Angliæ, sexu quidem fœmina, sed animo atque
virtute plus viro; quum temporibus suis Angliam alienigenæ min-
ime gravabant.[29]

(In the year of Our Lord's incarnation 1290, which is the nineteenth
year of King Edward's reign, the Lady Eleanor the younger, queen
of England, left this world at the vill of Harby, near Lincoln; whose
soul God keep. Seeing that I have said a little of her excellent quali-
ties, on account of grief at her death and the sorrow of my heart,
I have thought it fitting to add her genealogy briefly and truthfully,
so that when a diligent investigator shall examine the uprightness of
her forefathers, how virtue shone forth and how piety was resplend-
ent in them, he may recognise how natural it may be to abound in
riches, to blossom with virtues, to be made famous by victories, and
what is more than all these, to shine in the Christian faith and the
prerogative of justice. For to know oneself to come from the best
of those whose nobility of blood accords with merit, is the greatest
incentive to preserve the best qualities. It ever shames a noble spirit
to be found degenerate in its posterity, and it is against the nature
of things that bad fruit should sprout from a good root. Howbeit
she did not lose a kingdom but changed it, abandoning the temporal
and attaining the eternal, her passing was tearfully mourned by not
a few. For she was a pillar of all England, by sex a woman but in
spirit and virtue more like a man. In her days, foreigners troubled
England but little. As the dawn scatters the shadows of the waning
night with its rays of light, so by the promotion of this most holy
woman and queen, throughout England the night of faithlessness
was expelled.)

As this passage demonstrates, the complications of Eleanor's life
were lost and replaced by an idealised vision of femininity and
queenship: the memories fabricated by the crosses superseded
the historical reality. The crosses were and are untimely: they are

embedded in historical process, but at the same time stand outside those processes, initiating rather than reflecting ways of understanding her life, creative rather than representative.

The cross in medieval culture: tradition and performance

In his astounding construction programme, Edward was simultaneously working in and breaking with a deep tradition. The landscape of thirteenth-century England was marked by wayside and market crosses and still bore the traces of Anglo-Saxon devotion to the cross in the form of imposing stone sculptures such as those at Bewcastle, Hexham, Ruthwell and Sandbach. As Elizabeth Hallam details, these works stood alongside later constructions such as the stone cross near the Strand in London which was said to have been erected by William II to commemorate his mother Queen Matilda (d. 1083) and a cross built by Henry III in Merton, Surrey, in memory of his cousin William of Warenne (d. 1240). By the mid-1290s, Edward I had erected a cross in Reading for his sister Beatrice and another near Windsor which commemorated his mother, Eleanor of Provence.[30] But nothing on the scale of the construction programme of the Eleanor Crosses had been executed before.

In Christian cultures the cross is a symbol that connects people, communities and temporal moments. It is a multivalent sign that speaks of submission and victory, death and life, self and other, stillness and movement, trauma and redemption. Perhaps the most celebrated English meditation on the 'life' of the cross is the Old English poem known as *The Dream of the Rood* in which the cross is imagined to speak for itself and recounts the tortuous process by which Christ was raised upon it. The obscure relationship between the *Dream* and the Ruthwell Cross, which shares some language with the *Dream* among its inscriptions, provides an indication of the rich traditions of thought and ritual which revolved around the cross in early medieval culture.[31] Catherine Karkov writes of the Ruthwell Cross that, 'spoken words always suggest a body and a self that are present' and these texts and objects turn (physical or textual) wood and stone into living beings which engage their audience through oral performance.[32] As Karkov suggests, these texts are invitations to participate in the narratives of the crucifixion and its commemoration, narratives which speak of the past but unfold in the present.[33]

There is a rich interplay of self and other, subject and object, past and present, history and memory, threaded through these representations that can also be detected in other early and late medieval representations of the cross. At the church of St Paul in Jarrow, Northumberland, for instance, there is a cross inscribed with Latin text which can be translated as 'In this special sign life is returned to the world.'[34] The cross dates from the late seventh to the early eighth century and is therefore contemporary with Bede. As with the *Dream of the Rood* and the Ruthwell Cross, the text invites readers to participate in a community of worship. The Jarrow Cross locates its meanings in a tradition of Christian thought that can be traced, via Rufinus' translation of Eusebius' *Ecclesiastical History*, to Constantine's vision of the cross at the Battle of Milvian Bridge in 312.[35] This was a narrative freighted with significance in early medieval Northumbria and Bede's depiction of St Oswald's victory at Heavenfield in 634 is explicitly modelled on the story of Constantine at Milvian Bridge. According to Bede, the wooden cross raised by Oswald was the first monumental cross constructed in England.[36]

Like *The Dream of the Rood* and the Ruthwell Cross, a number of later texts imagine what the cross would say if it were able to express itself through speech and gesture. The Middle English poem *The Dispute between Mary and the Cross*, for instance, stages a debate between the two key witnesses of Christ's death – his mother and the cross. The *Dispute* also illustrates the important association of the cross and women, which is also seen in *The Dream of the Rood* and, most famously, the stories of Constantine's mother Helena's search for the true cross.[37] Again, in these stories the cross performs the function of drawing other people into the narratives of Christ's death. The animate nature of the cross is important, too, as it introduces other subjectivities, other voices, into the narratives of the event. Even outside scenes of Christ's death, the cross is imagined as animate and signifies as a sign of social, religious and sometimes royal power. An early thirteenth-century Latin Life of King Harold II, for example, explains that Harold stopped at the church at Waltham on his way to fight William the Conqueror and experienced, as Stephen Matthews writes, 'perhaps his greatest spiritual triumph, for, when he bowed to the cross as he left the church, the cross itself bowed back to him'.[38] What unites these texts is the manner in which they mediate between personal and collective identities, and their interest in the performative utterance, the ability of speech and gesture to create new subject positions as it blurs the lines between subject and object. Their narratives mark these crosses as more than mere objects, their wood and stone enlivened by spiritual truth and authority. They insist on the copresence of apparently absent beings, histories and temporal moments.

While the Eleanor Crosses self-consciously took a place among these long traditions, they were more directly related to two other contemporary building projects: the montjoies built to commemorate Louis IX and the shrine of Little St Hugh. The montjoies, described by John Zukowsky as 'freestanding flèche-like structures with sculptured niches … often surmounted by a cross',[39] were built to mark Louis' funerary journey from Notre Dame in Paris to Saint-Denis in the early 1270s and, like the Eleanor Crosses, were erected at sites where the funeral procession paused in its journey.[40] The montjoies provide a precedent for the ways in which the Eleanor Crosses blur the lines between spiritual and secular power. The shrine of Little St Hugh in Lincoln Cathedral, on the other hand, was funded by Edward in the direct aftermath of Eleanor's death. Stories of the martyrdom by crucifixion of Little St Hugh by the Jews of Lincoln in 1255 circulated widely in the Middle Ages – it is mentioned briefly, for instance, in Chaucer's 'Prioress's Tale' – and the two principal sources of the narrative both claimed that the child's body was acquired by the Dean and Chapter of Lincoln Cathedral and buried in the choir. Archaeological and antiquarian evidence suggests that the shrine, now destroyed, was designed and built in the early 1290s and decorated, like the Eleanor Crosses, with heraldic arms identifying Edward's munificence. Like the crosses, the shrine featured a complex architectural tabernacle, which bears few resemblances to other contemporary shrines, and David Stocker suggests that the shrine 'displays such close acquaintance with the Eleanor Crosses that it has be considered alongside them'.[41]

Examining the shrine and the crosses alongside one another brings Edward's intentions into focus. Anthony Bale describes the shrine as 'an act of memorialising and historicising the Lincoln Jews with an atemporal, fantastical, murderous image'[42] and it is clear that the Eleanor Crosses work from the same historicising and memorialising impulse, but with a very different purpose. They create an atemporal, fantastical image of an ideal Christian queen but, in their flurries of Christian ornament, the crosses reveal an anxiety about Eleanor's Jewish connections. Alongside the crosses, the memorial to Little St Hugh works hard to unbind the shared history of the Jews and the royal family. It defines the Jews as of the past and their past as other – expelled – from the Christian present. That is to say that it confirms their expulsion from England and, in turn, from English history. Even as they claim to represent the past, the memorials look to a future based on national and racial fantasy.

Memory and pilgrimage, temporal and spiritual

Another perspective on some of the meanings the Eleanor Crosses held in medieval England is provided by the fourteenth-century Luttrell Psalter. A monument that bears a striking resemblance to an Eleanor Cross appears in the margin of fol. 159v, beside the text of Ps. 88.7–10 (see Figure 2.6). The cross appears to be held aloft by a man while another, much smaller, man sits on his head. The smaller man leans against the steps of the stone structure making a gesture of befuddlement or awe. The monument is defined by the images of journeys, pilgrimages and memorials which surround it and the pages offer a rich meditation on humility, worship and discipline. The peak of the cross is associated with the word 'nubibus' (clouds) and if the reader's gaze passes directly over to the top of fol. 160 their attention is drawn to the line 'Tui sunt caeli et tua est terra orbem terrae et plenitudinem eius tu fundasti' (Yours are the heavens, and yours is the earth: the world and the fullness thereof you have founded). This association, which locates heaven at the top of the page, is confirmed by the text and images at the bottom of it. The text located in the lowest parts of the page is concerned with humility. The text in the lower registers of fol. 159v reads 'Tu humiliasti sicut vulneratum superbum' (You have humbled the proud one), and these lines are glossed by an image of a bull endowed with what Janet Backhouse calls 'somewhat inadequate legs'.[43] The bull's comically puny legs stand in contrast to the strength with which God disperses his enemies in the lines directly above. In the lower margin of fol. 160r the snail relates to the lines 'Beatus populus qui scit iubilationem Domine in lumine vultus tui' (Blessed is the people that knows jubilation. They shall walk, O Lord, in the light of your countenance) and signifies as an easily decoded sign of humility.

In the right-hand margin, above the snail and directly opposite the monumental cross, is an illustration of four men rowing a boat which is simultaneously being pulled – apparently in the opposite direction – by two men on the shore. This image speaks to the first

2.6 The Luttrell Psalter (British Library Add. MS 42130), folios 159v–160r

words of Ps. 88.13, 'Aquilonem et mare tu creasti' (You created the north and the sea), which are situated directly beside it. Michelle Brown has suggested that one of the rowers can be identified as Sir Geoffrey Luttrell, the patron of the Psalter, struggling to journey 'towards humility (the snail)' but being 'pulled back by his sins (his fellow oarsmen)', although it might equally be suggested that Sir Geoffrey is attempting to row to heaven but is being pulled back to earth.[44]

As this reading suggests, the ways the images interact with the text is key to the meanings the pages generate. As a whole, the scheme of the pages works to lead the viewer to read the illustrations in a clockwise manner from the peak of the monument to the boat, round to the snail and the bull, and back up to the peak of the cross.[45] This cognitive movement, suggested by the direction of travel of the three kinetic images and the form of the cross itself, speaks of the repetitive and meditative process of reading in the Middle Ages.[46] In the context of the Eleanor Crosses this optical journey around the page brings to mind pilgrimage and the journey the Queen's body took on its final journey to London.

Lucy Freeman Sandler suggests that the presence of the 'free-standing polygonal structure' of the Eleanor Cross might be explained by the phrase 'in circuitu' (round about), which appears twice in this passage.[47] There is another, albeit more prosaic explanation, however, and that is that the figure of the cross speaks of the place Eleanor's funeral rites occupied within the memories of the Luttrell family and the artist of the Psalter. The Luttrell family seat was in Irnham, a Lincolnshire village within easy reach of the three crosses at Lincoln, Grantham and Stamford. Although Geoffrey Luttrell was only fourteen at the time of Eleanor's death, it can be assumed that the Luttrells, as significant local gentry with established ties to the royal family, played some role in or at least were aware of the early stages of the funeral procession.[48] As Eleanor's bier made its way from Grantham to Stamford it would have travelled along what is now the A1 road, which runs just over half a dozen miles from Irnham. The illustration pays homage to the memory of the Queen constructed by the crosses and to Edward I's reign.

The cross also draws the Lincolnshire landscape into the visual scheme of the book and brings the local into the global Christian world. It marks the Luttrells' immediate environment as a point on the map of western Christendom and this is where the crosses' representation in the Psalter may chime with one of their primary purposes. The scallop shells used as line fillers on folio 159v bring to mind the idea of pilgrimage as they evoke the journey to Santiago de Compostela; they perhaps even mark out the crosses as potential sites of pilgrimage. Certainly, pilgrimage was an important part of the Luttrells' spiritual world: Sir Geoffrey's will made provision for contributions to particular images and shrines and in 1350 his daughter Beatrice applied for a licence to travel abroad as a pilgrim.[49] The final point of all these journeys is to follow the monument's cross on the page of the psalter up through the clouds to heaven. Movement – on pilgrimage, to the monuments, to heaven, through space and time – is key; and movement can be read, understood and replicated. As Nuala Johnson writes, monumental statues serve as 'points of physical and ideological orientation' around which 'circuits of memory are organized' and these circuits signify in the landscape, in everyday life and on the page.[50]

In this representation the Eleanor Crosses bring together the spiritual and the temporal as they infuse the physical world with religious meaning. In his commentary on the Gospel of St John, Thomas Aquinas used the lines inscribed on these pages of the

Luttrell Psalter to confirm God's control of nature and the way in which 'the movement of the things of nature toward a certain end indicates the existence of something higher by which the things of nature are directed to an end and governed'.[51] Like Aquinas, the crosses are interested in hierarchy and power but they also purposefully bind the political and the spiritual together. They celebrate spiritual and royal power and draw no distinction between the two. The crosses defined relations among people but also among places – they provided secular and spiritual as well as geographical and cultural orientation. As each singular cross encouraged their readers to consider their path to heaven, together the crosses marked out the path to secular authority: Westminster.

Early modern ruination and recreation

In London, the Cheapside Cross became an important civil site and played a key role in the celebrations following Henry V's victory at Agincourt in 1415.[52] In 1441 the Lord Mayor of London had it refurbished, while in the sixteenth century it was regilded for the coronations of Anne Boleyn in 1533 and Edward VI in 1547.[53] John Elder reports that in 1554 at the coronation of Mary I's consort, Philip of Spain, the couple passed through Cheapside and, 'perceiving the crosse thereof, which was with fine gold richely gilded, they staied a litle looking thereon, which was (no doubt it is) unto them a right excellent view, where also the kinges highnes, perceiving the crucifix in the top thereof, very humblie put of his cap'.[54] In the 1550s Anton van den Wyngaerde included a detailed representation of Charing Cross in his topographical view of London and it also takes a prominent place in the 1561 Agas Map. As Elder's account makes clear, however, while the crosses functioned as sites of civic and royal importance, over two decades after the beginning of the Reformation they still signified as symbols of religious devotion, too. And as the revolutions of the Reformation continued, Cheapside Cross in particular became the focus of puritan fury until it was brought down in May 1643. Charing Cross met a similar fate in 1647 when it was destroyed and, according to William Lily, its 'stones converted to pave before White-Hall'.[55]

For Edward Dering, a Church of England clergyman and evangelical preacher writing in the last quarter of the sixteenth century, the cross at Cheapside represented all that had to be destroyed in order to bring into being the new Protestant future. Dering saw the

cross as symptomatic of the 'childish', 'vaine' and 'idle ... wicked-
nesse of our forefathers' and the 'spiritual enchantments' which
'bewitched' them such as the works of 'Bevis of Hampton, Guy of
Warwick [and] Arthur of the rounde Table'. These works needed
to be 'sacrificed' and their burning would 'sanctify' Cheapside
itself. 'The place it selfe doeth crave it', Dering wrote, 'and holdeth
up a gorgeous idol, a fitte stake for so good a fire.'[56] The destruc-
tion of the 'spiritual enchantments' of the Middle Ages is justi-
fied in Dering's text by a weird agency that emanates around and
through the cross itself – Cheapside 'craves' the fire, as it offers
up its 'gorgeous idol'. James Simpson suggests that '[t]he question
of idolatry is inherently the question of historical distinctions and
continuities', but Dering's rhetoric illustrates the frayed borders
of the distinctions he attempts to write.[57] In order to justify his
beliefs Dering has to attribute extraordinary powers to the cross.
As Bruno Latour illustrates in his study of iconoclasm, science and
faith, this is a common manoeuvre of anti-fetish writing. Latour
writes that in such tracts, 'the fetish, far from being drained of
its efficacy, always seems to act in a way as to shift, muddle, invert
and perturb the origins of belief, as well as the very certainty that
mastery is possible'.[58] Dering attributes powers to the cross appar-
ently never before imagined. He magnifies the cross in order to
destroy it.

   As a synecdoche of an abjected past, Cheapside Cross continued
to attract the attention of reformers and iconoclasts throughout the
last decade of the sixteenth century. Following one attack in the
mid-1590s the Lord Mayor of London wrote to the Privy Council
to request guidance on whether and how to restore the cross. The
Mayor reported that 'Such defacement as had happened was very
small, and not easily discerned by passers-by unless pointed out to
them by those that knew it', but it seemed that certain 'light per-
sons ... had pilfered a little lead from the arms and crosses in the
lower part, which were easiest to break away.' Even as he reports
the damage, the Mayor notes that the cross has become something
of a talisman for 'strangers and other superstitious people' who
'mislike' the state and the new religion. 'Passing by the Cross',
these people 'knelt down to the images there, and daily gave idola-
trous worship thereunto, both in bending their knees, uncovering
their heads, and other outward shows of reverence.'[59] At the turn
of the seventeenth century the City requested further guidance
on what to do with their troublesome monument and turned to
George Abbot, Vice-Chancellor of Oxford University and later

Archbishop of Canterbury. Abbot advised that some of the sculptures on the cross were indeed associated with the 'highest points of popery' and recommended that an obelisk be set up in its place.[60]

Abbot's advice was not followed and controversies and occasional assaults continued to dog the cross. His letter was republished in 1641 as the debates around the cross reignited in a flurry of textual activity. As David Cressy notes, 'Pamphleteers repeatedly wrote of the Cross as a sentient being, as if it had a voice and social identity of its own.'[61] In Richard Overton's *Articles of high treason exhibited against Cheap-side crosse*, for instance, the author's personification of the cross is infused with misogyny and sexual fear. Overton calls the cross 'Babels whore' and remarks that the results of her treatment by iconoclasts has made her look 'as she'd got the pox' which means that 'woe' will come 'to him that next takes up her smock'.[62] In another text the cross is described as 'one of the jewels of the Whore of Rome'.[63] More than simply an object of horror and ridicule, however, the cross is continually imagined to exert agency. *The Downe-fall of Dagon*, an anonymous pamphlet printed to celebrate the destruction of the cross which rehearses its history and the reasons why it was pulled down, attributes the power of causing superstition to the cross and expresses a fear that it might control people's imagination:

> [D]ivers ignorant people who have been misled and misinformed in the Protestant Religion, have by such like Images been seduced and made believe that praying to severall Saints, desiring them and instigating them, that they would solicite and speake to our Saviour in their behalf, that our Saviour would make intercession to his father for the mitigation and for the forgivenesse of their sins ... So this Crosse hath been a great meanes to cause superstition and idolatry from time to time in worshipping and adoring it, as many people have done as they passe by it; for divers people both men & women hath been seen by severall honest, ancient, and good Inhabitants dwelling neare the place, that sundry sorts of people have by three o clock in the morning come barefoot to the Crosse, and have kneeled down, and said something to themselves, crossed their fore-head and the breast, and so risen and making obeysance, went away.[64]

As in Dering's writing against the cross, in *The Downe-fall of Dagon* the stone is animated and ascribed with agency. The cross is 'a great meanes to cause superstition and idolatry', drawing people towards it in worship and adoration in the middle of the night. In order to kill the past, these writers have to animate it. The image

of the worshippers at prayer at three o'clock in the morning illus-
trates their lateness, defines them as out of sync and untimely.
This image is double-edged, however, because as it associates the
worshippers with darkness it also produces an idea of repetition
as it invokes the rhythm of night and day. While Dering and *The
Downe-fall of Dagon* promise an end to such recursions, they are
both haunted by the possibility of return and repetition.

One sign of the inevitability of return is the fact that various
pamphlets that took part in this debate gave the Eleanor Crosses a
voice in a manner which recalls the medieval tradition represented
by *The Dream of the Rood* and *The Dispute between Mary and the
Cross*. One further seventeenth-century example, Henry Peacham's
A Dialogue between the Crosse in Cheap and Charing Crosse, allowed
the crosses to speak back against their accusers. As in the literature
of the iconoclasts, the crosses are imagined to be female and, amid
a great deal of punning, Cheap tells her 'deere Sister of the Strand'
that 'I feare my utter ruine and destruction is at hand'. Charing
replies: 'Sister of West-Cheape, Crosses are incident to us, and all
our kindred; the time hath beene when I have been Cross'd too, but
I have been free, without these fourscore and odd years.'[65] The per-
sistence of the anthropomorphism of the cross, on both sides of the
seventeenth-century debate and in medieval literature, recalls again
psychoanalytic theories of trauma. In her discussion of Freud's
thinking on repetition and trauma, Cathy Caruth highlights how
repetitions reveal truths that individuals cannot fully acknowledge
or know, and particularly how trauma relates to voice. While her
work examines individual experiences, Caruth's thinking invites us
to think about how the voices of the crosses represent traumatic
experience at the level of the collective as the 'enigma of the other-
ness of a human voice that cries out'.[66] The returns to the crosses
reveal traumas in collective identity, wounds 'in the mind's experi-
ence of time, self, and the world' and the crosses serve as a location,
a proxy, that voices the trauma while at the same time ensuring that
it remains inaccessible.[67] Just as the crosses bore witness to the pre-
sent absence of the Jews and Jewish history in the 1290s, in the
1640s they reveal the pre-Reformation other within the Puritan self.

Repetition and remembering

The later histories of the crosses demonstrate that restora-
tion can be no less transformative than destruction. By the
mid-nineteenth century Eleanor's reputation had significantly

improved. This upturn relied in part on renewed reverence for her crosses, but can be explained by three further factors, too: first of all, a legend that Eleanor saved Edward's life by sucking poison from a wound caused by 'a Moor with a poyson'd sword' in Acre while they were on Crusade found wide acceptance in historical works following William Camden's account of it in *Britannia*;[68] secondly, the accumulation of historical distance and the rise of the antiquarians meant that the stakes in the debate were altered and lowered; thirdly, Queen Victoria's reign prompted an unprecedented interest in queenship. As a result of all this Eleanor and her crosses were attributed new cultural meanings and a new place in cultural memory. Her reputation reached new heights following the 1840 publication of the first volume of the Strickland sisters' wildly successful *Lives of the Queens of England*. The Stricklands returned to the image of Eleanor created by the cross. Although they discount the Acre legend, the Stricklands imagine that Eleanor 'must have been a model of feminine beauty' in order to 'have inspired in the heart of her renowned lord an attachment so deep and true'.[69] The crosses, too, are 'models of architectural beauty'.[70]

Another event occurred in 1840 which further reformed the cultural meanings of the Eleanor Crosses. As part of the reaction against the Oxford Movement, it was decided that a monument should be raised to commemorate the deaths of Thomas Cranmer, Hugh Latimer and Nicholas Ridley, Anglican bishops who were tried for heresy and burned at the stake in 1555. The Oxford Martyrs' Memorial, unveiled in 1843, was designed by George Gilbert Scott and explicitly based on the Eleanor Crosses (see Figure 2.7).[71] This is iconoclasm as appropriation. In Scott's project medieval culture is transformed to signify Protestant memory. The Martyrs' Memorial constitutes a key moment in the history of the Gothic Revival as it reimagined the relationship between the style and religious history.[72] Scott's work was enormously influential and almost immediately another Eleanor Cross was commissioned by Jesse Watts-Russell of Ilam, Staffordshire, in memory of his late wife Mary.[73] In the 1860s the Ellesmere Memorial in Walkden, Salford, was erected to commemorate the local philanthropist Lady Harriet, Countess of Ellesmere.[74] The design also influenced countless later monuments, including the 1903 Boer War Memorial at Cheltenham College and many memorials to the First World War.[75]

2.7   The Oxford Martyrs' Memorial, by George Gilbert Scott (1843)

These varied works constitute what Alexander Nagel and Christopher Wood call 'a diachronic chain of replicas' that brings the Protestant present and future into contact with the Catholic medieval past.[76] This chain works across time as the monuments inform one another's meanings. As T. S. Eliot writes in 'Tradition and the individual talent', 'what happens when a new work of art is created is something that happens simultaneously to all the works of art which preceded it'.[77] By the mid-nineteenth century the Eleanor Crosses were part of a chain of monuments that spoke of mourning, loyalty and royalty. The Catholic language of the crosses, of pilgrimage and the cult of the cross, is reformed and this means that even as their purpose is defined by their immediate context, their meanings cannot be explained by historical context alone. The different – and occasionally conflicting – traditions, memories, hierarchies and events that can be traced in these medieval and modern monuments generate a heterogeneous sense of time.

This complex relation to history and temporality meant that the forms of the crosses were particularly attuned to the production of ideas of timelessness and, along with the success of Scott's work and A. W. N. Pugin's energetic campaign, the new relevance of the Eleanor Crosses meant that Gothic was legitimised as a national, albeit contradictory, style, to such a degree that at the death of another royal consort there appeared to some only one suitable form of memorial.[78] On 25 December 1862 the *London Daily News* printed a letter signed 'JA (Temple)'. JA wrote to make a suggestion regarding 'the most fitting form of commemorating the character and eminent virtues of the illustrious Prince whose mortal remains have but now been consigned to their final resting place'. Albert, the Prince Consort, had died on 14 December 1861 and a public meeting had taken place at Mansion House as early as 14 January 1862 to discuss a suitable memorial.[79] At the time of JA's letter no decision had been announced. His letter recalls how 'Being in the vicinity of Northampton a few weeks since, I renewed a visit to Queen Eleanor's Cross, a spot to which I had been a stranger for more than thirty years' and that 'Becoming absorbed at the once by the interest of old associations connected with it, I was struck by the analogy of the circumstances surrounding this tribute of royal affection, which, after the lapse of 600 years, still survives to commemorate the romance of his reign in the loss of his beautiful Queen by the brave and good King Edward I.' It is worth quoting JA's letter at length:

[T]he sight of Queen Eleanor's Cross, as I last looked upon it, in all its picturesque, with a group of peasants and children seated upon the steps at its foot, taking rest upon their return to market, has, I own, prompted the indulgence of a gentle thought that, in the centuries yet reserved for the history of our country, future pilgrims will be found wending their way to the good Prince Albert's Cross, to be erected let us hope, in some spot consecrated by the interest he took in the vicinity, there to repeat to their – it may be our – children's children how that, in the domestic life of Queen Victoria and the Prince Consort, no uncertain charm of endearment

bound together their royal hearts, no false lustre shone from their
union, whilst of the Prince they will be justified in their assurance
that he never swerved from the position that fortune assigned him,
nor failed to perform those duties which belonged to the station to
which he was summoned from the land of his birth to the country
whose pride it was, and now is, to have adopted him among the wor-
thiest of her sons.

The scene JA imagines, of peasants and children resting on the
steps of the cross, of secular, royalist pilgrims and perfected mas-
culinity, is a scene of an idealised Middle Ages rather than the mid-
nineteenth century. Like the Old English *Ruin*, the letter brings
the past into presence and traffics in affective memory rather than
objective history. The scene is untimely in the sense that it cannot
be securely located within a single historical moment and it legiti-
mises the identities and ideologies it represents – of social order
and masculine hierarchy – as timeless in turn. JA's meditation on
the Northampton Cross produces a vision of the future which fol-
lows the terms of a past invented by the crosses themselves. This
sense of repetition and return is confirmed by the image of the
'future pilgrims' continually 'wending their way to the good Prince
Albert's Cross'.[80]

The following March the plans for the monument were formally
announced and JA got his wish. As *The Times* reported, the Albert
Memorial was to be built by George Gilbert Scott and was 'to be
what is called an Eleanor Cross, something similar to the Martyrs'
Memorial at Oxford or the monument erected to Sir Walter Scott
at Edinburgh'.[81] Even as the Scott Monument is invoked, it is
clear that the Eleanor Crosses were seen as the primary influence,
even by those who were less than enthusiastic about Scott's plans.
The Builder, for instance, the influential trade newspaper for the
construction industry, wrote that they could not 'resist asking
whether it is exactly what all wish who are striving for the honour
of nineteenth-century advance, that wanting an Albert Memorial
we should be forced to take an "Eleanor Cross". There is surely
something humiliating in the admission.'[82]

During the Martyrs' Memorial project, Scott was open about
the influence the Eleanor Crosses had exerted on him and in his
memoirs he recalled that he 'thoroughly knew and had sketched
in detail all of the three [surviving] Eleanor Crosses by the time
I was nineteen years old'.[83] He was similarly forthcoming in the
explanatory remarks he submitted with his proposal for the Albert

Memorial which were quoted by the *Morning Post* in an article reporting the progress of the monument:

> In describing the general character or 'motive' of the work, Mr Scott said, 'I have not hesitated to adapt in my design the style at once most congenial with my own feelings, and that of the most touching monuments ever erected in the country – the exquisite "Eleanor Crosses" … I would further suggest that this style has a peculiar appropriateness in the present instance from the circumstance that its perfect revival has been up to the present time the one great characteristic of the history of architecture during the reign of Queen Victoria.'[84]

The Eleanor Crosses are the vehicle that allows Scott to draw an uncomplicated connection between the Victorian and the medieval in his vision, even if Scott's design itself did not bear a close resemblance to the crosses (see Figure 2.8). Ideas of time, memory and history intersect to mark out the contours of a collective identity, an identity that is at once new and legitimised as, like Scott's monument, a 'perfect revival'.

A similar temporal reflex is evident in a work dedicated to the surviving monuments to Eleanor. *Memorials to Queen Eleanor*

2.8 The Albert Memorial, London, by George Gilbert Scott (1872)

was published in 1864 and was edited by John Abel, likely the
'JA' whose letter was published in the *Daily News*. It was illus-
trated by beautifully composed photographs of the crosses at
Geddington, Northampton and Waltham as well as Eleanor's tomb
at Westminster. In his preface, Abel wrote:

> The sepulchral monuments raised by Edward I to the memory of
> Queen Eleanor, to mark the resting-places of her remains, as they
> were mournfully borne along from Harby, in Nottinghamshire,
> where she died, to the tomb prepared for them in Westminster
> Abbey, must be objects of interest to Englishmen at all times – how
> much more so at a moment when history, repeating herself as it
> were, by the removal of another Royal Consort – 'the silent father of
> our kings to be' – there has devolved upon the architectural genius
> of our countrymen, the conception and the execution of a work of
> kindred character with these beautiful crosses.[85]

For Abel, the work of mourning brings together past, present and
future. The uncertainty of the future – and the shock of the trau-
matic death of Albert – calls for a return to what he imagines to
be the settled, uncontested traditions of the past. And as he turns
towards that past, he creates it.

This is the context in which E. M. Barry was commissioned
to build a monument that paid homage to the public trauma and
joined in with their mourning – a moment when, as Abel put it,
history seemed to be 'repeating herself'. Although never explicitly
linked with Albert, the rebuilding of Charing Cross enters into the
logic of the debates that followed his death. It is of its time, even
as it disguises its own historicity.

The other significant achievement of Barry's new cross was to
connect the new railway station at Charing with an idealised vision
of the past.[86] The building of the railways had caused massive dis-
ruption in London and, at times, prompted mass panic. Charles
Dickens' *Dombey and Son* (1846–48) provides a celebrated example
of the feelings the building of the railways provoked. The imagery
speaks of a world turned upside down and of unnatural and inhu-
man processes:

> Here a chaos of carts, overthrown and jumbled together, lay topsy-
> turvy at the bottom of a steep unnatural hill; there, confused
> treasures of iron soaked and rusted in something that had actually
> become a pond ... Everywhere were bridges that led nowhere; thor-
> oughfares that were wholly impassable; Babel towers of chimneys,
> wanting half their height; temporary wooden houses and enclosures,

in the most unlikely situations; carcases of ragged tenements, and fragments of unfinished walls and arches, and piles of scaffolding, and wildernesses of bricks, and giant forms of cranes, and tripods straddling above nothing.[87]

For Ian Carter, the railway in *Dombey and Son* signifies modernity, 'jumbling together (not always in comfortable proximity) the many shifts in material conditions and consciousness which Victorian social critics identified as they struggled to make sense of a world changing its contours before their eyes'.[88] As much as it presents a memory of the medieval past then, Barry's Charing Cross expresses anxieties about the present and future.

The new Charing Cross was also a masterful stroke of marketing for the hotel and train company as it proved to be the focus of an avalanche of positive news stories. The *Illustrated London News*, for instance, produced a print and the cross was reproduced on advertisements for the hotel and on postcards.[89] But it was not greeted with universal acclaim. As noted earlier, *The Builder* derided the plan to reconstruct the cross and described the restoration as an anachronism and – quite literally – a waste of space. The single notice of the cross's completion published by the journal was a short, cryptic fragment, with the final phrases in Italian, signed by 'Q.':

> Dear to the shareholders, this cross
> Uplifts its head on high:
> 'Why stand it there?' the critic asks,
> And Echo answers, 'Why!'
> 'Carissima croce! Cha fatte la?'
> 'Non so, car'amico, en verita.'[90]

The Italian might be explained by the Renaissance style of the hotel in front of which the cross was placed, but the poem is deeply ambiguous. This ambiguity – or senselessness – is indeed an important part of the poem's meanings: the cross is asked why it stands there and replies that, in truth, it doesn't know. It voices the unspeakable contradictions expressed by Barry's cross, which is itself a sign of the unknowable, irregular and non-linear rhythms of time, memory and culture. *The Builder*'s wariness of the monuments speaks of a desire, in Dipesh Chakrabarty's words, to 'ascribe an underlying structural unity to historical process',[91] a desire that is frustrated by the tangled temporalities of the new old cross at Charing.

The production of timelessness

Two crosses erected in the last decades of the nineteenth century, St Augustine's Cross (1884), which stands in Thanet, Kent, and the Cædmon Memorial (1898), which stands in Whitby, North Yorkshire, form part of the chain initiated by the Eleanor Crosses, although neither is explicitly connected to Eleanor's memory or her memorials. St Augustine's Cross supposedly marks the very place where King Æthelberht first met Augustine and his missionaries in 597, while the Cædmon Memorial stands in the churchyard of St Mary's Church, Whitby, and celebrates the life of the man Bede names as the first English Christian poet.

St Augustine's Cross (see Figure 2.9) was erected by Granville George Leveson-Gower, 2nd Earl Granville. Lord Granville, a former Foreign Minister, was at the time Lord Warden of the Cinque Ports and as such had use of Walmer Castle, just fifteen miles down the coast from Ramsgate. As a result of the time he spent in eastern Kent, he became interested in the stories surrounding the arrival of St Augustine in 597. In a news report celebrating the new memorial, the *Birmingham Daily Post* noted that the monument stands in the very 'spot where the meeting between the king and the missionary took place', a location that can be identified by local memories of 'a gigantic oak' that stood there 'until the last fifty years'. The location is also marked by 'a natural spring of pure water' within 'a few yards' of the tree and it is said that 'with the water from that natural spring Augustine performed his first baptism'.[92] In another contemporary report, *The Tablet* quoted a local historian, Robert Bubb (whose work is said to have inspired Granville), as stating that the oak 'stood on a quarter of an acre of ground at least, and its principal branches were fifty inches in girth'.[93] Both articles name the field in which the tree stood as 'Cotmansfield' and suggest that this name can be defined as 'the field of the man of God', which they both take to be another sign that Granville identified the correct location. The articles form an authorising discourse of the monument from a combination of natural and national history and local cultural memory.

The other key source of authority is what *The Tablet* calls 'the famous Saxon crosses of Sandbach',[94] although, as the *Birmingham Daily Post* admits, because they are 'mutilated by time and ill-treatment, there is much difficulty in determining the meaning of the groups of figures [they] present' (see Figure 2.10). The *Daily Post* article continues to state that, 'Mr Ormerod, the historian

2.9   St Augustine's Cross, Pegwell Bay, by John Roddis (1884)

of Cheshire, does not attempt to give an interpretation; nor does Mr Rimmer in his work on ancient stone crosses. But it was necessary for the sculptor in reproducing the work to act on some definite theory, for otherwise he could carve nothing but a collection of meaningless forms.'[95] The article is not interested in ambiguity even as it notes that a strict reproduction of the Sandbach Crosses would result in 'a collection of meaningless forms'. Meaning belongs to – and in – the present rather than the past. But the Anglo-Saxon crosses provide what Stephanie Trigg terms the 'mythic capital' that legitimises the new cross.[96] The *Birmingham Daily Post* similarly hedges its analysis when it suggests that 'With the possible exception of some of the figures, [St Augustine's Cross] is a strict imitation of the original at Sandbach.' The memories and identities created by the cross are brought into being as a result of a negotiation between past and present. The true complexity of the past, revealed in this case by the 'meaningless forms', 'mutilation', 'ill treatment' and mysterious histories of the Sandbach Crosses, is acknowledged even as it is elided in order to invoke a transcendent source that secures the meaningfulness and coherence of the present.[97]

The design of the St Augustine's Cross, by John Roddis, is clear and sparse. The north side is decorated with images of the twelve apostles, which are mirrored on the south side by images

2.10   The Sandbach Crosses

of fourteen Christian martyrs. The top half of the east side of the cross, which faces the road, is decorated with what the *Birmingham Daily Post* called 'Runic ornament', while the lower half contains diamond-shaped panels showing St Alban, St Augustine and St Æthelberht. The carvings on the west side of the cross illustrate the principles of the Christian story: the Annunciation, the Virgin and Child, Christ's Crucifixion and the Transfiguration. As this suggests, despite the claims of the *Birmingham Daily Post*, the Sandbach Crosses influenced the design of the cross only in the most general way. A short passage of Latin, composed by Dr Henry Liddell, Dean of Christ Church, Oxford, is carved into the base of the cross and is now also displayed in front of the cross in both Latin and English:

> After many dangers and difficulties by land and sea Augustine landed at last on the shores of Richborough in the Isle of Thanet. On this spot he met King Ethelbert, and preached his first sermon to our own countrymen. Thus he happily planted the Christian faith, which spread with marvellous speed throughout the whole of England. That the memory of these events may be preserved among the English G G L-G Earl Granville, Lord Warden of the Cinque Ports has erected this monument, AD 1884.

The manner in which Liddell's text glosses over the complex and violent history of Christianity in Britain is instructive. The monument privileges continuity over rupture and uses its repetition of the forms of early medieval sculpture to press home its ideological intent. However, even as it asserts a vision of seamless history, the contrasts and joins are visible.

Liddell's reticent account of the history of Christianity in Britain brings us to the key context of St Augustine's Cross – its ambivalent position as an Anglican monument to pre-Reformation history. While the Roman Catholic Relief Act was passed in 1829, anti-Catholic sentiment remained common in English society throughout the nineteenth century and Granville's own life illustrates the sometimes blurred boundaries between Anglicanism and Catholicism in British society. His first marriage had been to Marie-Louise Pellina, who was Roman Catholic, and the marriage went ahead only after the couple agreed to his family's demand that any male children of the marriage were to be brought up Anglican. Pellina and Granville were also required to stage two ceremonies on their wedding day, one at the Spanish Chapel and the other at Devonshire House in Piccadilly.[98] Although he never converted, Granville's sister, Lady Georgiana Fullerton, did convert to Catholicism in 1846 following her father's death.[99]

As Gerald Parsons writes, the nineteenth century saw great changes to the social position of Catholics in England:

> From a position of official civil disability and overt suspicion and hostility from much of the non-Catholic population, and from a definitely marginal status within the overall religious life of England, Wales and Scotland, Roman Catholicism moved in the Victorian period to a position of civil equality and calm acceptance by the majority of the British people, and to a position within the religious life of the nation which – though it was not to become clear until the twentieth century – amounted to being the major alternative to the established churches of England, Wales and Scotland.[100]

St Augustine's Cross forms part of this process by simultaneously celebrating the Roman missionaries who brought Christianity to Britain and what its plaque describes as the 'marvellous speed' with which it spread 'throughout the whole of England'. To use Fradenburg's words, the cross enables 'the crossing-over of difference into identity, the unfamiliar into the familiar'. But this was not a seamless process. Indeed, shortly after the unveiling of the cross Granville's sister, Lady Georgiana, felt it necessary to explain to the *Journal of Rome* that the cross was not erected by the English Catholic community but her brother, 'one of their Protestant countrymen', and her remarks were considered significant enough to be reprinted in *The Times*.[101]

The cross's peculiar relation to the Catholic community of England was brought to the fore just over a decade after its creation. In July 1897 the Archbishop of Canterbury, Frederick Temple, led a group of over 150 prelates on a pilgrimage to commemorate the thirteen hundredth anniversary of St Augustine's arrival in England. They travelled to St Augustine's Cross. The pilgrimage was at once deeply traditional and unmistakably of its time. A train was chartered from Charing Cross, which the Archbishop joined at Canterbury, and after 'serious delay and inconvenience' the pilgrims disembarked at the main road that led to the field in which the Cross stood. The *Morning Post* recorded that 'The Bishops present were thoroughly representative of the whole Anglican Episcopate – the Metropolitans of India, Capetown, Australia, Canada, West Indies.'[102] In another contemporary account, the

Daily News reported that 'There were at least a hundred vehicles of all sorts, from the carriages of the country gentry to the donkey cart of the smallest tradesman, while there was a record show of bicycles.'[103] The choir sang 'Onward, Christian Soldiers' as the party walked towards the cross and onlookers lined both sides of the road.

Two months later another party set off for the cross. This event is recorded in two photographs published in the edition of *The Graphic*, a London-based weekly newspaper, published on September 25 1897 (see Figure 2.11). This pilgrimage was led by Cardinal Vaughan, Archbishop of Westminster, and should be understood as the Catholic response to the Anglican pilgrimage of July. One photograph shows Vaughan walking to the commemoration service, while the other is a group shot of the pilgrims sitting in front of the cross. These images capture the incongruity of the pilgrimage. There is a humour – an absurdity – to these photographs generated by a clash of traditions, times and technologies. The cleric's vestments and accoutrements sit uncomfortably in an image that reminds a modern viewer of a portrait of a sports team. The cross in the background – at this point only thirteen years old – further complicates the ideas of time, history and belief that the faithful perform.

The Cædmon Memorial (see Figure 2.12) was built at the direction of Hardwicke Drummond Rawnsley, a canon at Carlisle Cathedral and later one of the founders of the National Trust. Rawnsley announced the plan for the memorial in a letter to *The Times* that explained the cross would 'take the form of a beautiful cross of Anglian design, based upon the four contemporary crosses of the VIIth century workmanship – namely, the Ruthwell, the Bewcastle, the Rothbury, and the Acca cross at Hexham', and encouraged interested parties to contribute to the costs of design and construction.[104] As Matthew Townend writes, the memorial 'exemplifies many of the key features of nineteenth-century medievalism: a combination of scholarship and creativity, inspiration and elaboration; a preoccupation not just with England's medieval past, but with the literary products of that past; and a conviction that the medieval, or medievalist, had a public role to play in contemporary culture'.[105] In Stuart Hall's terms, the Cædmon Memorial played a role in the process – begun, the monument suggests, by Bede in the eighth century – of 'storying' the 'various random incidents and contingent turning points' of English history 'into a single, coherent, narrative'.[106] Like St Augustine's Cross, it

An Artistic Causerie

By M. H. SPIELMANN

WITHIN A memoir, is mind to the honour of a great artist the enthusiasts who initiate it should surely so arrange that the scheme is a fitting one, and not make the portrait or the means of providing the memorabilia with some "long-felt want." If Sir David Wilkie is to receive the homage of Pilhenie, it would be well that the tribute take one of the well-known forms which is universally associated with the honouring of the great dead; but the idea of acquiring in David Wilkie's name a second-hand ball "in fairly good repair," providing it with a memorial tablet, a caretaker, and a cottage all complete, does not seem to commend itself as a worthy, or even as a single-minded, proposal. Of course the people of Pilhenie want a ball; and no doubt the prospective caretaker will applaud the proposal. But why deny to David Wilkie's name?

I am asked on what grounds it is believed that the new picture in the National Gallery by John Beteu represents Edmund Betts. The identification of the portrait is due to the late Sir George Scharf, who informed Mr. George Richardot, R.A. (then owner of the picture), that the subject of it was "Edmund Betts, of Barrow, Suffolk, third son of Sir William Butts, Physician to Henry VIII," and specially remembered as one of the characters in Shakespeare's Play of Henry VIII. Edmund Butts married a daughter of Henry Bures, of Acton, in Suffolk, and their daughter married Sir Nicholas Bacon, ; Dr. Butts, the father, occurs in Holbein's picture of Henry VIII, granting the Charter to the Barber Surgeons"—the picture recently offered by that Guild for a good, and most wisely refused, in view of its condition and its repairing. Sir George Scharf added that he had already met a similar likeness of the same youth on panel, with the same age and date; and a coat-of-arms—so that the matter was placed beyond doubt. This discovery was the more interesting as, when the picture was exhibited at the Old Masters in 1877, no one knew who was the painter and none could guess at the author, and both the picture itself stood for more light. It may be added that the picture is dated 1545.

The works of Marie Bashkirtseff are coming to the hammer at last, after, it is said, being first sent on tour in those countries most likely to attract persons to visit them out of curiosity or admiration. The degree of excellence to which the gifted young painter attained, as much through emulation as by natural development, justifies no little interest in the event, but whatever her actual achievements merit the exceptional honour they receive in the Luxembourg at Paris may well be doubted. Without question, the influence and companionship of Bovier-Lepage counted for something in her accomplishment, though not so much, perhaps, as has been suggested. It is at least pleasant to note that the just reputation of the unhappy girl has suffered no eclipse, even through the absurd attempt to add to the interest of her career by deducting—as was proved some time ago—two years from her actual age. Had Marie lived her work would certainly have displayed proved merit of an extraordinary kind, and perhaps would have surpassed that of her school-rival.

who is now making a considerable mark in the French world of art —the Swiss lady, Mlle. Breslou.

"A Sapporist of the Death Duties" conveys to me his opinion that "it is absurd to suppose that any taxation could have the effect of suddenly driving works of art out of the country or, in fact, of influencing any art at all." He very properly does not directly challenge the facts themselves as specifically stated and quoted by me. But if he really thinks that no practice of art can be "influenced" by taxation, direct or indirect, I can convince him, perhaps, by producing the case of gem-engraving—now, to all intents and purposes, a lost art in England. The gem-sculptors and engravers were artists highly esteemed in their day, when the wearing of engraved seals at the fob was a fashion indulged in by all who would be known for men of taste. Such a one as Thomas Warner, pupil of the still more famous William Brown, and partner of Harris, who were never without lucrative employment, and were as highly esteemed as Burch and Marchant before them. These men were "appointed" to the Royal service, and their works were

engaily competed for by the rich and applauded by those who could afford only to admire. All at once Mr. Pitt's Administration imposed the watch tax. The measure gave at the time so severe a check to the watch trade, that the engraver of seals—which, of course, were themselves an advertisement to every passer-by that the wearer of these little works of art was carrying a watch—was fatally hit. Gem-sculptors forthwith deteriorated to the mere cutting of arms and cyphers, and certain of the producers of the art within a very short time were thrown upon the art-charities of London, and their craft was completely wiped from off the list.

The death of Monsieur Falize, the official goldsmith to the French Government, robs the world of an artist of the very front rank. His goldsmithery, so more craftsmanship, was equalled by the purity and charm of his decorative design. The olive branch of beaten gold, embellished by medallions by Messieur Roty, which Monsieur Félix Faure recently placed upon the tomb of Alexander III., was the last, as it was one of the most refined, of his works, designed with that perfect taste which seemed him the position and headship of all the art-goldsmiths of France, official or otherwise.

The loving-cup, or drinking-cup, which helped to draw all Paris to the Old Salon a couple of years ago—it was perhaps the most remarkable work in the Champs Elysées in whatever section—has never been surpassed, so far as I am aware, in all the qualities that make up a chef-d'œuvre of goldsmithery and enamelling. As an enameller he was especially successful, and trained his craftsmen to a high pitch of perfection. Some years ago he showed me with infinite pride a gem enamel he had just completed—the largest of the finest class ever executed—which he hoped was destined to repose in the cabinet of a world collector in England. Now that he has gone it will be M. Lalique, I imagine, who will take his place: a young artist whose name, unknown to the world this time last year, is now on everyone's lip.

Richardson's Theatre

IN the early part of this century, though fairs were still an institution outside London, only one, Bartholomew Fair, was held within the City boundary. On September 3rd each year Smithfield was given up to the holding of this fair until 1855, when it was finally stopped. It was the custom for one of the attorneys of the Lord Mayor's Court to accompany the Lord Mayor in his State coach from the Mansion House to Smithfield on the day of the fair, and there to read the proclamation of the fair. The proclamation dusk mainly with the selling of food and drink, and set forth that "All manner of sellers of Wine Ale, or Beer sell by measures ennacted, as by Gallon, Bottle, Quart or Pint upon pain that will be thereof. And that no person sell any Bread but is be good and wholesome for Man's Body upon pain that will fall thereof. And that no manner of Cook, Pyebaker, nor Huckster sell, nor put to sale, any manner of Victual except it be good and wholesome for man's body upon pain that will fall thereof." All kinds of things were sold at the stalls—gingerbread, toys, hazel nuts, garters, pocket-books, and trinkets, the prizes of the goods varying from a halfpenny to half-a-sovereign. But the great attraction at the fair were the shows of all kinds. Menageries, travelling theatres, peep-shows, &c. were, being skeletons, mermaids, and other curiosities were to be seen for a small coin. One of the best of the travelling shows was Richardson's Theatre. The outside of this show was about 30 feet high and too feet in width. The platform on the outside was very elevated, the back was lined with green baize and festooned with deeply fringed crimson curtains. A band of ten performers, in scarlet dresses, similar to those worn by bandsmen, used to perform on trombones, clarionets and drums; while the actors and actresses, in their gayest costumes, paraded before the admiring crowd, with the object of attracting a good audience. The plays were always brief, and no scenery was used; performances done and the audience had left, than another audience would press in to hear another performance. Inside the theatre the seats consisted of rows of planks rising gradually from the ground at the end. In front of the stage was a band of five violin players, and when the seats were filled the space between the bottom row and the band used to be occupied with spectators, so that there were at least a thousand persons present at a performance. The charge for the entertainment were, boxes 1s., pit 1s., and gallery 6d. Most of the other shows were cheaper, some costing only a penny.

CARDINAL VAUGHAN AND HIS ATTENDANTS ON THE WAY TO THE COMMEMORATION SERVICE
THE ST. AUGUSTINE CELEBRATIONS AT EBBS FLEET
From a Photograph by Gunn and Stewart, Richmond

Cardinal Persial   Cardinal Vaughan
A GROUP OF ECCLESIASTICS TAKEN IN FRONT OF ST. AUGUSTINE'S CROSS
THE ST. AUGUSTINE CELEBRATIONS AT EBBS FLEET
From a Photograph by Gunn and Stewart, Richmond

2.11   *The Graphic*, 25 September 1897

celebrates English exceptionalism and the unfolding of God's will on English soil. The monuments create memories of a static and uncontested past while their endeavours reveal the processes and dialogues – in and between past and present – that define the past and visions of it.

2.12   The Cædmon Memorial, Whitby (1898)

The design of the Cædmon Memorial, like that of St Augustine's Cross, self-consciously brings together biblical and English history. The front panel is decorated with named portraits of Christ, David, Hild and Cædmon above a short piece of text that reads: 'To the glory of God and in memory of Cædmon the father of English sacred song fell asleep hard by 680.' The text of Cædmon's *Hymn*, in Anglo-Saxon minuscule and Northumbrian runes, is inscribed in the margins of the narrower sides of the monument while a Modern English translation is provided on the rear panel (see Figure 2.13). The medieval is decoration, literally in the margins.

The Cædmon Memorial was unveiled on 21 September 1898 by the Poet Laureate, Alfred Austin. Although little known today,

2.13   Old English text in the margins of the Cædmon Memorial

Austin had published his homage to King Alfred the Great, *England's Darling*, two years earlier and, as its allusions to the Anglo-Saxon Chronicle, *The Battle of Maldon* and the Alfredian Preface to Gregory the Great's *Pastoral Care* make clear, was well read in Anglo-Saxon literature and culture.[107] It is striking then to read Austin's begrudging celebration in his speech of 'the somewhat rudimentary verse of Cædmon' that he suggests 'possesses the tentative and hesitating character of yet imperfect dawn'. Austin's language recalls *The Downe-fall of Dagon*'s account of the idolaters worshipping the Cheapside Cross at three o'clock in the morning discussed earlier. Both imagine the past as existing in the darkness of the night as opposed to the enlightened present. As in *The Downe-fall* there is a suggestion of recursiveness in this image that Austin corrects with an evolutionary notion of Cædmon's relation to English poetry, which causes him to adjust the epithet inscribed on the memorial to describe Cædmon as 'the half inarticulate father of the English poets yet to be'.[108] His description of Hild's role in Cædmon's career is equally provocative:

> It was a woman, a woman who was both shelter and inspiration; and
> I have sometimes thought it not too fanciful to say that Cædmon was

Hild's Laureate. I have observed with some surprise that in these later days a sort of crusade has been organised for the extension of the influence of woman. I should have thought that quite impossible, seeing that from the days of Adam she has really inspired and sympathised with man's feelings, his aspirations and his activities. It is woman who trains us to speak; it is woman who teaches us to pray; and it is woman, indeed it is woman, who stimulates us to sing.[109]

Austin's use of the first-person plural pronoun, 'us', is revealing as it directs attention once again to the creation and sustenance of personal and collective identities. Poetry and, by implication, history is made by men, even if inspired by women. Once again the medieval is used as a vehicle to elucidate contiguity between difference and identity, to mark out subject positions. As the monument works to essentialise and mythicise the beginnings of Christian English poetry, as it promotes a timeless notion of English nationhood and a singular national identity, Austin attempts to imagine social relations as occupying that same timeless, unchanging, now of the contemporary medieval. He also directs us, however, to the insight that this vision of the medieval past is the very first experience of that past.[110]

The Cædmon Memorial, then, along with St Augustine's Cross, returns us to the ideas of accuracy, authenticity and originality with which this chapter began. To borrow Judith Butler's language, these crosses are copies without an original and their 'imitation does not copy that which is prior, but produces and *inverts* the very terms of priority and derivativeness'.[111] They destabilise the binary between repetition and remembrance, the fake and the real, medievalism and medieval studies, medieval and modern. Freud's errors were perhaps not errors at all, then, but insights into the crosses' histories and meanings, gestures towards their unknowable pasts and futures and the continuities and discontinuities that characterise their history. Similarly, the discourses of authenticity that surround these crosses simply underscore the nebulous nature of the concept. Authenticity is invoked as a means of producing ideas of difference and similarity between peoples, places and times which rely on clean distinctions the crosses themselves question. The histories of the crosses unravel the very claims they are put to work to support. What unites all the crosses encountered in this chapter is their performance as sites of ideological and institutional discourse – of power, religion, the legitimacy of the state, personal and collective identity and the nature of change. In the next chapter, we will continue to examine how acts of medievalist cultural memory think through the fragmentation of the Middle Ages and the transformations of modernity and use the invocations of the medieval past as a means of restricting access to the future.

Notes

1 Sigmund Freud, 'First lecture', in *The Standard Edition of the Complete Psychological Works of Sigmund Freud*, James Strachey (ed. and trans.) in collaboration with Anna Freud, assisted by Alix Strachey and Alan Tyson, vol. 11 (London: Hogarth Press and the Institute of Psycho-analysis, 1957), pp. 9–21, pp. 16–7.
2 See 'The psychopathology of everyday life', in *The Standard Edition of the Complete Psychological Works of Sigmund Freud*, James Strachey (ed. and trans.) in collaboration with Anna Freud, with the assistance of Alix Strachey and Alan Tyson, vol. 6 (London: Hogarth Press and the Institute of Psycho-analysis, 1960), particularly 'Misreadings and slips of the pen', pp. 106–33.
3 Margreta de Grazia, 'The modern divide: From either side', *Journal of Medieval and Early Modern Studies* 37 (2007), 453–67, p. 453.
4 This is confirmed by the frequency with which Freud's mistake is repeated. See Cora Kaplan, *Victoriana: Histories, Fictions, Criticisms* (Edinburgh: Edinburgh University Press, 2007), p. 15: 'erected in memory of Richard Plantagenet's beloved Queen'; and Margaret Iverson, *Beyond Pleasure: Freud, Lacan, Barthes* (University Park, PA: Pennsylvania State University Press, 2007), p. 108: 'Charing Cross, an ornate stone cross outside the railway station in London, is the last remaining memorial set up along the path of the cortege taking the coffin of the queen of a thirteenth-century Plantagenet king to Westminster.'
5 Freud, 'First lecture', p. 16.
6 See *The Oxford Dictionary of Phrase and Fable*, 2nd edn, ed. Elizabeth Knowles (Oxford: Oxford University Press, 2005), p. 135.
7 A. D. Mills, *A Dictionary of British Place-Names* (Oxford: Oxford University Press, 2003), p. 107.
8 Sigmund Freud, 'Remembering, repeating and working-through (further recommendations on the technique of psycho-analysis)', in *The Standard Edition of the Complete Psychological Works of Sigmund Freud*, James Strachey (ed. and trans.) in collaboration with Anna Freud, assisted by Alix Strachey and Alan Tyson, vol. 13 (London: Hogarth Press and the Institute of Psycho-analysis, 1958), pp. 145–56, p. 150. Emphasis in the original.
9 Adam Phillips, 'Close-ups', in Mark Salber Phillips, Barbara Caine and Julia Adeney Thomas (eds), *Rethinking Historical Distance* (Basingstoke: Palgrave Macmillan, 2013), pp. 84–91, p. 87.

10 'Annales prioratus de Dunstaplia, AD 1–1297, from MS Cotton Tiberius A.X.', in Henry Richards Luard (ed.), *Annales Monastici*, vol 3: *Annales prioratus de Dunstaplia and Annales monasterii de Bermundeseia* (London: Longmans, Green, Reader, and Dyer, 1866), p. 362.

11 For an overview of the medieval crosses see R. Allen Brown, H. M. Colvin and A. J. Taylor, *The History of the King's Works*, vols 1 and 2: *The Middle Ages* (London: Ministry of Public Building and Works, 1963), pp. 479–85 and Jonathan Alexander and Paul Binski (eds), *Age of Chivalry: Art in Plantagenet England* (London: Royal Academy of Arts, 1987), pp. 361–4.

12 John Carmi Parsons, 'Ritual and symbol in English medieval queenship to 1500', in Louise O. Fradenburg (ed.), *Women and Sovereignty* (Edinburgh: Edinburgh University Press, 1992), pp. 60–77, p. 68.

13 Fradenburg, 'Introduction: Rethinking queenship', *Women and Sovereignty*, pp. 1–13, p. 5.

14 John Carmi Parsons, *Eleanor of Castile: Queen and Society in Thirteenth-Century England* (London: Macmillan, 1995), p. 122.

15 David Carpenter, *The Struggle for Mastery: Britain 1066–1284*, The Penguin History of Britain (London: Allen Lane, 2003), p. 42.

16 Paul Brand, 'Jews and the law in England, 1275–90', *English Historical Review* 115 (2000), 1138–58, p. 1140.

17 Carpenter, *Struggle for Mastery*, p. 488.

18 Marc Morris, *A Great and Terrible King: Edward I and the Forging of Britain* (London: Windmill Books, 2009), p. 226.

19 See Joe and Caroline Hillaby, *The Palgrave Dictionary of Medieval Anglo-Jewish History* (Basingstoke: Palgrave Macmillan, 2013), pp. 189–94.

20 Parsons, 'Appendix I: Queen Eleanor's lands', *Eleanor of Castile*, pp. 157–97.

21 *Registrum epistolarum Fratris Johannis Peckham, Archiepiscopi Cantuariensis*, 3 vols, ed. C. T. Martin (London: Longman, 1882–85), vol. 2, pp. 619–20, p. 619. Translated by Parsons, *Eleanor of Castile*, p. 120.

22 *Registrum epistolarum Fratris Johannis Peckham*, ed. Martin, vol. 3, pp. 937–8. Translated by Parsons, *Eleanor of Castile*, pp. 120–1.

23 *The Chronicle of Walter of Guisborough, Previously Edited as the Chronicle of Walter of Hemingford or Huemingburgh*, ed. Harry Rothwell (London: Royal Historical Society, 1957), p. 212. See also Parsons, *Eleanor of Castile*, p. 120.

24 Parsons makes a similar point, *Eleanor of Castile*, p. 154.

25 Parsons, *Eleanor of Castile*, pp. 109–13.

26 For a succinct and detailed description of Eleanor's memorials see Alexander and Binski (eds), *Age of Chivalry*, pp. 361–6.

27 Paul Binski, *Medieval Death: Ritual and Representation* (London: British Museum Press, 1996), p. 110.

28 Emmanuel Levinas, *Totality and Infinity: An Essay on Exteriority*, trans. Alphonso Lingis (London: Martinus Nijhoff Publishers, 1979), p. 193.

29 'Opus Chronicorum (MS Cotton Claudius D vi)', in Henry Thomas Riley (ed.), *Johannis de Trokelowe et Henrici de Blaneforde, monachorum S. Albani, necnon quorundam anonymorum chronica et annales, regnantibus Henrico tertio, Edwardo primo, Edwardo secundo, Ricardo secundo, et Henrico quarto* (London: Longmans, Green, Reader, and Dyer, 1866), pp. 3–62, pp. 49–50. Translated by Parsons, *Eleanor of Castile*, 216–17.

30 Elizabeth Hallam, 'Introduction: The Eleanor Crosses and royal burial customs', in David Parsons (ed.), *Eleanor of Castile 1290–1990: Essays to Commemorate the 700th Anniversary of her Death, 28th November 1290* (Stamford: Paul Watkins, 1991), pp. 9–22, p. 18.

31 See Éamonn Ó Carragáin, *Ritual and Rood: Liturgical Images and the Old English Poems of the Dream of the Rood Tradition* (London: British Library, 2005), pp. 7–8.

32 Catherine Karkov, *The Art of Anglo-Saxon England* (Woodbridge: Boydell Press, 2011), p. 145. See also Fred Orton and Ian Wood, with Clare A. Lees, *Fragments of History: Rethinking the Ruthwell and Bewcastle Monuments* (Manchester: University of Manchester Press, 2007), pp. 144–69.

33 Catherine Karkov, 'Art and writing: Voice, image, object', in Lees (ed.), *Cambridge History of Early Medieval English Literature*, pp. 73–98, p. 91.

34 See Rosemary Cramp, *Corpus of Anglo-Saxon Stone Sculpture*, vol 1: *County Durham and Northumberland* (Oxford: Oxford University Press, 1984), pp. 112–13; George Hardin Brown, 'Bede and the cross', in Karen Louise Jolly, Catherine E. Karkov and Sarah Larratt Keefer (eds), *Cross and Culture in Anglo-Saxon England: Studies in Honor of George Hardin Brown*, Medieval European Studies IX (Morgantown: West Virginia University Press, 2007), pp. 19–35; and Ó Carragáin, *Ritual and the Rood*, p. 32. On sculpture in Anglo-Saxon Jarrow see Richard N. Bailey, *England's Earliest Sculptors*, Publications of the Dictionary of Old English 5 (Toronto: Pontifical Institute of Mediaeval Studies, 1996), pp. 30–6.

35 Rufinus, *Historia ecclesiastica*, IX.9, 1, ed. T. Mommsen, Eusebius Werke 2.2 (Leipzig, 1908), pp. 827–9. See also Ian Wood, 'Constantinian crosses in Northumbria', in Catherine E. Karkov, Sarah Larratt Keefer and Karen Louise Jolly (eds), *The Place of the Cross in Anglo-Saxon England*, Publications of the Manchester Centre for Anglo-Saxon Studies (Woodbridge: Boydell Press, 2006), pp. 3–13; Calvin B. Kendall, 'From sign to vision: The Ruthwell Cross and the *Dream of the Rood*', in Karkov, Keefer and Jolly (eds), *The Place of the*

Cross in Anglo-Saxon England, pp. 129–44; and Sandra McEntire, 'The devotional context of the cross before AD 1000', in Paul E. Szarmach and Virginia Darrow Oggins (eds), *Sources of Anglo-Saxon Culture*, Studies in Medieval Culture 20 (Kalamazoo, MI: Medieval Institute, 1986), pp. 345–56.

36 Bede, *Ecclesiastical History*, pp. 215–19. See also Douglas Mac Lean, 'King Oswald's wooden cross at Heavenfield in context', in Catherine E. Karkov, Robert T. Farrell and Michael Ryan (eds), *The Insular Tradition* (Albany: State University of New York Press, 1997), pp. 79–98. J. M. Wallace-Hadrill links Bede's story of Oswald's cross to the Jarrow Cross and Rufinus' account of Constantine's vision in *Bede's 'Ecclesiastical History of the English People': A Historical Commentary* (Oxford: Clarendon Press, 1988), p. 89.

37 See 'The Dispute between Mary and the cross', in Susanna Greer Fein (ed.), *Moral Love Songs and Laments* (Kalamazoo, MI: Western Michigan University, 1998), pp. 87–160. On the connection between the cross and women see Ó Carragáin, *Ritual and Rood*, pp. 308–11. On the Anglo-Saxon traditions see Mary-Catherine Bodden, *The Old English Finding of the True Cross* (Cambridge: D. S. Brewer, 1987).

38 Stephen Matthews, 'The content and construction of the *Vita Haroldi*', in Gale R. Owen-Crocker (ed.), *King Harold and the Bayeux Tapestry*, Publications of the Manchester Centre for Anglo-Saxon Studies (Woodbridge: Boydell Press, 2005), pp. 65–92, p. 68. I would like to thank Professor Owen-Crocker for this reference.

39 John Zukowsky, 'Montjoies and Eleanor Crosses reconsidered', *Gesta* 13 (1974), 39–44, p. 39. On the cult of St Louis see M. Cecilia Gaposchkin, *The Making of Saint Louis: Kingship, Sanctity, and Crusade in the Later Middle Ages* (Ithaca, NY: Cornell University Press, 2008).

40 Robert Branner makes an important distinction, however, when he notes that although it seems likely that the montjoies were designed as part of a sustained campaign to secure Louis' canonisation, there is no evidence the Eleanor Crosses had such ambitions. See Robert Branner, 'The montjoies of St. Louis', in D. Fraser, H. Hibbard, M. Lewine (eds), *Essays in the History of Architecture presented to Rudolf Wittkower on his Sixty-Fifth Birthday* (London: Phaidon Press, 1967), pp. 13–16, p. 15. See also Joseph Hunter, 'On the death of Eleanor of Castile, consort of King Edward the First, and the honours paid to her memory', *Archaeologia* 29 (1841), 167–91 and Joan Evans, 'A Prototype of the Eleanor Crosses', *Burlington Magazine* 91 (1949), 96–9.

41 David Stocker, 'The shrine of Little St Hugh', in T. A. Heslop (ed.), *Medieval Art and Architecture at Lincoln Cathedral* (London: British Architectural Association, 1996), pp. 109–18, p. 115.

42 Anthony Bale, *The Jew in the Medieval Book: English Antisemitisms, 1350–1500* (Cambridge: Cambridge University Press, 2006), pp. 137–8.

43 Janet Backhouse, *Medieval Rural Life in the Luttrell Psalter* (London: British Library, 2000), p. 33.
44 Michelle Brown, *The Luttrell Psalter: A Facsimile* (London: British Library, 2006), p. 44.
45 See Michael Camille, *Mirror in Parchment: The Luttrell Psalter and the Making of Medieval England* (London: Reaktion, 1998), p. 166.
46 See Michael Clanchy, *From Memory to Written Record: England 1066–1307* (Oxford: Blackwell, 1993), pp. 194–5.
47 Lucy Freeman Sandler, 'The word in the text and the image in the margin: The case of the Luttrell Psalter', *Journal of the Walters Art Gallery* 54 (1996), 87–99, p. 96.
48 See Robert W. Dunning, 'Luttrell (Lutterell) family (*per. c.* 1200–1428, gentry', in *Oxford Dictionary of National Biography* (Oxford: Oxford University Press, 2004), www.oxforddnb.com/view/article/54529?docPos=1, accessed 24 October 2017.
49 See Camille, *Mirror in Parchment*, p. 136 (on the will) and p. 157.
50 Nuala Johnson, 'Cast in stone: Monuments, geography and nationalism', *Environment and Planning D: Society and Space* 13 (1995), 51–65, p. 63.
51 Thomas Aquinas, *Commentary on the Gospel of St John: Chapters 1–5*, trans. Fabian Larcher and James A. Weisheipl with an introduction and notes by Daniel Keating and Matthew Levering (Washington, DC: Catholic University of America Press, 2010), p. 2.
52 Maurice Keen, *English Society in the Later Middle Ages, 1348–1500* (London: Penguin, 1990), p. 115.
53 John Stow, *A Survey of London. Reprinted from the Text of 1603*, ed. Charles Lethbridge Kingsford, 2 vols (Oxford: Clarendon, 1908), vol. 1, p. 266.
54 John Elder, 'John Elder's letter describing the arrival and marriage of King Philip, his triumphal entry into London, the legation of Cardinal Pole, &c. To Lord Robert Stuart, c. 1554', in John Nichols (ed.), *The chronicle of Queen Jane, and of two years of Queen Mary, and especially of the rebellion of Sir Thomas Wyat: written by a Resident in the Tower of London* (London: Camden Society, 1850), pp. 136–66, p. 149.
55 William Lilly, 'Observations upon the life and death of King Charles I', in T. Davies (ed.), *The Lives of those Eminent Antiquaries Elias Ashmole, esquire, and Mr William Lilly, written by themselves ...* (London: T. Davies, 1774), p. 255. On the destruction of the cross and Robert Harley's committee, see Julie Spraggon, *Puritan Iconoclasm during the English Civil War* (Woodbridge: Boydell Press, 2003), pp. 84–6 and Margaret Aston, *England's Iconoclasts*, vol. 1: *Laws against Images* (Oxford: Oxford University Press, 1988), p. 76. For a detailed partisan account of the destruction of Cheapside Cross see John Vicars, 'Magnalia Dei Anglicana', in *Jehovah-Jireh, God in the Mount: or,*

England's Parliamentary Chronicle (London: J. Rothwell and T. Underhill, 1646), pp. 326–7.

56 Edward Dering, *A briefe and necessary catechisme or instructio(n). Very needfull to be known of al housholders. Wherby they may teach & instruct ther famelies, in such pointes of Christian religion as is most meete. With prayers to the same adioyning* (Middelburg: Printed by Richard Schilders, 1590), n.p.

57 James Simpson, *Under the Hammer: Iconoclasm in the Anglo-American Tradition* (Oxford: Oxford University Press, 2010), p. 71.

58 Bruno Latour, *On the Modern Cult of the Factish Gods*, trans. Catherine Porter and Heather MacLean (Durham, NC: Duke University Press, 2010), p. 11.

59 William Henry Overall and Henry Charles Overall (eds), *Analytical Index to the Series of Records known as the Remembrancia. Preserved among the Archives of the City of London. A.D. 1579–1664* (London: E. J. Francis & Co., 1878), pp. 65–6, p. 66.

60 *Cheap-side cross censured and condemned by a letter sent from the vice-chancellour and other learned men of the famous Universitie of Oxford* (London: Printed by A. N. for I. R., 1641), p. 3.

61 David Cressy, *Travesties and Transgressions in Tudor and Stuart England: Tales of Discord and Dissension* (Oxford: Oxford University Press, 2000), p. 235.

62 Richard Overton, *Articles of high treason exhibited against Cheap-side cross. With the last will and testament of the said crosse. And certaine epitaphs upon her tombe. By R. Overton. Newly printed and newly come forth; with his holinesse priviledge, to prevent false copies* (London: Printed for R. Overton, 1642), p. 4.

63 *Cheap-side cross censured and condemned*, p. 14.

64 *The Downe-fall of Dagon, or, The taking downe of Cheap-side crosse this second of May, 1643* (London: Printed for Thomas Wilson, 1642), n.p.

65 Ryhen Pameach (Henry Peacham), *A dialogue between the crosse in Cheap, and Charing Crosse. Comforting each other, as fearing their fall in these uncertaine times* (London, 1641), n.p.

66 Cathy Caruth, *Unclaimed Experience: Trauma, Narrative, and History* (London: Johns Hopkins University Press, 1996), p. 3.

67 Caruth, *Unclaimed Experience*, p. 4.

68 William Camden, *Camden's Britannia, 1695: A Facsimile of the 1695 edition published by Edmund Gibson (translated from the Latin), with an introduction by Stuart Piggott and a bibliographical note by Gwyn Walters* (Newton Abbot: David & Charles, 1971), p. 320. For an account of the transmission of this legend see Parsons, *Eleanor of Castile*, pp. 223–4.

69 Agnes Strickland, *Lives of the Queens of England from the Norman Conquest* (Philadelphia: Blanchard and Lea, 1852), p. 428 (on the Acre legend) and p. 445 (on Eleanor's beauty and Edward's love).

70 Strickland, *Lives of the Queens*, p. 447.

71 See Nicola C. Smith, 'George Gilbert Scott and the Martyrs' Memorial', *Journal of the Warburg and Courtauld Institutes* 42 (1979), pp. 195–206.

72 On the anti-Catholicism of the Memorial see Andrew Atherstone, 'The Martyrs' Memorial at Oxford', *Journal of Ecclesiastical History* 54 (2003), 278–301.

73 On the Ilam Cross see Nikolaus Pevsner, *Staffordshire*, The Buildings of England (London: Penguin, 1974), pp. 152–3. Although he did later complete work for Watts-Russell, Scott was not responsible for the cross. See David Cole, *The Work of Sir Gilbert Scott* (London: Architectural Press, 1980), p. 215.

74 Clare Hartwell, Matthew Hyde and Nikolaus Pevsner, *Lancashire: Manchester and the South East*, The Buildings of England (London: Yale University Press, 2004), pp. 668–9.

75 On the Cheltenham memorial (1903) see David Verey and Alan Brooks, *Gloucestershire 2: The Vale and the Forest of Dean*, The Buildings of England (New Haven: Yale University Press, 2002), p. 249. On medievalist First World War memorials see Stefan Goebel, *The Great War and Medieval Memory: War, Remembrance and Medievalism* (Cambridge: Cambridge University Press, 2007), p. 239.

76 Alexander Nagel and Christopher Wood, *Anachronic Renaissance* (New York: Zone Books, 2010), pp. 29–30.

77 T. S. Eliot, 'Tradition and the individual talent', in *The Sacred Wood: Essays on Poetry and Criticism* (New York: Alfred A. Knopf, 1921), pp. 42–53, p. 44.

78 On Pugin see Rosemary Hill, *God's Architect: Pugin and the Building of Romantic Britain* (London: Allen Lane, 2007).

79 'The speakers at the meeting', *The Times* (15 January 1862), p. 9. On Albert's death and mourning see John Wolfe, *Great Deaths: Grieving, Religion, and Nationhood in Victorian and Edwardian Britain* (Oxford: Oxford University Press for the British Academy, 2000), pp. 192–204.

80 JA (Temple), 'Prince Albert's cross', *Daily News*, 25 December 1862, p. 3.

81 'We have lately described ...', *The Times*, 28 March 1863, p. 11. It is, as Stephen Bayley suggests, intriguing that Gilbert Scott never once referred to Brown's designs in his writings on architecture. See Stephen Bayley, *The Albert Memorial: The Monument in its Social and Architectural Context* (London: Scholar Press, 1981), p. 20.

82 'Designs for the national Albert memorial', *The Builder*, 4 April 1863, p. 233.

83 George Gilbert Scott, *Personal and Professional Recollections*, ed. Gavin Stamp (Stamford: Paul Watkins, 1995), p. 59.

84 'The national monument to the Prince Consort', *Morning Post*, 5 December 1864, p. 2.

85 John Abel, *Memorials of Queen Eleanor, Illustrated by Photography: with a short account of their history and present condition* (London: Published for the Proprietor, 1864), n.p. The quotation is taken from Alfred Lord Tennyson's 'Ode sung at the opening of the International Exhibition'.

86 On Charing Cross see Oliver Green, *Discovering London Railway Stations* (Oxford: Shire Publications and London Transport Museum, 2010), pp. 82–7.

87 Charles Dickens, *Dombey and Son*, ed. Andrew Sanders (London: Penguin, 2002), p. 79.

88 Ian Carter, *Railways and Culture in Britain: The Epitome of Modernity* (Manchester: Manchester University Press, 2001), p. 90.

89 *Illustrated London News*, 9 December 1865, p. 560.

90 Q., 'On the new cross at Charing', *The Builder*, 19 August 1865, p. 594.

91 Dipesh Chakrabarty, *Provincializing Europe: Postcolonial Thought and Historical Difference* (Princeton: Princeton University Press, 2008), p. 12.

92 'The landing of St Augustine in England: An interesting memorial', *Birmingham Daily Post*, 22 July 1884, p. 4.

93 'St Augustine's Cross in the Isle of Thanet', *The Tablet*, 27 September 1884. Article reprinted in the appendix to the second volume of Edmond Fitzmaurice, *The Life of Granville George Leveson Gower, Second Earl Granville*, 2nd edn (London: Longmans, Green, 1905), pp. 509–12, p. 509.

94 'St Augustine's Cross in the Isle of Thanet', p. 510.

95 The works referred to are George Ormerod, *The history of the county palatine and city of Chester … incorporated with a republication of King's Vale Royal and Leycester's Cheshire antiquities*, 3 vols (London: Lackington, 1816–19) and Albert Rimmer, *Ancient Stone Crosses of England* (London: Virtue & Co., 1875).

96 Stephanie Trigg, *Shame and Honor: A Vulgar History of the Order of the Garter* (Philadelphia: University of Pennsylvania Press, 2012), p. 35.

97 On the Sandbach Crosses see Jane Hawkes, *The Sandbach Crosses: Sign and Significance in Anglo-Saxon Sculpture* (Dublin: Four Courts Press, 2002).

98 Muriel E. Chamberlain, 'Gower, Granville George Leveson-, second Earl Granville (1815–1891), politician', *Oxford Dictionary of National Biography*; online edn, January 2008, www.oxforddnb.com/view/article/16543?docPos=2, accessed 24 October 2017.

99 Solveig C. Robinson, 'Fullerton (*née* Leveson-Gower), Lady Georgina Charlotte (1812–85), novelist and philanthropist', *Oxford Dictionary of National Biography*; online edn, January 2008, www.oxforddnb.com/view/article/10242/?back=,16543, accessed 24 October 2017.

100 Gerald Parsons, 'Victorian Roman Catholicism: Emancipation, expansion and achievement', in Gerald Parsons (ed.), *Religion in Victorian Britain*, vol. 1: *Traditions* (Manchester: Manchester University Press and the Open University, 1988), pp. 146–84, p. 175.

101 'Latest intelligence', *The Times*, 13 October 1884, p. 5.

102 'The Augustinian celebration. Prelates at Ebbsfleet', *Morning Post*, 3 July 1897, p. 8.

103 'The landing of St Augustine in Kent', *Daily News*, 3 July 1897, p. 6.

104 H. D. Rawnsley, '"Caedmon Memorial" at Whitby', *The Times*, 8 February 1898, p. 8.

105 Matthew Townend, 'Victorian medievalisms', in Matthew Bevis (ed.), *The Oxford Handbook of Victorian Poetry* (Oxford: Oxford University Press, 2013), pp. 166–83, p. 167.

106 Stuart Hall, 'Whose heritage? Un-settling "the heritage", re-imagining the post-nation', in Jo Littler and Roshi Naidoo (eds), *The Politics of Heritage: The Legacies of 'Race'* (London: Routledge, 2005), pp. 23–35, p. 25. See also Robert Hewison, *The Heritage Industry: Britain in a Climate of Decline* (London: Methuen, 1987).

107 On Victorian attitudes to King Alfred see Joanne Parker, *'England's Darling': The Victorian Cult of Alfred the Great* (Manchester: Manchester University Press, 2007) and Simon Keynes, 'The cult of King Alfred', *Anglo-Saxon England* 28 (1999), 225–356.

108 *The Cædmon Memorial. Being a description of the cross, with explanation of lettering and figures thereon* (Whitby: Horne & Son, 1899), p. 10.

109 *The Cædmon Memorial*, p. 13.

110 Caruth expresses a similar idea in *Unclaimed Experience*, p. 14.

111 Judith Butler, 'Imitation and gender insubordination', in Henry Abelove, Michèle Aina Barale and David M. Halperin (eds), *The Lesbian and Gay Studies Reader* (London: Routledge, 1993), pp. 307–20, p. 313.

3
Medievalist double consciousness and the production of difference: Medieval bards, cultural memory and nationalist fantasy

Thomas Gray's 1757 poem 'The Bard' sits at the centre of a complex network of medievalist cultural memory. Gray was an accomplished scholar and historian as well as poet, familiar with many works of medieval as well as Classical literature, and his poem was first published at his good friend Horace Walpole's press at Strawberry Hill. An image of Walpole's astonishing medievalist building is printed on its title page (see Figure 3.1). Strawberry Hill was built between 1749 and 1776 and was the first house built in the Gothic style without any medieval origins of its own.[1] 'The Bard' charts a similar course between fact and fiction, the critical and the creative, history and cultural memory. It poses, like the Eleanor Crosses, complex questions regarding authenticity and the relationship between history and memory.

The poem claims to tell the story of the last Welsh bard, a figure who is presented as the voice of a lost people, speaking of and from the past, but the poem also draws on the Arthurian tradition and speaks eloquently of contemporary concerns. The classical form civilises the poem's medieval interests. The poem's preface, which tells its readers that, 'The following Ode is founded on a Tradition current in Wales, that EDWARD the First, when he compleated the conquest of that country, ordered all the Bards, that fell into his hands, to be put to death', reveals its interests in history and memory.[2] When Gray suggests that the tradition is 'current' in Wales, he implies that Wales is not quite on the same temporal plane as England and, by implication, not quite in the present. This 'denial of coevalness', to use Johannes Fabian's term, is also a denial of social agency: Gray's vision of the medieval past is structured by contemporary power relations and the colonial history of England and Wales.[3]

In English culture, the bard is a figure always caught between modernity and the Middle Ages. While there were thriving

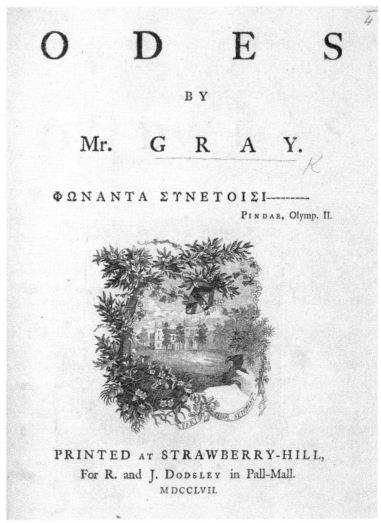

3.1 Title page of Thomas Gray's *Odes* (1757)

traditions of public poetry in medieval Ireland, Scotland and Wales, there is little evidence of bardic performance in Anglo-Saxon or medieval English sources.[4] Indeed, the word 'bard' only entered the English language in the fifteenth century as a loanword from the Celtic vernaculars of Ireland, Scotland and Wales.[5] This linguistic history reveals the main concerns of Gray's poem – the relations among the nations of the British Isles and the importance of cultural memory to ideas of nationhood. His poem asks how the medieval past informs the contours of national identity. This chapter takes this question as its focus and explores how acts of memory express nationalist fantasies of wholeness and exclusion. It begins in Britain but traces a transnational network of cultural memory that encompasses Hungary and Denmark. It examines how works of memory that promote ideas of nationhood according to medieval structures always reveal, as Jeffrey Jerome Cohen, Kathleen Davis, Patrick Geary, Sharon Kinoshita and others have demonstrated, the arbitrariness and precarity of racial and national boundaries, even as they attempt to secure them through the production of difference.[6] The very limits of the work medievalist cultural memory can achieve demand its repetition and reiteration. The questions Gray's poem raises regarding the relationship between the medieval past and the modern nation remain central concerns of medievalist cultural memory.

Medievalist nation building

On 15 June 2015, David Cameron, Prime Minister of the United Kingdom, attempted to explain the relevance of the medieval past to twenty-first-century Britain in a speech at Runnymede in Surrey to mark the eight hundredth anniversary of the signing of Magna Carta, the celebrated charter signed by King John that put certain limits on the sovereign's power. Cameron made a case for the continuing significance of Magna Carta – and the importance of cultural memories of the medieval past in twenty-first-century Britain – premised on the connection between the charter, the landscape of Britain and the British nation, declaring that 'We talk about the "law of the land" and this is the very land where that law – and the rights that flow from it – took root.' He approached Magna Carta not as a historical document to be studied and interrogated but as a piece of cultural memory, with self-evident value and meaning. So what was significant about the document, for Cameron, was not its historical context or even its contents, but its influence. Again, this claim was bound up in a celebration of British national identity and, implicitly, its imperial history:

> What happened in these meadows eight centuries ago is as relevant today as it was then. And that relevance extends far beyond Britain. All over the world, people are still struggling to live by the rule of law and to see their governments subject to that law. The countries that have these things tend to be the long term successes. Those who

don't tend to be the long term failures. And what is taken for granted here in Britain, what is sewn into the fabric of our nation, so deep we barely even question it is what others are crying out for, hoping for, praying for.

Cameron looked back to Magna Carta, and the Middle Ages more broadly, as a site of pure ideological origin, a source of the instruments that define modern British national identity and a cause of the continued prosperity and power of the nation. While the histories of the Eleanor Crosses reveal the transformations of medieval culture as it is used to generate collective identities, Cameron saw Magna Carta as an essential, unchanging foundation of British culture. For Cameron, 'Magna Carta is something every person in Britain should be proud of.'[7] But exactly what Magna Carta is or was, or what it achieved or intended, was left unsaid.

Cameron's medievalist thinking requires no interrogation of the culture of the Middle Ages, allows no room for the complexity or indeterminacy of history – such as the fact that the 1215 Magna Carta was annulled by Pope Innocent III the same year – but he presents a rich sense of the continuing presence of medieval culture in the twenty-first century, although on the condition that that history is understood as over and settled.[8] While he is keen to present Britain as an archetypically modern nation, 'a long term success' in which the people and the government are governed by law, the very qualities of modernity in this instance are located in the Middle Ages. Those countries that, for Cameron, are 'long term failures' are presumably not just not quite modern, but also lack a Middle Ages. So Cameron presents a model of historical time that is at once supercessionary, as Britain has left the Middle Ages while other countries have not; nonlinear, as the social and cultural forms and practices of the Middle Ages continue to define British life, even as that past is passed and uninterrogated; and nonidentical with itself, as some apparently contemporary nations have not quite left the Middle Ages. Like Gray's preface, Cameron denies 'coevalness' to those countries he defines as 'long term failures'. For Cameron, the Middle Ages is simultaneously inside and outside modernity. As I will explore below, Gray's poem engages similar structures of thought.

There is some provocative overlap between the Prime Minister's thoughts on the importance of Magna Carta and the historian Sharon Turner's thoughts on the value of the Anglo-Saxon past.

In his monumental *History of the Anglo-Saxons*, first published in 1799, Turner writes that:

> Though other invaders have appeared in the island, yet the effects of the Anglo-Saxon settlements have prevailed beyond every other. Our language, our government, and our laws, display our Gothic ancestors in every part: they live, not merely in our annals and traditions, but in our civil institutions and perpetual discourse. The parent-tree is indeed greatly amplified, by the branches grafted on it from other regions, and by the new shoots, which the accidents of time, and the improvements of society, have produced; but it discovers yet its Saxon origin and retains its Saxon properties.[9]

Like Cameron's speech, Turner's reflection on the importance of the medieval past appropriates the language of the natural world to express nationalist sentiment. Unlike Cameron, Turner encouraged the examination of that past, but he did so with a clear sense of its contemporary meaning and function. For both the historian and the politician, there is a doubleness about the idea of the Middle Ages, as what is valuable about the medieval past is, first of all, that it is over, but also that it continues to define the present.

In Paul Freedman and Gabrielle Spiegel's terms, Cameron and Turner offer examples of the 'dual consciousness' of the Middle Ages, conceptions of the medieval past 'as a place and time of non-origin (that is, the dark period constructed in and by the Renaissance) and that of origin (the origin of the modern state)'.[10] Moreover, in both Cameron and Turner's thinking, there is an implicit suggestion that the Middle Ages defines social identities as well as institutions. This sense that the Middle Ages is at once present and absent, inside and outside modernity, and informs modern subject positions, ethnic and racial identities, is what I am calling 'medievalist double consciousness'. W. E. B. Du Bois coined the term 'double consciousness' to describe how an individual might feel that their identity was composed of several parts. He used it to speak of the experience of African Americans, living in a white culture but always feeling alien, as Du Bois put it, 'always looking at one's self through the eyes of others'.[11] What Du Bois described as the 'two-ness' of this experience speaks eloquently to the doubleness of medieval culture identified by Freedman and Spiegel, but his phrasing draws attention to the construction of subjectivity that I will argue is often implicit in medievalist thinking. There are significant differences between Du Bois' formulation and my deployment of his language. Medievalist double consciousness is not a feeling but rather a projection, a means of identifying a problem, undermining or bolstering a social identity. Using Du Bois' language reminds us that, in Homi Bhabha's words, 'What is at issue is the performative nature of differential identities', because when Cameron speaks of the self-evident value of Magna Carta, he reveals his own comfort and unquestioned belief in an idea of a benign, triumphant Britishness.[12] Similarly, when Turner celebrates the Anglo-Saxon past in the context of the British Empire, he offers his history to those who ruled rather than those who were subjugated in the Empire. Both these visions of the medieval past, then, are produced by and produce historically and culturally situated personal and collective identities, which are in turn expressed in hierarchical language: some people and nations are 'long term successes', others are not; those who enjoy such success have 'Saxon' or medieval 'origin' or 'properties'; those who do not, do not. Medievalist double consciousness offers a fantasy of wholeness and exclusion. It is a means of producing difference and marks some people, some places and some nations as abject. How might a citizen of the Commonwealth respond to Turner's Anglo-Saxonism? How might a non-Briton, a citizen of one of the countries Cameron identifies as a 'long term failure', respond to his paean to Magna Carta? If the medieval is open and relational, Cameron and Turner suggest that not everyone can enjoy equal access to it.

Since the rise of romantic nationalism in the eighteenth century, the idea of the Middle Ages has occupied a crucial role in formulations of the idea of the nation. On the one hand, many social scientists and historians have claimed that nationhood is a uniquely modern phenomenon and have used the Middle Ages as a foil against which to define complex and vital modernity. For Benedict Anderson, for instance, the people of the Middle Ages enjoyed an 'unselfconscious coherence' that meant that collective identities were self-evident and undisputed.[13] On the other hand, however, as Ernest Gellner writes, the 'self-image of nationalism involves the stress of folk, folklore, popular culture' and other traces of culture commonly located in the Middle Ages.[14] The modern popularity of the Eleanor Crosses provides one piece of evidence in support of this insight. Again, then, the Middle Ages is constructed as simultaneously subject and other: origin and non-origin. This is the structure of thought demonstrated by David Cameron's reflections on Magna Carta: Britain is modern because it had, and because it left, a Middle Ages. So the very possibility of a modern sense of nationhood relies on medievalist double consciousness.

The idea of the Middle Ages has also been used to define the social, ethnic and racial identities of the people who occupy nations. Medievalist double consciousness is implicitly present in both Cameron's and Turner's thinking, but a more explicit example is evident in the first published history of English poetry, Thomas Warton's *History of English Poetry*, which first appeared in 1774. Warton claimed that what he called 'Saxon' was a 'language subsisting on unformed principles, and polished by poets and theologians, however corrupted by the Danes [it] had much perspicuity, strength and harmony' before it was undermined by French.[15] Warton seems to have known little Old English and began his history with the Norman Conquest, but he nevertheless understood the Anglo-Saxon past as a point of pure origin, even as he constructed it as a non-origin by eliding it from his history. Moreover, for Warton, this origin was both cultural and racial. As John Niles indicates, Warton 'tends to construe the evolution of the English language during the period after the Conquest as a process of corruption and, indeed, miscegenation'.[16] As with Cameron and Turner, Warton uses an idea of medieval culture to produce hierarchical differences between peoples and nations in the present, without allowing medieval culture to actually take an active presence in the present.

While Warton offers one of the clearest and earliest examples of racialised medievalist thinking, other instances are not hard to find. In *Ivanhoe*, his enormously successful and influential novel of 1819 set in late twelfth-century England, for instance, Walter Scott wrote that 'four generations had not sufficed to blend the hostile blood of the Normans and Anglo-Saxons, or to unite, by common language and mutual interests, two hostile races'.[17] Like Cameron and Turner, Warton and Scott offer a Middle Ages mediated by the idea of the nation and racial thinking. They offer a model of medievalist cultural memory in which fantasies of cultural and ethnic origin flourish. As we will see, Gray's 1757 poem at once anticipates these performances of cultural memory and engages medieval structures of difference established during the English conquest of Wales in the late thirteenth century. 'The Bard' looks both backwards and forwards as it contemplates the history of Welsh culture and its relationship with England, the English and the British.

Thomas Gray's British-Welsh bard

Gray's poem produced a nationalist fantasy of wholeness and exclusion. The poem begins with a bard standing, with 'hagged eyes … and hoary hair / Streamed like a meteor' on a rock in Snowdonia 'o'er old Conway's flowing flood'.[18] Below him Edward I's army is making ever further progress into Wales. Acknowledging his inevitable defeat, the bard delivers a prophecy to Edward that confirms his and his line's eventual doom. The bard's declaration and the poem both begin with the exclamation 'Ruin seize thee, ruthless King!' (1), before promising that although Edward is currently 'fann'd by Conquest's crimson wing' (3) his military and political victories will not be enough 'To save thy secret soul from nightly fears, / From Cambria's curse, from Cambria's tears!' (7–8).

The bard summons 'a grisly band' (44) of his fellow poets, 'Avengers of their native land' and they speak together, 'in dreadful harmony', to 'weave with bloody hands the tissue' of Edward's line (46–8). Their voices proceed through 300 years of English history to deliver a curse to Edward that foresees Edward II's 'shrieks of death' ringing 'through Berkeley' castle (55), the 'terrors' of the violence of the hundred years' war that Edward III fought with France (60), the crimes of Richard III, a 'bristled boar in infant gore' (93), and the 'usurper' Henry VI (90). After this whirlwind celebration of the fall of Edward's House of Plantagenet, the bards turn their attention to the rise of the House of Tudor and Henry VIII's accession to the throne, which they celebrate fulsomely. 'No more our long-lost Arthur we bewail', the bards proclaim, 'All-hail, ye genuine kings, Britannia's issue, hail!' (109–10). For Gray's bards, then, the fact that the House of Tudor was of Welsh origin signifies a victory over their conquerors. Despite the fact that Henry's reign also saw the union of England and the Principality of Wales in the 1536 Act of Union and the 1542 Laws of Wales Act, which can be seen as conclusive acts of conquest, the bards read it as a glorious resolution. For other communities in Wales, the experience would have been very different, as the 1536 legislation sought to 'extirpate all the singular uses and customs' of the Welsh and attempted to ensure that 'no person or persons that use Welsh speech or language shall have or enjoy any manner of office or fees'.[19] Gray's bards, however, demonstrate an 'unselfconscious coherence' as they speak together to tell a unified story of Welsh culture and history.

As the bards' prophecy reaches into the sixteenth century they celebrate the reign of Elizabeth I, 'Her lion-port, her awe-commanding face, / Attemper'd sweet to virgin-grace' and the poetry of Spenser, Shakespeare and Milton (116–17). This is fitting, as the future the bards forecast is the past of the history plays of Shakespeare and Marlowe. The precise terms on which the medieval is permitted to signify are defined by the concluding lines of the poem when, having delivered his and his grisly band's prophecy and recorded history up to Gray's present day, the bard has served his purpose and takes his leave:

> 'Enough for me: With joy I see
> The different doom our Fates assign.
> Be thine Despair, and scept'red Care,
> To triumph, and to die, are mine.'
> He spoke, and headlong from the mountain's height
> Deep in the roaring tide he plung'd to endless night. (139–44)

The final destiny of the bard adds a further layer of complexity to the temporalities of the poem. Once the poem comes to an end the bard is not merely the last voice of an extinguished people, but a voice that is itself always already dead. The voices of the Welsh bards are doubly extinguished, first by Edward's massacre, and finally, ultimately, by the bard's suicide. The only thing that enables Gray's bard to speak is the promise of death.

The pastness of the bards is confirmed by the political content of their speech. As Peter Lord notes, it is Arthur rather than Llewelyn that Gray's bards imagine as their lord.[20] When they exclaim that 'No more our long-lost Arthur we bewail. / All-hail, ye genuine kings, Britannia's issue, hail!', the bards turn to cultural memory rather than historical fact. The bards' fantasies of an independent Wales and a Britain not dominated by England are necessarily mythic and unreal and can thus be subsumed into the Britain of the eighteenth century, which was of course dominated by England.[21] As with the medievalist remakings of *The Ruin* and the Eleanor Crosses, medieval culture in 'The Bard' is always already mediated. Unlike those other examples, however, upon closer examination the history at the centre of Gray's poem refuses final interpretation.

Gray found the story of Edward's massacre of the bards of Wales in Thomas Carte's 1738 *General History of England*. Of Edward's conquest of Wales, Carte writes that:

> The onely sort of men among the Welsh, that had reason to complain of Edward's severity, were the Bards, who used to put those remains of the antient Britains in mind of the valiant deeds of their ancestors: he ordered them all to be hanged as inciters of the people

to sedition. Politiks in this point got the better of the king's natural lenity: and those, who were afterwards entrusted with the government of the country, following his example, the profession became dangerous, gradually declined, and in a little time, that sort of men was utterly destroyed.[22]

As with Gray's history of Anglo-Walsh relations, this is a decidedly English vision of British history. The 'onely' tells us that Carte saw Edward's conquest as, on balance, a very good thing for the people of Wales.

Carte's own source for the story was a work called *The History of the Gwydir Family* written by Sir John Wynn, a Welsh landowner and historian, between 1590 and 1614.[23] Wynn's history was designed to secure his family's pedigree and claimed to trace their lineage back to the eleventh-century king of Gwynedd, Gruffudd ap Cynan. In reality, his family's rise could only be traced back with any confidence to a landowner named Maredudd ab Ieuan ap Robert who lived between 1465 and 1525. In his *History*, Sir John Wynn quotes an early fifteenth-century poem by the bard Rhys Goch Eryri before stating that:

> This is the most ancient story I can find extant which is addressed to any of my ancestors since the reign of Edward I, who caused all our bards to be hanged by martial law as stirrers of the people to sedition, whose example being followed by the governors of Wales until Henry IV's time was the utter destruction of that sort of men.

This statement is the sum total of the evidence for Edward I's purge of the bards. Today it is recognised as myth rather than history and not even mentioned by either Michael Prestwich or Marc Morris in their lengthy studies of Edward.[24] Indeed, it is unclear whether Gray himself believed the story to be historically true or merely a curiosity of cultural memory.[25] Wynn too seems to recognise that he is treading on thin ice and offers a fascinating meditation on historiography as a means of justifying his methods:

> [T]here is no certainty or very little of things done other than what is to be found in the Prince's records which now, by tossing the same from the Exchequer at Caernarfon to the Tower and to the offices in the Exchequer at London, as also by ill-keeping and ordering of late days, are become a chaos and confusion for any man to find things in order as were needful for him to have who would be ascertained of the truth of things done from time to time. I have, to my charge, done what I could but for my travail have reaped little or nothing as you see.[26]

For Wynn it is the custodians of the history who have brought chaos to it. He sees himself as repairing the past, undoing the 'ill-keeping and ordering of late days', as he remakes it according to his own image.

There is another significant connection between the Wynn family and Gray's 'Bard'. Although Gray began the poem in 1754, he didn't complete it for three years. As he himself told it, it was a performance by a real-life Welsh bard which provided the inspiration required to finish it. This bard was John Parry, a Welsh musician known as Parry Ddall (or Blind Parry).[27] Parry played the triple harp and was also a scholar who edited important collections of early Welsh music, as well as resident harpist to Sir Watkin Williams Wynn, a relation of Sir John Wynn's. When Watkin Williams Wynn inherited Sir John's estates and took his name in 1719 he became the greatest landowner in Wales.[28] Parry lived at the Wynn family estate Wynnstay, near Wrexham, and would travel with Wynn to London to play before groups of powerful and influential people, including Handel and the Prince of Wales. And it was his performance in Cambridge in the spring of 1757 that apparently prompted Gray to complete his poem. Gray wrote to William Mason that Parry 'scratched out such ravishing blind harmony, such tunes of a thousand years old, with names enough to choke you, as have set all this learned body a-dancing' and set his ode 'in motion again'.[29] As with the 'grisly band' of bards Gray writes in his poem, Parry Ddall's performance collapsed time. The performance of 'tunes of a thousand years old' brought, for Gray, the bardic past into the present.

This part of the story is well known and is to some degree a self-fashioned moment of Romantic inspiration. But it reveals a fascinating network of friendship and cultural exchange. These ties – between Parry, Sir John Wynn, Watkin Williams Wynn and Gray – are defined by inheritance, influence and patronage. They cut across the national boundary between England and Wales, but are governed by the boundaries of class. So Gray's composition of 'The Bard', and the stories he told of it, speak of a precise historical and cultural context. That is to say that, as with the history the bard delivers to Edward, what is striking is not the untimeliness of this medievalist vision, but its timeliness.

The timeliness of Gray's work is confirmed by its contemporary reception. The immediate critical response was mixed but the poem exerted a strong cultural influence. Many commented on the obscurity of the poem and George Colman published a pastiche titled 'To obscurity'.[30] Other responses were more positive. The *Critical Review* judged that, 'The subject is exquisitely chosen, and the piece executed by the hand of a master',[31] while the *Monthly Review* wrote that, 'The circumstances of grief and horror in the preparation of the votive web, and the mystic obscurity with which the prophecies are delivered, will give as much pleasure to those who relish this species of composition, as any thing that has hitherto appeared in our language, the Odes of Dryden himself not excepted.'[32] The third act of James Boaden's 1798 drama *Cambro-Britons* was based on Gray's poem and countless paintings took up the theme of the ancient bard throughout the eighteenth and nineteenth centuries, including works by Benjamin West (1778), Thomas Jones (1794), J. M. W. Turner (1800), William Blake (1809) and, most famously, John Martin (1817). Gray's work was folded into the general fascination with ancient literary remains prompted by the Ossian poems, published by James MacPherson from 1760.[33]

The modern critical reception of Gray's poem has largely focused on its relationship to ideas of Britain and Britishness. Howard Weinbrot suggests that it is a poem about British national identity, a work of cultural patriotism that celebrates insular literary culture and expresses 'the public voice of the nation'.[34] For Paul Odney, 'Gray's Bard becomes the symbolic figure of Britain's cultural genius, establishing the origins of native poetic tradition and reasserting the national role of the poet-hero.' Odney recognises, however, the Englishness of the poem's reading of Welsh history and 'the artificial and invented nature of nationalistic historiographies'.[35] Katie Trumpener notes how many English writers, like Gray, removed bardic literature from its social and political contexts. Trumpener writes:

> For nationalist antiquaries, the bard is the mouthpiece for a whole society, articulating its values, chronicling its history, and mourning the inconsolable tragedy of its collapse. English poets, in contrast, imagine the bard (and the minstrel after him) as an inspired, isolated, and peripatetic figure. Nationalist antiquaries read bardic poetry for its content and its historical information … English poets are primarily interested in the bard himself, for he represents poetry as a dislocated art, standing apart from and transcending its particular time and place. The late-eighteenth-century bardic revival gives new emphasis to the social rootedness and political function of literature, as to the inseparability

of literary performance from specific institutions and audiences.
English writers insist, in contrast, on literature's social and politi-
cal autonomy.[36]

In rewriting the pseudo-history of Edward's massacre of the
bards, Gray was able to create an idea of British national iden-
tity that incorporated both English savagery and Welsh cultural
riches, without weakening the English dominance of Britain and
Wales and without allowing Wales significant cultural and political
power. It is an act of appropriation that creates a cultural memory
of the Welsh bards which signifies on English terms.[37] It is the idea
of the medieval that allowed Gray to do this, as Edward's massacre
could be at once acknowledged and dismissed as a relic of the bar-
baric Middle Ages, while the poetry of the Welsh bards could simi-
larly be celebrated and contained as occurring in, and being limited
to, a medieval period that is decidedly over. Gray exports violence,
conquest and inequality to the Middle Ages and thus removes it to
a pre-political time, beyond contest and resolution in the present.
Gray's bard typifies the concept of medievalist double conscious-
ness, as he is, from an English perspective, simultaneously origin
and other and functions to mark out some identities as living and
thriving in modernity, while banishing others to the past. This
move relies on an idea of the Middle Ages as stable, whole and
monolithic, but Gray's poem actually speaks to acts of medieval
cultural memory which reveal how ideas of difference and power
intersected in the Middle Ages and undercut Gray's vision of the
'unselfconscious coherence' of the medieval past.

Glastonbury, Arthur, the Welsh, the British and the English

Gray's poem situates itself precisely in the context of Edward's
conquest of Wales, which was the culmination of England's
long-standing imperial ambitions and was preceded by a decade
of heightened tensions. In 1277 Edward had signed the Treaty
of Aberconway with the Welsh prince Llywelyn ap Gruffudd.[38]
Llywelyn had been encroaching on English lands throughout the
1270s and was declared an outlaw on 12 November 1276. He only
agreed to sign the treaty once Edward's troops had effectively sur-
rounded him, almost one year into the English king's campaign.
The treaty significantly reduced Llywelyn's power and political
heft and marked the successful completion of the first stage of
Edward's conquest of Wales, which was total by 1284.

Rather than a particular military action, however, Gray's poem speaks to an act of political ceremony performed by Edward and his queen in 1278. In the spring of that year Edward and Eleanor travelled to Glastonbury to pay homage to King Arthur and Queen Guinevere. The texts and intertexts of the Arthurian tradition are the finest example of the construction of cultural memory in the Middle Ages. From the early Celtic works to Geoffrey of Monmouth's *History of the Kings of Britain* to Thomas Malory, Chrétien de Troyes, Wolfram von Eschenbach, Marie de France, Geoffrey Chaucer and John Lydgate, the tradition flourished across time, space, form, genre and media. The texts of Arthur, like Magna Carta, came to be, and continue to signify as, a canonical cultural memory. Edward and Eleanor's enthusiasm for the Arthurian tradition is well known, but on this occasion they came not to celebrate or perpetuate the king's memory, but to confine it to the past.[39] They arrived in April 1278 to participate in the reburial of Arthur and Guinevere.

The particular meaning of Arthur and Guinevere at this moment was defined by the importance of Arthur to ideas of Welsh nationhood. As Nicholas Higham writes, 'The Glastonbury "recovery" [of Arthur] was part of an appropriation of the idea of Arthur from its Welsh origins by the Anglo-Norman elite who now held power across most of Britain and parts of Ireland and the Continent.'[40] Edward and Eleanor's reburial of the bones laid Arthur to rest and disabled him 'as a symbol of Welsh resistance to Anglo-Norman domination'.[41] The continuing significance of Arthur to Welsh cultural identity, combined with Edward's imperial intentions, means that, as Marc Morris suggests, Edward and Eleanor's solemnities at Glastonbury 'can hardly be interpreted as anything other than an exercise in propaganda directed squarely at the Welsh'.[42]

The events that unfolded in April 1278 were recorded by a chronicler of Glastonbury Abbey, Adam de Damerham, who offers a scene attuned to questions of privilege and custody.[43] Adam explains how the bodies understood to be Arthur and Guinevere were exhumed and then writes of how Edward and Eleanor returned the remains to the ground:

> Dominus Rex ossa Regis, Regina ossa Reginae, in singulis pallis preciosis inuoluta, in suis cistis recludentes, et sigilla sua opponentes, praeceperunt idem sepulcrum ante maius altare celeriter collocari, retentis exterius capitibus et genis utriusque propter populi

deucionem, apposita interius scriptura hujusmodi: Haec sunt ossa nobilissimi regis Arturi, quae anno incarnacionis dominicae milles- imo ducentesimo septuagesimo octauo, terciodecimo Kalend Maii, per dominum Edwardum, regem Angliae illustrem, hic fuerunt sic locata.[44]

(The king enclosed the king's bones again in their chest, wrapped in a single precious pall, while the queen did the same for the queen's bones. They marked them with their seals and directed the tomb to be placed speedily before the high altar, while the heads and knee-joints of both were kept out for the people's devotion. This was the inscrip- tion put on the inside: 'These are the bones of the most noble King Arthur which were placed here on 19 April in the year of the Lord's Incarnation 1278 by the illustrious Lord Edward, King of England.')

Adam's report records a scene that speaks clearly to the political needs of the participants. When Edward and Eleanor mark the bones with their 'sigilla' (seals) they quite literally placed a seal on the past. This is an act of appropriation rather than homage. Their ritualised performance attempts to put a limit on the power of Arthurian memory. As they rebury the storied king and queen, historical truth, cultural memory and future power are transmitted from the bones of Arthur and Guinevere to the bodies of Edward and Eleanor. Edward and Eleanor's reburial of the bones was a performance of cultural memory, a staged and deliberately plotted event designed to transform the identities of the participants.

The temporalities of Edward and Eleanor's performance are complex. The ritualised public event allowed the royals to simul- taneously associate themselves with Arthurian legend and finally put a seal on the king's imagined return. In one moment they attempted to refashion both past and future. The meanings of their performance are further enriched, however, by the manner in which it repeats events that took place at Glastonbury just under a hundred years earlier. So, just as Gray's poem creates a network of memory that uses Edward's conquest of Wales as a point of origin, so Edward and Eleanor's reburial of Arthur created a network of memory that engaged an earlier act as a source of authority and origin.

The monks of Glastonbury Abbey first claimed to hold the bones of Arthur and Guinevere in the aftermath of a fire that destroyed their abbey in 1184 and their putative grave became an important site of pilgrimage. In 1191 Henry II ordered that the remains be exhumed and the monks later commissioned Gerald of Wales to record the excavation.[45] Gerald writes that, although 'phantasticum' (fantastical) legends reported that Arthur remained alive, the discovery proved at last that he and Guinevere were both dead and buried, at Glastonbury. He records the discovery of the bodies as follows:

> Cum autem aliqua indicia corporis ibi inveniendi ex scripturis suis, aliqua ex litteris pyramidus impressis, quanquam nimia plurimum antiquitate deletis, aliqua quoque per visiones et revelationes bonis viris et religiosis factas, maxime tamen et evidentissime rex Angliæ Henricus secundus, sicut ab historico cantore Britone audierat antiquo, totum monachis indicavit, quod profunde, scilicet in terra per xvi. pedes ad minus, corpus invenirent, et non (in) lapido tumulo sed in quercu cavata. Ideoque tam profunde situm corpus, et quasi absconditum fuerat, ne a Saxonibus post necem ipsius insulam occupantibus, quos tanto opera vivens debellaverat et fere ex toto deleverat, posset nullatenus inveniri.[46]

> (Indeed, there had been some evidence from the records that the body might be found there, and some from the lettering carved on the pyramids (although that was mostly obliterated by excessive antiquity), and also some that came from the visions and revelations made by good men and the devout. But the clearest evidence came when King Henry II of England explained the whole matter to the monks (as he had heard it from an aged British poet): how they would find the body deep down, namely more than 16 feet into the earth, and not in a stone tomb but in an oak-hollow. The body had been placed so deep, and was so well concealed, that it could not be found by the Saxons who conquered the island after the king's death – those whom he had battled with so much exertion while he was alive, and whom he had nearly annihilated.)

Two elements of Gerald's account are of particular significance. First of all, when he reports that the monks were told of the location of the grave by Henry II the whole episode receives a kind of royal approval, but when he writes that Henry himself learnt of the site from a 'cantore Britone' (British poet), Gerald complements this royal association with a claim to indigenous knowledge. The unnamed British poet stands in for the Welsh who had claimed Arthur as a figurehead and a symbol of resistance against English imperial ambitions. Secondly, when Gerald explains that the bodies were buried so deep that the king's body was concealed from the Saxons he came so close to defeating, he offers a very literal image of historical distance. Gerald is fascinated by the mediation of historical knowledge – by bards or earth or royalty, the monks of the abbey or Gerald himself – and how access to the past is determined by privilege. As I will explore in this chapter, Gerald's invocation of the 'cantore Britone' fits into a larger pattern of thought that stretches from the Middle Ages through to modernity, a network of memory of which Gray's 'Bard' is an active participant. As with Gerald's British poet, medieval bards of modernity are often mere ciphers, constructions of cultural memory that are designed to support claims to national or ethnic dominance.

Gerald's account of the rediscovery of Arthur and Guinevere contains another melancholy note. As he describes how a woman's bones were found in a different section of the tomb from Arthur's, he adds that it was also, 'ubi et trica comæ muliebris flava cum integritate pristina et colore reperta fuit, quam ut monachus quidam avide manu arripuit et sublevavit, tota statim in pulverem decidit'[47] (where a lock of a woman's hair was discovered pristine with its original colour, but when a certain monk snatched it greedily with his hand and raised it up, at once all of it crumbled into dust). Again, then, Gerald offers a scene that illustrates how access to the past is dependent on privilege. The unfortunate monk, perhaps driven by desire or awe but according to Gerald acting 'avide' (greedily), destroys a tangible trace of the past in his enthusiasm. Phillip Schwyzer writes that the message of this scene 'could not be more clear. However vivid and beautiful the vision of past glory that dances before the eyes nothing awaits those who foolishly grasp at it but the bitterness of a second, still more absolute loss.'[48] Gerald offers his readers a cautionary tale about the correct custody of the past. As with *The Ruin* and the Eleanor Crosses, the writing of history and the construction of cultural memory in this moment is as much about what is out of touch and beyond recall as what is brought into the present.

The scenes at Glastonbury in 1191 and 1278 are fine examples of Freedman and Spiegel's sense of dual consciousness, even though they occur in the Middle Ages rather than modernity. The ceremonies defined the mythic king and queen as non-origins of Welsh collective identity, while at the same time the ritualised performances were presented as an origin of the English dominance of the myths of Arthur and the people of Wales. They also reveal the compromised subjectivity of the Welsh who lived under English rule, the 'two-ness' and 'double consciousness' generated by English domination of Welsh culture. There is little sense of 'unselfconscious coherence'. The important role of ethnic identity in these scenes is confirmed by the presence of the 'cantore Britone', who is perhaps a figure of divided loyalties, perhaps another cipher performing what the narrative required. The ceremonies at Glastonbury reveal one instance of how racial and ethnic origins were contested in the Middle Ages, how ideas of essence and collective identity were produced, how the past was figured as both inside and outside the present, but they also speak to how cultural memories of the Middle Ages have formed, and been formed by, nationalist discourses in the modern world. They are examples of what Jeffrey Jerome Cohen describes as how 'Medieval texts reflect and participate in the creation of human hierarchies with lived effects.'[49] In the next section of this chapter we will see how the reception of Gray's poem perpetuated the hierarchies that Edward and Eleanor worked to establish.

Evan Evans' Welsh bards

Sarah Prescott has explored the cultural work Gray's bard was put to from a Welsh perspective. For Prescott, 'Gray's poem incorporates the Welsh tradition of the massacre of the bards into a poem which offers a version of Anglo-Britishness that ultimately dilutes the original nationalist force of the myth.' Prescott notes that Gray's bard, MacPherson's fictional Ossian and other literary adaptations and appropriations of the figure of the British bard enjoyed greater success and popularity than the medieval material antiquarians discovered and published.[50] Indeed, as the Ossian case exemplified, it was often extremely difficult to distinguish between the real and the fake, the premodern and the modern. The tension between adaptation and original, or history and cultural memory, is exemplified in the work of Evan Evans (1731–88). Evans was a Welsh churchman, scholar and poet and is best known today for his work on early Welsh poetry.[51] For my purposes, however, it is his English-language poem, 'Paraphrase of the 137th Psalm', that is of most relevance. Evans' poem attracted a great deal of critical and popular attention and offers a Welsh nationalist vision that incorporates Gray's appropriation of its literary tradition.

The full title of Evans' poem is 'A Paraphrase of the 137th Psalm, alluding to the Captivity and Treatment of the Welsh Bards by King Edward I' and rather than the rivers of Babylon, the bards in this text stand beside the 'inhospitable flood' of the 'willowy Thames'.[52] These bards are remembering 'injured Cambria' rather than Zion and their harps 'silent, neglected, and unstrung … upon the willows hung' (9–10). While Psalm 137 asks 'How can we sing

the songs of the Lord / while in a foreign land?', in Evans' poem
the bards are commanded to sing by their 'insulting foe' (13) but
refuse:

> What, – shall the Saxons hear us sing,
> Or their dull vales with Cambrian music ring?
> No – let old Conway cease to flow,
> Back to her source Sabrina go:
> Let huge Plinlimmon hide his head,
> Or let the tyrant strike me dead,
> If I attempt to raise a song
> Unmindful of my country's wrong.
> What, shall a haughty king command
> Cambrian's free strain on Saxon land?
> May this right arm first wither'd be,
> Ere I may touch one string for thee,
> Proud monarch; nay, may instant death
> Arrest my tongue and stop my breath,
> If I attempt to weave a song,
> Regardless of my country's wrong! (21–36)

Evans uses the Welsh landscape here in a manner that brings
to mind Gray's association of his bard with Snowdonia, but his
treatment of the landscape has a markedly different effect to
Gray's.

In both 'The Bard' and the 'Paraphrase of the 137th Psalm',
the landscape functions as a means of confirming medievalist
cultural memory, as it does in David Cameron's reflections with
which I began this chapter. However, not all of Gray's authenticat-
ing uses of the landscape achieve the desired effect. For instance,
Gray's claim that his bard stood 'o'er old Conway's foaming flood'
and addressed Edward and his troops as they marched along 'the
steep of Snowdon's shaggy side' would strike anyone familiar with
the landscape of north Wales as very odd, as they would know that
the river flows through a broad valley. The political significance
of the landscape in Evans' poem is clear. Indeed, the bards draw a
direct link between their voices and the landscape when they ask
'shall the Saxons hear us sing, / or their dull vales with Cambrian
music ring?' (21–2). Indeed, these bards would rather 'Conway
cease to flow' (23) than they sing for their Saxon conquerors. It
is also significant that while Evans quotes Gray's line describing
the bard 'High on a rock o'er Conway's flood', he doesn't mention
Snowdon; instead Evans refers to 'Conway's banks and Menai's

streams' (65). This reference to Welsh topography brings in the final lines of the poem:

> On Conway's banks and Menai's streams
> The solitary bittern screams;
> And, where was erst Llywelyn's court,
> Ill-omened bards and wolves resort.
> There oft at midnight's silent hour,
> Near yon ivy-mantled tower,
> By the glow-worm's twinkling fire,
> Tuning his romantic lyre,
> Gray's pale spectre seems to sing,
> 'Ruin seize thee, ruthless King.' (65–74)

While perhaps it is Evans' quotations from Gray that are most striking, the differences between Evans' poem and 'The Bard' are also significant. In these lines, for instance, it is important that Evans refers directly to Llywelyn rather than Arthur, a gesture that seems to show that this bard directs his gaze towards history rather than cultural memory. Combined with Evans' use of the Welsh landscape, this marks his poem as a self-consciously nationalist text. However, Evans' use of Gray's poem threatens to undercut these aspirations.

The appearance of Gray's opening line as Evans' final line is particularly provocative and offers itself as evidence of the compromised position Welsh culture occupied following the English conquest. James Mulholland, however, suggests that 'Evans used Gray's Welsh bardic voice to legitimize his own.' For Mulholland, 'Evans did not undermine Welsh cultural development by quoting Gray; he accelerated it by making the poetics of printed voice collaborative and reciprocal.'[53] Mulholland's reading acknowledges the asymmetrical power relations that existed between Gray and Evans, determined by the relationship between England and Wales, but also notes that Welsh cultural practitioners enthusiastically appropriated Gray's text. In 1798 a bardic festival in London awarded a prize for the best Welsh translation of Gray's poem and in 1822 W. Owen Pughe published his own translation of the poem into Welsh.[54] Pughe's translation is remarkably close to the source text and maintains, as Mulholland illustrates, Gray's visual presentation of the different voices.[55] Mulholland concludes that:

> By disseminating their own adaptations of Gray's voices, Welsh authors devised significant vehicles by which to enact politically that which they wrote about. Gray is presented both as an important

origin and an authenticating figure for the national history that Welsh authors hoped to intensify with their own writing and performances. That this history is ostensibly one of the English invading Wales does not change the fact that for them an English author had become the best-known critic of this history and one of the most successful exponents of a resistant Welsh national identity.[56]

Mulholland's reading works hard to uncover Welsh agency and self-determination in this tradition. But his efforts cannot disregard the inequalities in power that existed between the countries and the cultures. As he sets out the compromises and ambivalences of nationalist Welsh literature written in the wake of Gray's 'Bard', Mulholland's reading chimes with Helen Fulton's thinking on medieval Welsh literature. Drawing on the work of Homi Bhabha, Fulton reminds us that national identities are not stable, that they are interpellations of individuals rather than natural categories. Fulton emphasises the ambivalence of Welsh attitudes towards the English and highlights the fact that the two identities do not exist in a binary structure. She notes that, 'medieval Welsh identity was in large part constructed by the "other" of Englishness, an otherness that was both desired and feared'.[57] While Fulton is writing here of medieval Welsh poetry, her work also speaks to the poems of Gray, Evans and Pughe. Following Mulholland, it is possible to read the poems of Evans and Pughe as an attempt to incorporate the other of Gray's Englishness into a nationalist Welsh identity. But the continuing presence of Gray's English bard in these poems, as well as Gray's language and imagery, takes us back to Edward and Eleanor's performance at Glastonbury and reveals the fundamental inequality and persistence of colonial relations.

At Glastonbury, Edward and Eleanor took part in a ritualised act of Arthurian cultural memory that simultaneously identified them with and against the Welsh. As they acknowledged the mythic power of Arthur and Guinevere, they appropriated that power and remade it for their own political purposes. When Gray takes up the Edwardian conquest of Wales he engages an Arthurian tradition that has English dominance woven through it, English dominance that is military, political and cultural. This dominance exists in the present while Gray's bard, the story of Edward's massacre of the Welsh bards and the radical hope the bard's curse expresses, exist in a closed-off medieval past. Gray makes this clear when he notes that the story is only 'current in Wales', a place, the reader is invited to conclude, non-contemporary with Gray and England.[58] So this cultural memory of the bard represents not the power the past might exert to transform the present, but the power of the present to define the past and expresses an inequality of power similar to that between England and Wales. It is this compromised subjectivity that Evans and Pughe attempt to rehabilitate, but they are unable to navigate the networks of power, time and history that Gray lays down. Homi Bhabha writes that 'Colonial mimicry is the desire for a reformed, recognizable Other, *as a subject of a difference that is almost the same, but not quite.*'[59] The labours of Evans and Pughe attempt to overcome this not-quite-ness, what Du Bois would describe as 'two-ness', an inferiority that is determined and expressed by the medieval-ness of their culture and the figure on which they pin their hope, Gray's bard. This bard is a synecdoche of Welsh culture, medieval and modern. In their treatment of the figure of the bard, Gray, Evans and Pughe acknowledge the cultural power of the medieval past while at the same time insisting on its fundamental malleability, its essential emptiness. Thus the medieval past itself becomes a site of '*a difference that is almost the same, but not quite*', in Fulton's words a site of 'an otherness that was both desired and feared', but a site which is always reconfigured precisely according to the power relations of the present.

To return to Gray's poem's primary context, it emerges from a cultural moment defined by a medievalist and Gothic aesthetics. The image of Strawberry Hill on the title page of Gray's volume marks it out as emerging from a milieu particularly invested in medieval culture and the cultural work the medieval might be put to in the present. According to Lytton Strachey, Horace Walpole, the designer and owner of Strawberry Hill and Gray's great friend, 'liked Gothic architecture, not because he thought it beautiful but because he found it queer'.[60] Susan Bernstein glosses Strachey's use of the term queer by writing that, 'The queerness of the Gothic consists in its simultaneous participation in and resistance to signification. It moves across – *quer* – the demarcation line between history and fantasy, referent and reified signifier.'[61] The same can be said of Gray's bard and his Welsh intertexts. 'The Bard' simultaneously participates in and resists a number of powerful cultural structures, but the manner in which Gray's poem activates and preserves atavistic approaches to identity and power, while lacking a sustaining, stable meaning, ensured that it could not provide an answer to those questions, or alternative cultural structures, beyond the political possibilities of the present. As Gray's poem appeared to query, but ultimately reinforced, the demarcation lines between past and present, so it could be used to produce and reinforce demarcation lines of cultural and ethnic difference.

The Hungarian bards of Wales

As I noted above, it is hard to overestimate the cultural influence of Gray's poem, in Britain and beyond. In this section of the chapter I will explore another appropriation of Gray's text, a poem entitled 'A Walesi Bárdok' (The Bards of Wales) and written by the Hungarian poet János Arany, which brings the relationship between cultural memories of the medieval bard and discourses of nationalism into greater focus and demonstrates how medievalist cultural memory can form, and be formed by, transnational networks of influence. Arany wrote 'A Walesi Bárdok' in 1857, by which time he was an established poet, critic and translator. He was familiar with many aspects of British culture and had translated some of Shakespeare's works into Hungarian. Aside from 'A Walesi Bárdok', his most famous work today is his medievalist lyric trilogy 'Toldi'.[62] Arany was moved to write his poem when he and other poets were requested to write texts celebrating the 1857 visit of the Austro-Hungarian emperor Franz Josef I to Hungary. This was the first visit by Franz Josef since his empire's defeat of the Hungarian revolution of 1848 and the subsequent war of independence.[63] As with Evans' poem, 'A Walesi Bárdok' presents an image of the British Middle Ages whose meaning depends on the precise context of its production. Arany disregards the English nationalism present in Gray's work and presents a text that engages forcefully with the subjugated Welsh.

As its context suggests, 'A Walesi Bárdok' is a meditation on tyranny and freedom. Although written at a moment of danger, it wasn't circulated until 1863, when Arany presented it as a translation of an Old English ballad in an attempt to avoid suspicion. When it was published, Arany inserted a note which precisely dated the composition of the poem to June 1857 and commented that 'A történelem kétségbe vonja, de a mondában erősen tartja magát, hogy I. Eduárd király, Wales tartomány meghódítása (1277) után, ötszáz walesi bárdot végeztetett ki, hogy nemzetök dicső múltját zöngve, a fiakat föl ne gerjeszthessék az angol járom lerázására' (Historians doubt it, but legend has it that after he conquered Wales in 1277, Edward I, King of England, had 500 Welsh singers executed to prevent them singing about their glorious past as this might have led to a rebellion against him amongst the sons of the singers).[64] Like Gray, Arany seems to be ambivalent about the historical truth of the story, but the power of his poem depends on its performance and reception, rather than the medieval past on which it draws. While Gray's poem is clearly a primary influence on Arany's text, it also reworks elements of Thomas Warton's 'The Grave of King Arthur'.[65] Like Warton's poem, 'A Walesi Bárdok' tells the story of a royal feast at Montgomery Castle held in the midst of Edward's conquest. After the meal Edward requests a performance by a Welsh bard:

> 'Ti urak, ti urak! Hát senkisem
>   Koccint értem pohárt?
> Ti urak, ti urak! … ti velsz ebek!
>   Ne éljen Eduárd?
>
> Vadat és halat, s mi az ég alatt
>   Szem-szájnak kellemes,
> Azt látok én: de ördög itt
>   Belül minden nemes.
>
> Ti urak, ti urak, hitvány ebek!
>   Ne éljen Eduárd?
> Hol van, ki zengje tetteim -
>   Elő egy velszi bárd!'[66]

> ('Now drink my health, you gentle sirs,
>   And you, my noble host! You Sirs …
> Welsh Sirs … you filthy curs,
>   I want the loyal toast!
>
> 'The fish, the meat you served to eat
>   Was fine and ably done.
> But deep inside it's hate you hide:
>   You loathe me, every one!
>
> 'Well, then, you sirs, you filthy curs,
>   Who will now toast your king?
> I want a bard to praise my deeds,
>   A bard of Wales to sing!')[67]

As each bard refuses to sing, the king sentences them to death. The poem ends with a desperate Edward driven mad by the ghosts of the murdered bards:

> Ötszáz, bizony, dalolva ment
>   Lángsírba velszi bárd:
> De egy se birta mondani
>   Hogy: éljen Eduárd. –
>
> 'Ha, ha! Mi zúg?… Mi éji dal
>   London utcáin ez?

Felköttetem a lordmajort,
  Ha bosszant bármi nesz!'

Áll néma csend; légy szárnya bent,
  Se künn, nem hallatik:
'Fejére szól, ki szót emel!
  Király nem alhatik.'

'Ha, ha! Elő síp, dob, zene!
  Harsogjon harsona:
Fülembe zúgja átkait
  A velszi lakoma ...'

De túl zenén, túl síp-dobon,
  Riadó kürtön át:
Ötszáz énekli hangosan
  A vértanúk dalát.[68]

(Five hundred went singing to die,
  Five hundred in the blaze,
But none would sing to cheer the king
  The loyal toast to raise.

'My chamberlain, what is the din
  In London's streets so late?
The Lord Mayor answers with his head
  If it does not abate!'

Gone is the din; without, within
  They all silently creep:
'Who breaks the spell, goes straight to hell!
  The King can't fall asleep.'

'Let drum and fife now come to life
  And let the trumpets roar,
To rise above that fatal curse
  That haunts me evermore!'

But over drums and piercing fifes,
  Beyond the soldiers' hails,
They swell the song, five hundred strong,
  Those martyred bards of Wales.)[69]

Whereas Gray's text is nestled in a network of class privilege that extended beyond national borders, like Evans' 'Paraphrase of the 137th Psalm', Arany's work is deeply nationalist.

Along with other poets such as Sándor Petőfi, Arany formed part of a cultural movement of romantic literature and art in which, as the historian Ivan Berend writes, 'romantic literature

and art in Central and Eastern Europe successfully propagan-
dized the main idea of enlightened romanticism: freedom, both
in social and national terms'. This movement, which sought to
use culture as a means of national self-expression, was entirely
self-conscious. In one letter to Arany, for instance, Petőfi stated
that they should aim to make 'the poetry of the people ... pre-
dominant in the realm of literature', concluding that, 'When the
people are prominent in poetry, they are very near to power in
politics.'[70] In 'A Walesi Bárdok', Arany used the figure of the
poet as a proxy for the people in a manner which recalls the 'can-
tore Britone' of Gerald of Wales as well as the work of Gray
and Evans. Indeed, Arany's text used the medieval past to
cloak its political aspirations. He attempted to give voice to the
'two-ness' of Hungarian culture's existence within the Austro-
Hungarian Empire.

While Gray's poem and Wynn's historiographical self-
indulgence can be looked upon as curiosities today in Britain, 'A
Walesi Bárdok' retains a deeper significance in Hungary. It remains
on the Hungarian school syllabus and children are expected to com-
mit it to memory. A statue of Arany stands in front of Hungary's
National Museum in Budapest. *In Quest of the Miracle Stag*, a col-
lection of English translations of Hungarian poetry published to
commemorate the eleven hundredth anniversary of the foundation
of Hungary and the fortieth anniversary of the Uprising of 1956,
describes Arany as 'Hungary's greatest epic poet and undoubtedly
most influential literary figure in the nineteenth century' and goes
on to state that:

> Arany was a man of immense probity and intellectual integrity. It
> is no exaggeration to rank him with the two great Germans, Goethe
> and Schiller, the Russian Pushkin, and the English John Milton.
> He became, in the truest sense, a teacher of his nation and a major,
> determining shaper of its literary standards for the next century and
> beyond. ... His heritage is still strongly and inspiringly alive in his
> native country.[71]

The heritage of 'A Walesi Bárdok' was most recently celebrated
during Hungary's presidency of the council of the European
Union in 2011. A number of projects celebrated the shared liter-
ary history of Hungary and Wales. A new symphony inspired by
the poem was composed by the Welsh composer Karl Jenkins[72]
and a Gorsedd Circle, a group of standing stones set out for the
National Eisteddfod in Wales, was constructed in Hungary.[73]

These works of cultural memory attempted to produce a cultural alliance between the two countries and draw the two cultures into contact.

While these projects attempted to establish progressive connections between the two nations, the poem is also used to produce difference between social, ethnic and racial groups within modern Hungary itself. For instance, on 23 October 2009 the actor György Dörner recited the poem at a rally for the far-right party Jobbik, known for its anti-Semitic and anti-Roma policies. Dörner is a figure well known in Hungary for the manner in which he uses his cultural activity to express far-right nationalist views. Indeed, in 2012, when he was appointed Director of the New Theatre in Budapest by the city's mayor, István Tarlós, another nationalist and noted anti-Semite, Dörner stated that, 'We want to use our own tools to make it possible to say proudly, I love my country, I am a Hungarian, a Christian Hungarian, and I live according to European Christian moral values.'[74]

The history of 'A Walesi Bárdok' illustrates the points of connection between nationalism and xenophobia and racism. As Berend laments, it is possible to draw a line between the nineteenth-century context of 'A Walesi Bárdok' and its modern uses:

> Theatrical emotion, heroic poses, and bombastic rhetoric became a requirement for discussing the national issue. Poets and writers continued to be self-appointed national prophets. Leadership required charisma, not modern rational political institutions and procedures. Temporarily declining birthrates or other socio-political crises immediately revived the fear of the extinction of the nation. Confrontations with other countries and political and economic losses in a difficult period, imagined or real, immediately generated a sense of betrayal. A critical remark about the backwardness of the nation or major policy mistakes made by a fellow citizen were often considered high treason. Self-pity, a kind of romantic-national Weltschmerz, became a national characteristic. The nation was often considered a victim surrounded by enemies. National feeling was mixed with xenophobia … Otherness generated suspicion and hostility. If the nation was at stake, reason was often suppressed by emotion. Because of its 'tribal' ethnocultural character, a romantic, deformed, and pathetic national consciousness in Central and Eastern Europe carried within it the seeds of xenophobic, exclusive, aggressive nationalism.[75]

As with the work of Gray and Evans, Arany queried but ultimately reinforced the structures that determined his subjecthood.

He sought to disrupt the structures which limited his own free-
dom, but his nationalist fantasy of wholeness relied on the exclu-
sion of others and the violence that Gray and Arany both imagine
in the past legitimised further violence in the present. As Berend
makes clear, this history is not unique to Hungary and this nation-
alist reimagining of medieval culture is not unique either. As work
by Louise D'Arcens and Clare Monagle, Kevin McDonald, James
Smith and others demonstrates, medievalist double consciousness
is an expression of cultural memory that can form, and be formed
by, nationalist violence.[76] It is a means of marking out some lives
and identities as belonging in the present and some as belonging in
an abjected past.

Locating *Beowulf* in the modern world

Racial, ethnic and nationalist readings and uses of medieval cul-
ture are present in the disciplinary history of medieval studies
as well as the political and creative archive of the Middle Ages.[77]
Indeed, the discipline of medieval studies developed along-
side the birth of nationalist thinking and the two are inextri-
cably linked. This is seen clearly in the early scholarly history
of the Old English poem known as *Beowulf*, during which the
early medieval poem was used to secure the identity of a mod-
ern nation-state and the *Beowulf*-poet was imagined to be a fig-
ure who might bring the people of the northern world together.
This focus on the figure of the poet – as in the work of Gerald
of Wales, Gray and Arany – expresses a desire for a singular,
pure voice of the past. While today *Beowulf* is most often under-
stood in relation to English national and literary history, Danish
national interests drove its early scholarly recovery.[78] Grímur
Jonsson Thorkelín, an Icelandic scholar who self-identified as a
Dane and whose studies were funded by the Danish crown, pub-
lished the first edition of the poem in 1815 and claimed *Beowulf*
as a work of the Danes. He also identified Beowulf as a prince
of the Scyldings and located his homeland in Jutland, northern
Denmark.[79] Moreover, as with Gerald of Wales, Thomas Gray
and János Arany, and no doubt influenced by the eighteenth-
century discourses of the medieval bard, he imagined the
Beowulf-poet as a conduit between the early medieval past and
his own contemporary moment and argued that the poet must
have been an eyewitness at the hero's funeral. Thorkelín prac-
tised an imperial model of history writing, in which Danish

cultural dominance was aggressively pursued. In the introduc-
tion to his edition Thorkelín wrote:

> Inter omnia monumenta veteris orbis Danici, qvæ tempus edax
> rerum nobis reliqvit, admirabile de Scyldingis Epos publici nunc
> juris factum eminet. Habemus enim hic irriguos fontes, unde reli-
> gionis poëseosqve notitia, et gentis nostræ rerum seculis III et IV
> gestarum series deduci possit.
>
> …
>
> Quod autem ad Scyldingidem nostram attinet, eam vere Danicam
> esse, nemo non ibit inficias, qvi observaverit auctorem rerum a
> Regibus HRODGARO, Beowulo et Higelaco gestarum oculatum
> fuisse testem, et in Boewulfi exseqviis encomiasten adfuisse. Cecidit
> autem Beowulfus in Jutia anno æræ nostræ CCCXL.
> Igitur hercle miror Hickesium Anglosaxonibus tribuisse carmen,
> qvod vates Danus Appolinis hyperborei igne calefactus fudit. At
> seduxit virum intergerrimum externa rei facies. Eqvidem non bene
> meminit lingvam, qva ante Wilhelmum I. utebantur Angli, fuisse
> communem tribus septentrionis populis, qvi vocati uno nomine
> Dani, omnes ore eodem dialectice solummodo differente loqveban-
> tur. Hujus si vel aliunde auctoritas nulla peti posset, plena sane hic
> in aprico cubat. Epos etenim hoc, qvale id nunc habemus, evidenter
> docet, idioma Anglosaxonicum esse revera Danicum, qvod Islandi
> extra solis vias fere jacentes hodiedum servant purum, et studiose
> colunt.[80]

(Among all the monuments of the ancient Danish world which
devouring time has left us, the epic of the Scyldings, now published,
stands out as an astonishing achievement. For here we have an over-
flowing foundation from which can be drawn knowledge about the
religion, poetry, and deeds of our people in the third and fourth
centuries.

…

That our poem of the Scyldings is indeed Danish will be clear to
anyone who sees that the author was an eyewitness to the exploits of
kings Hroðgar, Beowulf and Hygelac, and was the eulogizer at the
funeral of Beowulf, who died in Jutland in the year of our Lord, 340.
By Hercules! I am astounded that Hickes attributed to the Anglo-
Saxons a song that poured forth from the Danish bard, fired by the
flame of hyperborean Apollo. But appearances have led that most
impartial man astray. Obviously he does not remember that the lan-
guage spoken by the English before William I had been common to
three peoples of the north – all called by one name 'Danes' – who
spoke slightly different dialects of the same tongue. This fact is as

clear as the light of day, even if no other authority could be found for it. For our epic plainly teaches that the Anglo-Saxon idiom is actually Danish, a language cultivated and kept pure even to this day by the inhabitants of Iceland, who dwell almost beyond the path of the sun.)

Thorkelín's edition received a frosty reception, as his transcription, translation and reading of the poem were extremely faulty. Among his fiercest critics was the Danish scholar, pastor and poet Nikolai Frederik Severin Grundtvig, who published an eviscerating review of Thorkelín's work in 1817[81] and went on to produce two major works on *Beowulf*, a Danish translation entitled *Bjovulfs Drapa* (*Beowulf's Lay*)[82] in 1820 – the first published translation of the poem into a vernacular language – and a full edition in 1861 entitled *Beowulfes Beorh* (*Beowulf's Barrow*).[83] Despite his frustrations at Thorkelín's mistakes, Grundtvig shared some of his predecessor's convictions, including that the *Beowulf*-poet must have been present at the hero's funeral.

At the beginning of his 1861 edition, Grundtvig presented the reader with two poems of his own composition, one in Old English, one in Danish, printed side by side. The poems are hymns to Beowulf and the *Beowulf*-poet and express a hope that the poem might initiate reconciliation between England and Denmark. Both of Grundtvig's poems begin with a paraphrase of lines 2806–7 of *Beowulf*, in which the dying hero asks his loyal retainer Wiglaf to ensure that his people build and bury him in a barrow on a headland, 'þæt hit sæliðend syððan hātan / Bīowulfes Biorh' (lines 2806–7, so that seafarers then will call it Beowulf's Barrow).[84] Grundtvig's Old English poem goes on to hail the *Beowulf*-poet as a conduit of cultural memory and express his hope that the poem might cast the national histories and identities of England and Denmark in a new light:

Best þæt ge-munde,
mine gefræge,
se þe eall-fela
eald-gesegena
worn gemunde,
wigena bealdor,
Scope Beowulfes,
Scefinga leod;
hlæw he ge-worhte
æfter wines dædum,
in bæl-stede,

beorh þone hean,
micelne and mærne,
swa he manna wæs,
wigend weorð-fullost
wide geond eorðan,
þenden he burh-welan
brucan moste.
Se is wæg-liðendum
wide gesyne,
Beorh Beowulfes,
beorhtost geweorca,
mearcod to ge-mynde,
meaglum wordum!

Þær is on þam scennum
sciran goldes,
þurh run-stafas,
rihte gemearcod,
'þæt nu sceal Geataleodum
and Gar-Denum
sib-gemænum,
and-sacu restan,
inwit-niðas,
þe hie ær drugon,
sceal hring-naca
ofer heaðo bringan
lac and luf-tacen;
ic þa leode wat
ge wið feond ge wið freond
fæste geworhte,
æghwæs untæle
ealde wisan!'

God-fremmendra swylcum
gefeðe bið,
þæt seo Engla-þeod,
þegna-heap ær-god,
seo þe wiccung-dome
wrættum gebunden
for-gyteð and for-gymeð
þisne þe hire God seale,
wuldres wealdend,
weorðmynda dæl,
on eðel-londe,
oðre siðe,
gaste gefysed,

fugle gelicost,
wudu-holt wynlic
willsum geþence
Scede-londum in,
scopas and witan,
hæleða dream,
Dena and Wedera![85]

(The poet of Beowulf, a man of the Scefings, remembered all that best, so far as I have heard, he who remembered a great many ancient sagas, a leader of men. He made a barrow high and famous in memory of his friend's deeds, on the place of the funeral pyre, that high tumulus, since he was the most glorious warrior of all men through the world while he was able to enjoy his city's treasure. *Beowulfes Beorh* is seen from afar by seafarers, the most shining of structures, designed as a memorial in the mightiest of words. There on the panels of bright gold it was rightly written in runic letters 'that now peace must be enjoyed between the Geatas and the Danes, and strife must slumber, hostilities which they formerly experienced. The ring-prowed ship must bring over the waves gifts and tokens of affection. I know the people to be firmly disposed toward both friend and foe, altogether blameless in the ancient way.'

To such performers of good it will be granted that the English people, a troop good of old, who, though bound by works of art to the *wiccung-dome*, forget and neglect this portion of honour that God, the Lord of glory, gave to them in their native land on one occasion, will, urged by the spirit (most like a bird), think of the winsome, delightful forests in Scandinavia, poets and thinkers, the joy of heroes, of Danes and Geatas.)[86]

For Grundtvig, *Beowulf* offered a means of bringing people together. He read the poem for evidence of human and cultural contact and his scholarship was intended to generate a collective identity for the people of northern Europe, albeit defined by the Danes. The figure of the poet emerges for Grundtvig, as for Gerald, Gray, Arany and Thorkelín, as a bridge between the past and present and a bind that might secure a collective identity.

Grundtvig's desire for a new collective identity even more explicitly expressed in the Danish poem he presented at the beginning of his 1861 edition of *Beowulf*. In this poem Grundtvig writes of *Beowulf* as a 'fælles Kilde' (common source), a wondrous work 'Ligner mest en Konge-Hal' (similar to a royal hall), and he makes it clear the cultural work he hopes the poem will be put to:

Give Gud, at Anglers Æt,
Nu for Norden fremmed,

Mindes maatte Videslet,
Mindes Vane-Hjemmet,
Bryde af den Grændels-Haand
I det Pluddervælske,
Som uddrev med Anglers Aand
Hierte-Ordet 'elske'!
Ja, gid snart vi Svane-Sang
Høre maae frae 'Aven',
Hvori Aanden har sin Gang,
Uden Frygt for Paven!

(God grant that the clan of the Angles, now alienated from the north, might remember old Denmark, might remember the Vanir-home and tear off that Grendel-hand which drove out the gibberish of the heart's own word for 'love' along with the English spirit! Yes, may we soon hear the song of the swan of the Avon, in which the spirit goes its way without fear of the pope!)[87]

Grundtvig's two poems are not translations of one another. Like the translations of *The Ruin* we encountered in Chapter 1, they write around, alongside and through one another. They express the doubleness, the 'two-ness' of past and present, familiar and other and, for Grundtvig, English and Dane. For Grundtvig, it was not possible to read *Beowulf* without reading it through modern notions of ethnicity and nationhood. Grundtvig's medievalist double consciousness was expressed through languages that, like his visions of the past and present, are clearly related but not the same. As with Gray, Evans and Arany, Grundtvig's work delineated subject positions in the present as it attempted to rewrite the medieval past. As with those other works, Grundtvig's medievalist vision is an exercise in displacement – a means to express a culture's non-identification with itself, as well as an attempt to assuage it. Grundtvig's work was, however, much more influential than the other examples recounted in this chapter. From his work on the literature of the medieval north, as well as his religious and educational activity, Grundtvig constructed an idea of Denmark and Danish culture that still holds sway in the twenty-first century and he remains an important figure in contemporary Denmark and the history of the Danish nation.[88]

Claims about medieval heritage are often claims about social and political status and power. As Thorkelín and Grundtvig demonstrate, medieval studies can be as much about promoting social identities as promoting knowledge about the past, and the boundaries between medievalism and nationalism can be delicate.

The texts produced by the Norwegian terrorist Anders Behring Breivik demonstrate the relationship between Grundtvig's work in particular and later nationalist discourses. Breivik, who in July 2011 killed 77 people in attacks in Oslo and on the island of Utøya, wrote extensively of the culture of the north in the manifesto he circulated to the media before he committed his crimes. In one passage of his long, sketchy and ill-thought-out essay, Breivik turns to the English poet Ted Hughes' work. After claiming that Hughes is his 'favourite English poet', Breivik writes that 'Hughes was a Yorkshireman, and the blood of the Danes runs thick in the veins of Yorkshire. Especially in the North Riding – the closer one gets to Whitby, the more natural blond hair in evidence, and the more obvious the Danish place names.' Breivik quotes two of Hughes' poems, 'The Warriors of the North' and 'Thistles', in full, as well as a short section of 'Gog'. All of these poems meditate on the northern cultures celebrated by Grundtvig and reimagine the shared history of northern England and Scandinavia.[89]

For Breivik, however, what is significant about Hughes' poems and the medieval cultures of northern England and Scandinavia is that they provide a means of uniting against and excluding an other. Meaning resides primarily in the present rather than the past. Racist fantasies provide a means of drawing the complex webs of history and cultural memory together. Breivik writes that 'the Men of the North form the core of the Counterjihad' and suggests that 'They are already in action, clearing the back alleys of Anbar Province, riding point in Kabul, and forming up in self-organised groups to defend our borders.' He continues to claim that, 'As I've said before, it's not race that's the issue here, it's culture. The culture of the Danes, the Norsemen, the English, and the Celts. The culture of the hardy and self-reliant Men of the North, always ready to defend their ancient liberties with a ferocity that their enemies can scarcely imagine.'[90] The ease with which he moves between literary and cultural history and fantasies of racial and ethnic origin is striking and makes a strong case for the political importance of medieval studies. Breivik, like the nationalist appropriations of 'A Walesi Bárdok', offers a lesson in how medievalist cultural memory can reify social relations and how medievalist double consciousness can mark some lives as not belonging in the present. What medieval culture actually was perhaps becomes insignificant in this work. While Breivik might not be persuaded of his errors by learning of the history of medieval multiculturalism, just as the meanings of 'A Walesi Bárdok' in modern Hungary are immune from the shaky historiography on which Gray's poem was built, he nevertheless initiates a debate that medievalists cannot ignore and cannot refuse. Such claims to singular national, racial and ethnic origin must be countered by work that recognises the diversity of medieval Europe and the archive of the European Middle Ages.[91]

Performance and reproduction

The material covered in this chapter shares a conviction that medieval culture provides a means of defining and recognising the modern subject, as well as marking others who do not belong in the present. This process operates at different scales and has different effects in different times and places, from eighteenth-century Wales to nineteenth-century Hungary to twenty-first-century Norway. But it always expresses fantasies of wholeness and exclusion. To take one final example, in September 2013, the Isle of Sheppey in Kent, UK, staged a three-day festival in celebration of early medieval culture. People dressed in Viking costume for a parade down Sheerness High Street, a dramatic performance entitled *Vikings – Violence and Love* was staged at Minster Abbey, a replica Viking longboat was set alight on the estuary and a walk through Harty on the southeast edge of the island was complemented by performances of episodes from *Beowulf*. The celebration was recorded in a mural painted in Sheerness depicting the fight between Beowulf and Grendel (see Figure 3.2).[92]

As with the other material surveyed so far in this book, Sheppey's festival illustrates the complex interplay between scholarly and creative responses to the Middle Ages that defines modern cultural memory of the medieval, but it also reminds us again that affect and intuition structure responses to the Middle Ages as much as reasoned critical discourse. In Sheppey, as in Grundtvig's scholarship, *Beowulf* was used as a means of bringing people together, expressing common bonds and celebrating the pleasures of shared collective identity. Sheppey's celebrations, however, like Grundtvig's and Thorkelín's conviction that the *Beowulf*-poet was present at the hero's funeral, or Edward's massacre of the Welsh bards, had no basis in historical fact. Rather, this performance of cultural memory was predicated on a piece of erroneous philology that draws a connection between the 'brimclifu blican' (222, shining seacliffs) Beowulf sees as he approaches Denmark and the place name Sheerness which, it has been claimed, is possibly formed of

3.2 *Beowulf* mural at Sheerness

the Old English elements 'scir' and 'næss', meaning 'bright head-
land'.[93] *A Dictionary of British Place-Names* notes, however, that
an alternative source of the name Sheerness could be 'scear', an
Old English word that can be translated as 'plough-share'.[94] It is
the ambiguity of medieval sources that allows this kind of appro-
priation, but in the production of medievalist cultural memory
that ambiguity is systematically displaced as the past is trans-
formed into a stable, secure origin. The difference and uncertainty
of the past is transferred onto the others of the present. The past
becomes familiar even as it expresses alienation from the present.
As with Breivik, this is a debate the medievalist cannot refuse or
ignore. The people of Sheppey can lay claim to *Beowulf*, but they
cannot claim the poem doesn't belong to others too.

The events on Sheppey, like the poems of Evans and Arany and
the nationalist hopes of Thorkelín and Grundtvig, tell us more
about contemporary social conditions than medieval culture but
they still form part of the archive of the Middle Ages. In this
work, the production of medievalist double consciousness, the
idea of the Middle Ages becomes what it always was: a means
of producing difference in the present. The Middle Ages is not
a historical category in this material, but a means of outlining
subject positions, a means of establishing hierarchies, a means of
securing personal and collective identities. The circular logic, the
'two-ness' of medievalist double consciousness, ensures that these
patterns of thought reproduce themselves. To use Slavoj Žižek's

language, as these cultural forms are repeated, 'a retroactive effect is experienced as something which was already there from the beginning'.[95] As with Edward and Eleanor's performance at Glastonbury, we are left not with a continuous, stable, unchanging essence, but a performance of speculation, repetition and reiteration that generates a simulacrum of an origin, a fantasy of wholeness and exclusion. Excavating this imagined origin, as I have in this chapter with Gray's bards, for instance, leaves us not with a reassuring and comforting sense of linear historical time, progression or order, but with dislocation and untimeliness. In this sense, the Middle Ages has never been over, but is constantly becoming, as ideas of the medieval are deployed to suture or reveal fissures in the contemporary moment. The meanings of the Middle Ages are therefore not found in the past, or at least not wholly in the past, as they always reside in part in the moment in which they are produced or reproduced. In this chapter we have witnessed some of the potential of cultural memories of the Middle Ages to emphasise difference and embed hierarchical structures between peoples, to mark some people as untimely as a means of writing them out of the future. In Chapter 4 I will explore the potential of medievalist thinking to assuage the untimeliness of the human body. Where the works surveyed in this chapter share an insistence on the singularity of time and compound this with their commitment to a rigid understanding of social relations, the texts in the next chapter imagine – and sometimes struggle to come to terms with – echoes, repetitions and moments of contact that unfold in and across time, and gesture towards a radically open, unknowable but hopeful future.

Notes

1 On Walpole, Strawberry Hill and Gothic, see E. J. Clery, 'Horace Walpole, the Strawberry Hill press, and the emergence of the Gothic genre', *Ars et Humanitas* 5 (2010), 93–112.

2 A digital edition is available online at the Thomas Gray Archive: www.thomasgray.org/cgi-bin/view.cgi?collection=primary&edition=1757, accessed 24 October 2017.

3 See Johannes Fabian, *Time and the Other: How Anthropology Makes its Subject* (New York: Columbia University Press, 2002).

4 See Emily V. Thornbury, *Becoming a Poet in Anglo-Saxon England* (Cambridge: Cambridge University Press, 2014). On the relationship between Gray's poem and the antiquarian enthusiasm for bards see Nick Groom, *The Making of Percy's 'Reliques'* (Oxford: Oxford University Press, 1999), pp. 61–105.

5 'bard, n.1', *OED Online*, www.oed.com/view/Entry/15474?rskey=zaH sJ0&result=1&isAdvanced=false, accessed 24 October 2017.

6 See Jeffrey Jerome Cohen, *Hybridity, Identity, and Monstrosity in Medieval Britain: On Difficult Middles* (New York: Palgrave Macmillan, 2006), p. 4; Kathleen Davis, 'Time behind the veil: The media, the Middle Ages, and Orientalism now', in Jeffrey Jerome Cohen (ed.), *The Postcolonial Middle Ages* (New York: Palgrave, 2000), pp. 105–22; Patrick Geary, *The Myth of Nations: The Medieval Origins of Europe* (Princeton: Princeton University Press, 2002); Sharon Kinoshita, 'Deprovincializing the Middle Ages', in Rob Wilson and Christopher Leigh Connery (eds), *The Worlding Project: Doing Cultural Studies in the Era of Globalization* (Santa Cruz, CA: New Pacific Press, 2007), pp. 61–75.

7 Cameron's speech is archived online: www.gov.uk/government/speeches/magna-carta-800th-anniversary-pms-speech, accessed 24 October 2017.

8 On Magna Carta see David Carpenter, *Magna Carta* (London: Penguin Classics, 2015).

9 Sharon Turner, *The History of the Anglo-Saxons, from their first appearance above the Elbe, to the death of Egbert …* (London: T. Cadell, 1799), p. 2. See further Reginald Horsman, 'Origins of racial Anglo-Saxonism in Great Britain before 1850', *Journal of the History of Ideas* 37 (1976), 387–410.

10 Paul Freedman and Gabrielle Spiegel, 'Medievalisms old and new: The rediscovery of alterity in north American medieval studies', *American Historical Review* 103 (1998), 677–704, p. 679.

11 Du Bois, *The Souls of Black Folk*, ed. Gates and Oliver, p. 11. On double consciousness see Robert Gooding-Williams, *In the Shadow of Du Bois: Afro-Modern Political Thought in America* (Cambridge, MA: Harvard University Press, 2009), esp. pp. 66–95 and Frank M. Kirkland, 'On Du Bois' notion of double consciousness', *Literature Compass* 8 (2013), 137–48.

12 Homi K. Bhabha, *The Location of Culture* (London: Routledge, 1994), p. 313.

13 Benedict Anderson, *Imagined Communities: Reflections on the Origin and Spread of Nationalism*, rev. edn (London: Verso, 2006), p. 16.

14 Ernest Gellner, *Thought and Change* (London: Weidenfeld and Nicholson, 1964), p. 162. See further A. D. Smith, 'When is a nation?', *Geopolitics* 7 (2002), 5–32, who notes that, 'For the vast majority of analysts, some ancient and medievalist historians excepted, the nation and nationalism are modern; and "modern" means both relatively recent (since the French and American revolutions) and qualitatively novel' (p. 6).

15 Thomas Warton, *The History of English Poetry, from the Close of the Eleventh to the Commencement of the Eighteenth Century* (London: J. Dodsley, 1774), p. 2.

16 John D. Niles, *The Idea of Anglo-Saxon England 1066–1901: Remembering, Forgetting, Deciphering, and Renewing the Past* (Chichester: Wiley-Blackwell, 2015), p. 194.

17 Walter Scott, *Ivanhoe*, ed. Ian Duncan (Oxford: Oxford University Press, 1996), p. 26.

18 Thomas Gray, 'The Bard', in *The Complete Poems of Thomas Gray*, ed. H. W. Starr and J. R. Hendrickson (Oxford: Clarendon Press, 1966), pp. 18–24, lines 18–20 and 16, p. 19. Further references are given by line number.

19 See Norman Davies, *The Isles: A History* (London: Macmillan, 2000), pp. 417–18.

20 Peter Lord, 'Y Bardd – Celtiaeth a Chelfyddyd', in Geraint Jenkins (ed.), *Cof Cenedl VII: Ysgrifau hanes Cymru* (Llyandysdul: Gwasg Gomer, 1992), p. 97–131, p. 101.

21 On the construction of British identity in the eighteenth century see Linda Colley, *Britons: Forging the Nation, 1707–1837* (New Haven: Yale University Press, 1992).

22 Thomas Carte, *A General History of England: An account of all public Transactions from the Accession of Henry II, A.D. 1216, to the Death of Henry VII, April 22, A.D. 1509* (London: Printed for the Author, at his House in Dean's Yard, Westminster, 1747), vol. 2, p. 196.

23 See J. Gwynfor Jones, 'Wynn, Sir John, first baronet (1553–1627)', *Oxford Dictionary of National Biography*; online edn, October 2006, www.oxforddnb.com/view/article/30153, accessed 13 April 2016.

24 On the 1282–83 conquest of Wales see Morris, *A Great and Terrible King*, pp. 182–93 and Michael Prestwich, *Edward I* (London: Methuen, 1988), pp. 188–201. For a full account of the myth of the bards of Wales see Neville Masterman, 'The massacre of the bards', *Welsh Review* 7 (1948), 58–66.

25 See, for instance, Paul Odney, 'Thomas Gray's daring spirit: Forging the poetics of an alternative nationalism', *CLIO: A Journal of Literature, History, and the Philosophy of History* 28 (1999), 245–60, p. 255.

26 Sir John Wynn, *The History of the Gwydir Family and Memoirs*, ed. and trans. J. Gwynfor Jones (Llandysul: Gomer, 1990), p. 24.

27 Trevor Herbert, 'Parry, John (1710?–1782)', *Oxford Dictionary of National Biography*; online edn, May 2009, www.oxforddnb.com/view/article/21420, accessed 13 April 2016.

28 Peter D. G. Thomas, 'Wynn, Sir Watkin Williams, third baronet (1693?–1749)', *Oxford Dictionary of National Biography*; online edn, May 2008, www.oxforddnb.com/view/article/30155, accessed 13 April 2016.

29 Thomas Gray, 'Letter CXL to Mason', in Paget Toynbee and Leonard Whibley (eds), with corrections and additions by H. W. Starr, Correspondence of Thomas Gray, 3 vols (Oxford: Clarendon Press, 1971), letter no. 238, vol. 2, pp. 501–3, p. 501. Available online: www.thomasgray.org.uk/cgi-bin/display.cgi?text=tgal0271, accessed 24 October 2017.

30 'Two Odes' (London: H. Payne, 1760), illustrated with an image of a bearded bard playing his lyre.

31 *The Critical Review: Or, Annals of Literature* 4 (1758), p. 168.

32 *The Monthly Review* 17 (1757), p. 242.

33 See Howard Gaskill (ed.), *The Reception of Ossian in Europe* (London: Thoemmes Continuum, 2004).

34 Howard Weinbrot, *Britannia's Issue: The Rise of British Literature from Dryden to Ossian* (Cambridge: Cambridge University Press, 1993), p. 397.

35 Odney, 'Thomas Gray's daring spirit', p. 254.

36 Katie Trumpener, *Bardic Nationalism: The Romantic Novel and the British Empire* (Princeton: Princeton University Press, 1997), p. 6.

37 As Trumpener writes: English literature 'constitutes itself … through the systematic imitation, appropriation, and political neutralization of antiquarian and nationalist literary developments in Scotland, Ireland, and Wales', *Bardic Nationalism*, p. xi.

38 On Llywelyn see R. R. Davies, *The Age of Conquest: Wales 1063–1415* (Oxford: Oxford University Press, 2000), pp. 308–30. On the Treaty of Aberconway see *ibid.*, pp. 335–7. See also James Carley, 'Arthur in English History', in W. R. J. Barron (ed.), *The Arthur of the English: The Arthurian Legend in Medieval English Life* (Cardiff: University of Wales Press, 1999), pp. 47–57.

39 On Edward and Eleanor's Arthurian enthusiasms see Juliet Vale, 'Arthur in English society', in Barron (ed.), *The Arthur of the English*, pp. 185–96, esp. pp. 185–90, and R. S. Loomis, 'Edward I, Arthurian enthusiast', *Speculum* 1 (1953), 114–27.

40 N. J. Higham, *King Arthur: Myth-Making and History* (London: Routledge, 2009), p. 232.

41 Higham, *Arthur*, p. 230.

42 Morris, *Great and Terrible King*, p. 166. On the Welsh Arthurian tradition see Rachel Bromwich, A. O. H. Jarman and Brynley F. Roberts (eds), *The Arthur of the Welsh: The Arthurian Legend in Medieval Welsh Literature* (Cardiff: University of Wales Press, 1991). On the relationship between the Arthurian traditions and the borders of Britain, see Michelle R. Warren, *History on the Edge: Excalibur and the Borders of Britain* (Minneapolis: University of Minnesota Press, 2000).

43 Antonia Gransden, 'Damerham, Adam of (*d.* in or after 1291?)', *Oxford Dictionary of National Biography*; online edn, September 2013, www.oxforddnb.com/view/article/93, accessed 22 April 2016.

44 *Adami de Domerham Historia de rebus gestis Glastoniensibus*, ed. Thomas Hearne, 2 vols (Oxonii: E Theatro Sheldoniano, 1727), vol. 2, pp. 588–9.

45 On the excavation see Antonia Gransden, 'Glastonbury traditions and legends', in J. P. Carley (ed.), *Glastonbury Abbey and the Arthurian Tradition* (Cambridge: D. S. Brewer, 2001), pp. 29–53.

46 Gerald of Wales, 'Liber de principis instructione', 'Distinctio I', in *Giraldus Cambrensis opera*, ed. J. S. Brewer, James F. Dimock and George F. Warner, 8 vols, (London: Eyre and Spottiswood, 1891), vol. 8, pp. 127–8. See further Julia Crick, 'The marshaling of antiquity: Glastonbury's historical dossier', in Lesley Abrams and James P. Carley (eds), *The Archaeology and History of Glastonbury Abbey, Essays in Honour of the Ninetieth Birthday of C. A. Ralegh Radford* (Woodbridge: Boydell Press, 1991), pp. 217–43.

47 Gerald of Wales, 'Liber de Principis Intructione', p. 127

48 Philip Schwyzer, *Literature, Nationalism, and Memory in Early Modern England and Wales* (Cambridge: Cambridge University Press, 2004), p. 11.

49 Jeffrey Jerome Cohen, 'Race', in Marion Turner (ed.), *A Handbook of Middle English Studies* (Oxford: Wiley-Blackwell, 2013), pp. 109–22, p. 112.

50 Sarah Prescott, *Eighteenth-Century Writing from Wales: Bards and Britons* (Cardiff: University of Wales Press, 2008), p. 75.

51 See Evan Evans, *Some Specimens of the Antient Welsh Bards* (London, 1764) and Geraint H. Jenkins, 'Evans, Evan (1731–1788)', *Oxford Dictionary of National Biography* (Oxford: Oxford University Press, 2004), www.oxforddnb.com/view/article/8955, accessed 12 April 2016. See also Bethan M. Jenkins, *Between Wales and England: Anglophone Welsh Writing of the Eighteenth Century* (Cardiff: University of Wales Press, 2017).

52 Evan Evans, 'A paraphrase of the 137th Psalm, alluding to the captivity and treatment of the Welsh bards', *The Cambro-Briton* 2 (1820), 87–9, lines 1–2, p. 87. Hereafter cited by line number.

53 James Mulholland, *Sounding Imperial: Poetic Voice and the Politics of Empire, 1730–1820* (Baltimore: Johns Hopkins University Press, 2013), p. 73.

54 Mulholland, *Sounding Imperial*, pp. 73–4.

55 'Y bardd', in Reginald Heber, *Palestine, a poem, by Heber: and the Bard, an ode, by Gray, translated into Welsh by W. O. P* (London: Argrafiad E. Williams, 1822), pp. 41–57.

56 Mulholland, *Sounding Imperial*, p. 75.

57 Helen Fulton, 'Class and nation: Defining the English in late-medieval Welsh poetry', in Ruth Kennedy and Simon Meecham-Jones (eds), *Authority and Subjugation in Writing of Medieval Wales* (Basingstoke: Palgrave Macmillan, 2008), pp. 191–213, p. 199.

58 For an alternative tradition of Welsh writing see Jane Aaron, 'Bardic anti-colonialism', in Jane Aaron and Chris Williams (eds), *Postcolonial Wales* (Cardiff: University of Wales Press, 2005), pp. 137–58.

59 Bhabha, *The Location of Culture*, p. 86.

60 Lytton Strachey, 'Horace Walpole', in *Characters and Commentaries* (London: Chatto and Windus, 1933), pp. 32–44, p. 40.

61 Susan Bernstein, *Housing Problems: Writing and Architecture in Goethe, Walpole, Freud and Heidegger* (Stanford: Stanford University Press, 2008), p. 47.

62 On Arany see Albert Tezla, *Hungarian Authors: A Bibliographical Handbook* (Cambridge, MA: Belknap Press of Harvard University Press, 1970), pp. 36–52.

63 For an overview of the 1848 revolution see István Deák, *The Lawful Revolution: Louis Kossuth and the Hungarians, 1848–1849* (New York: Columbia University Press, 1979); István Deák, 'The revolution and the war of independence, 1848–1849' and Eva Somogyi, 'The Age of neoabsolutism', in Peter F. Sugar, Péter Hanak and Tibor Frank (eds), *A History of Hungary* (Bloomington: Indiana University Press, 1990), pp. 209–34 and 235–51. On the composition of 'A Walesi Bárdok' see Alice Freifeld, *Nationalism and the Crowd in Liberal Hungary, 1848–1914* (Baltimore: Johns Hopkins University Press, 2000), p. 150. On nationalism and poetry in nineteenth-century Hungary see József Szili, 'Nation-religion in nineteenth-century Hungarian poetry', *Hungarian Studies* 16 (2002), 3–28.

64 János Arany, 'A Walesi Bárdok', in Arany János, *Balladák*, ed. Földes Tamás (Budapest: Akkord Kiadó, 2009), pp. 86–90, p. 86. I'd like to thank Rachel Homer for help with Hungarian.

65 See E. Wyn Jones, 'The lame chick and the north star: Some ethnic rivalries in sport as reflected in mid-nineteenth-century Welsh broadsides', in Marjetka Golež (ed.), *Ballads between Tradition and Modern Times* (Ljubljana, Slovenia: Slovenian Academy of Sciences and Arts, 1998), pp. 93–100. Gabriella Hartvig suggests that Arany found the story of Edward's massacre of the bards in Hugh Blair's *A Critical Dissertation on the Poems of Ossian*. See Gabriella Hartvig, 'Ossian in Hungary', in Gaskill (ed.), *Reception of Ossian in Europe*, pp. 240–58, p. 235.

66 Arany, 'A Walesi Bárdok', p. 87.

67 Text taken from János Arany, 'The Bards of Wales', trans. Peter Zollman, in Adam Makkai (ed.), *In Quest of the Miracle Stag* (Chicago: Atlantis-Centaur), pp. 319–23, p. 320.

68 Arany, 'A Walesi Bárdok', p. 90.

69 Arany, 'Bards of Wales', trans. Zollman, pp. 322–3.

70 Iván Berend, *History Derailed: Central and Eastern Europe in the Long Nineteenth Century* (Berkeley: University of California Press, 2003), p 58.

71 Adam Makkai, 'János Arany, 1817–1882', in *In Quest of the Miracle Stag*, p. 291.

72 See 'Hungarian tale of 500 slaughtered Welsh bards inspires new symphony', *Wales Online*, 21 March 2013, www.walesonline.co.uk/news/wales-news/hungarian-tale-500-slaughtered-welsh-1809705, accessed 24 October 2017.

73 See 'Strengthening the link between Wales and Hungary', *Wales Online*, 27 March 2013, www.walesonline.co.uk/news/local-news/strengthening-link-between-wales-hungary-2056906, accessed 24 October 2017.

74 See Nick Thorpe, 'Protests usher in far-right theatre director in Hungary', *BBC News*, 2 February 2012, www.bbc.co.uk/news/world-europe-16843913, accessed 24 October 2017.

75 Berend, *History Derailed*, pp. 77–8.

76 Louise D'Arcens and Clare Monagle, ' "Medieval" makes a comeback in modern politics: What's going on?', *The Conversation*, 22 September 2014, http://theconversation.com/medieval-makes-a-comeback-in-modern-politics-whats-going-on-31780, accessed 24 October 2017; Kevin McDonald, 'ISIS Jihadis aren't medieval – they are shaped by modern Western philosophy', *Guardian*, 9 September 2014, www.theguardian.com/commentisfree/2014/sep/09/isis-jihadi-shaped-by-modern-western-philosophy, accessed 24 October 2017; James L. Smith, 'Medievalisms of moral panic: Borrowing from the past to frame fear in the present', *Studies in Medievalism* 25 (2016), 157–72.

77 See, for instance, Frantzen, *Desire for Origins*; Ian Wood, *The Modern Origins of the Early Middle Ages* (Oxford: Oxford University Press, 2013); and Eric G. Stanley, *The Search for Anglo-Saxon Paganism* (Cambridge: D. S. Brewer, 1975).

78 See, for instance, Fred C. Robinson, who writes that although *Beowulf* 'is usually seen as the first great masterpiece of English literature, from another perspective it may be said that by virtue of its large scale, refined style and lofty theme *Beowulf* is also the chief glory of early Germanic poetry at large'. '*Beowulf*', in Godden and Lapidge (eds), *The Cambridge Companion to Old English Literature*, pp. 142–59, p. 142.

79 On Thorkelín and *Beowulf* see Magnús Fjalldal, 'To fall by ambition – Grímur Thorkelín and his *Beowulf* edition', *Neophilologus* 92 (2008), 321–32. On Scandinavian nationalism and medieval studies see Robert E. Bjork, 'Nineteenth-century Scandinavia and the birth of Anglo-Saxon studies', in John D. Niles and Allen J. Frantzen (eds), *Anglo-Saxonism and the Construction of Social Identity* (Gainesville: University Press of Florida, 1997), pp. 111–32 and Wood, *Modern Origins of the Early Middle Ages*, pp. 162–4.

80 Translation by Robert E. Bjork and Taylor Corse in 'Grímur Jónsson Thorkelín's Preface to the first edition of *Beowulf*', *Scandinavian Studies* 68 (1996), 291–320, p. 299 and p. 303.

81 The review is translated in T. A. Shippey and Andreas Haarder (eds), '*Beowulf*': *The Critical Heritage* (London: Routledge, 1998), pp. 143–52.

82 The word 'drapa' indicates that Grundtvig is claiming a Norse heritage for the poem.

83 See Andreas Haarder, *Beowulf: The Appeal of a Poem* (Copenhagen: Akademisk Forlag, 1975), pp. 55–8.

84 *Klaeber's Beowulf and the Fight at Finnsburg*, 4th edn, ed. R. D. Fulk, Robert E. Bjork and John D. Niles (Toronto and London: University of Toronto Press, 2008), p. 96.

85 N. F. S. Grundtvig, *Beowulfes Beorh, eller Bjovulfs-Drapen* (Copenhagen: Schönberg, 1861), pp. iv–x.

86 Translation by Fred C. Robinson, 'The afterlife of Old English', in *The Tomb of Beowulf and Other Essays*, pp. 275–303, p. 301.

87 Translation by Robinson, 'Afterlife of Old English', p. 303.

88 See further John A. Hall, Ove Korsgaard and Ove K. Pedersen (eds), *Building the Nation: N. F. S. Grundtvig and Danish National Identity* (Montreal: McGill-Queen's University Press, 2015).

89 Ted Hughes, 'Thistles', p. 147, 'Gog', pp. 161–4, 'The Warriors of the North', p. 167, all in Paul Keegan (ed.), *Ted Hughes: Collected Poems* (London: Faber and Faber, 2003).

90 Anders Berhing Breivik, *2083: A European Declaration of Independence*. Available online: publicintelligence.net/anders-behring-breiviks-complete-manifesto-2083-a-european-declaration-of-independence, accessed 24 October 2017. See further Daniel Wollenberg, 'The new knighthood: Terrorism and the medieval', *Postmedieval: A Journal of Medieval Cultural Studies* 5 (2014), 21–33; Åsne Seierstad, *One of Us: The Story of a Massacre and its Aftermath*, trans. Sarah Death (London: Virago, 2016); and Aage Borchgrevink, *A Norwegian Tragedy: Anders Behring Breivik and the Massacre on Utøya*, trans. Guy Puzey (London: Polity Press, 2013).

91 See further Geraldine Heng, 'The invention of race in the European Middle Ages I: Race studies, modernity, and the Middle Ages', *Literature Compass* 8 (2011), 315–31 and 'The invention of race in the European Middle Ages II: Locations of medieval race', *Literature Compass* 8 (2011), 332–50; and the essays collected in Thomas Hahn (ed.), 'Race and ethnicity in the Middle Ages', *Journal of Medieval and Early Modern Studies* 31 (2001), 1–165; Cord J. Whitaker (ed.), 'Making race matter in the Middle Ages', *Postmedieval: A Journal of Medieval Cultural Studies* 6 (2015), 1–110; and the ongoing series of essays on 'Race, racism and the Middle Ages' collected at www.publicmedievalist.com/race-racism-middle-ages-toc/, accessed 24 October 2017.

92 See Andy Gray, 'Enjoying a creative voyage across Sheppey with the Vikings', *Kent Online*, 25 September 2013, www.kentonline.co.uk/sheerness/news/enjoying-a-creative-voyage-with-6459/, accessed 24 October 2017.

93 See Paul Wilkinson, '*Beowulf*: Some topographical considerations', in *Beowulf in Kent* (Faversham: The Faversham Society, 1998),

pp. 1–18, p. 5. See also www.faversham.org/history/people/beowulf. aspx, accessed 24 October 2017. Thanks to Patrick Wright for sharing this with me.

94 See Mills, *A Dictionary of British Place-Names*, p. 417.

95 Slavoj Žižek, *The Sublime Object of Ideology* (London: Verso, 2008), p. 104.

4
The language of gesture: Untimely bodies and contemporary performance

'Art' is the name of the possibility of a conversation across time, a conversation more meaningful than the present's merely forensic reconstruction of the past.

Alexander Nagel and Christopher Wood,
Anachronic Renaissance[1]

Uniquely among the surviving memorials to Eleanor of Castile, the Eleanor Cross at Northampton is decorated with open books (see Figure 4.1). The books were likely once illustrated, perhaps even with text, and may be an allusion to Eleanor's own learning. While the contents of the books is ultimately unknowable, their design suggests a belief, to use Alexander Nagel and Christopher Wood's words, in 'the possibility of a conversation across time' between the monument and the visitor – an embodied, affective conversation. As I explored in Chapter 2, the medieval tomb involved the mourner in what Elizabeth Valdez Del Alamo and Carol Stamatis Pendergast describe as an 'active, even an interactive, process' of meaning-making.[2] These conversations contradict a simplistic past–present dualism, but are always precisely situated in time and place. Regardless of the age of the monument, this conversation always takes place in the viewer's present. Time is not collapsed, but bridged, and multiple presents – the present of the monument's making and the present of the viewer's interpretation most obviously – come together. We cannot know precisely what the cross might have communicated to a medieval viewer, but we can be sure that the cross was designed to draw people in to it, to determine their movements, to initiate contact across time.

This chapter takes this kind of coming together of bodies as its starting point. It is prompted by two works of twenty-first-century art that engage in affective conversations with medieval material and visual texts. Elizabeth Price's 2012 film *Woolworths Choir of 1979* constructs an archive of gesture that brings together medieval

4.1   Detail of the Eleanor Cross at Northampton

visual culture and twentieth-century social history. The film insists
on the continuing presence of medieval culture and expresses a
radical hope for collective belonging as it seeks to expose and
redress historical inequalities. Michael Landy's *Saints Alive* (2013)
reimagines the temporal and affective potential of the visual and
textual cultures of medieval hagiography. His work brings the
twenty-first-century viewer literally into contact with representa-
tions of medieval saints, seeking to generate affective contact across
time. While the previous chapter charted the manner in which
modern texts reinscribed the difference and inequality recorded
in medieval texts, Price and Landy challenge the normative struc-
tures established in their medieval sources. They not only provide

another example of the continuing cultural energy of the Middle Ages, but also demonstrate how engaging with medieval culture has the potential to radically disrupt contemporary social practices.

This chapter traces a network of cultural memory around and across Price's and Landy's work and their medieval sources. It begins with an examination of representations of untimely bodies in a group of medieval monuments, the very monuments that stand at the centre of Price's film, and explores the structures of time these works create. While Chapters 2 and 3 explored material that attempted to mitigate the untimeliness of cultural memories of the Middle Ages and excavated the fragments, fissures and fragility of cultural memory, the material encountered in this chapter embraces untimeliness, anachrony and fragmentation, in a manner that recalls but does not repeat some of the translations and appropriations of *The Ruin* explored in Chapter 1. The medieval material Price and Landy direct us to insists that a body might remain present and animate, vital and full of meaning, through time, long past an individual's death. In this process, the body becomes a locus of narrative, social and cultural memory and generative of embodied and experiential knowledge. This insistence refocuses our apprehension of time to emphasise duration rather than period and to explore, as I have in the previous chapters of this book, the possibility of affective connection across time. My exploration of the vitality and temporality of the body in medieval effigies and Price's film is qualified and developed through analysis of the Middle English poem *St Erkenwald*, an example of the kind of hagiography that Landy's work responds to. *St Erkenwald* tells a story of a body out of time. It worries about what happens when the past interrupts the present and, while Price and Landy explore the radical consequences of such temporal collisions, the poem ultimately attempts to entrench previously established structures of time and authority.

The material brought together in this chapter is unified by an interest in the temporal and communicative possibilities of the body. I do not suggest that the texts, sculptures or art works I discuss reveal a network of influence. But what they do share is an interest in the language of gesture and the relationship between the body and time.[3] I have borrowed my methodology from the practice of the art historian Aby Warburg and in particular the unfinished project often referred to as the *Mnemosyne Atlas*. It was Warburg's great ambition, sadly never fulfilled, to trace the transfer of gestures and culture from antiquity to the Renaissance.

Before his death in 1929, Warburg did manage to create a number of panels that explore the temporalities of gesture. In one completed panel, known as Panel 46, for instance, Warburg collated images that revealed variations of images of a fruit-bearing nymph from antiquity to the Renaissance. In others, he traced changes in the representation of the planet Mars, representations of nymphs and Virgil's Neptune.[4] For Warburg, the value of this project was that it revealed how images of great symbolic power emerged in antiquity and reappeared, reanimated, in later times and places. As Christopher Johnson writes:

> Dating from Ancient Babylon to Weimar Germany, these symbolic images, when juxtaposed and then placed in sequence, were meant to foster immediate, synoptic insights into the *Nachleben* of pathos-charged images depicting 'bewegtes Leben' (life in motion). A summa of symbolic images, *Mnemosyne* strove to make the ineffable process of historical change and recurrence immanent and comprehensible.[5]

My own ambitions are more restricted. The images, works and texts I assemble in this chapter reveal one history of the medieval in motion, one means of approaching the continual returns of the Middle Ages in modernity, one archive of the continuing presence of the medieval. My method is not exhaustive but suggestive and determined by the work of Price and Landy.

Where my intentions are more clearly aligned with Warburg's is in my belief in the emancipatory potential of this material. As Jan Assmann writes, for Warburg 'cultural collective memory has an emancipatory, rather than an enslaving function'. It offered a means of reimagining social and psychic reality and Warburg believed that, 'With the assistance of cultural objectification, man is able to free himself from the phobic pressures of reality. He can free himself from his fear of demons and of being overwhelmed by the senses.'[6] The material collected in this chapter tells a story of humans pushing against the barriers of linear time, habits of periodisation and other normative structures, working to explore the possibilities of continued presence across time. The bodies we encounter in this chapter are always already archaic, but also oriented towards the future. Thus they are able to resist the temporal structures that have formed, and been formed by, much of the material explored in this book. As I have shown so far, the idea of the Middle Ages is often defined by a doubleness, a two-ness, which allows it to signify on condition of closure. In this chapter, we encounter bodies that refuse these conditions and instead embrace their untimeliness and express radical hope in the generation of collective, affective relations across time.

The bodies of the unknown knight: sculptural relationscapes

The Woolworths Choir of 1979 begins in the medieval church before expanding its gaze to encompass other archives of gesture. I will examine the film in more detail below, but for now will unpick the medieval gesture that sits at the centre of Price's network of memory. Like the Eleanor Cross at Northampton, a martial effigy that survives in Dorchester Abbey, Oxfordshire (see Figure 4.2), attempts to initiate a conversation with its viewers. This outsized, intimidating figure reclines, legs crossed, as if at rest, but his hand is on his sword, as if he might draw it and leap into action at any moment. These two gestures – legs crossed and hand on sword – are provocative but ambiguous. As with the book at Northampton, while it is clear that they might communicate something urgent and meaningful, exactly what they might say is unknown and unknowable. But what is clear is that this effigy creates a sense of vigorous physicality and even generates a possibility of movement. It creates a male, martial identity. The body exerts a palpable presence, even in death. It is perfected. This knight might just snap back into action if the viewer steps too near, looks too closely. The effigy incorporates the viewer into its dynamic production of meaning because it is the viewer's body, as it leans in, that creates the possibility, the opportunity, for the effigy to spring into movement.

This sculpture structures the opening movement of Price's film and the hand gesture becomes the point of contact that brings Price's divergent archives together. As Price's shot pauses on one large, particularly striking monument – the effigy at Dorchester Abbey – the narration describes 'Whole human figures / Which lie recumbent / But with an animated attitude / The greatest expression confined / To a conspicuous twist / To a twist / Of the right wrist' (see Figure 4.3). Price's text draws on and echoes the fullest academic study of secular thirteenth-century effigies, H. A. Tummers' *Early Secular Effigies in England: The Thirteenth Century*, published in 1979, while the image of the monument is taken from the National Monuments Record.[7] As in the translation history of *The Ruin* excavated in Chapter 1, Price's film demonstrates how critical and creative responses to medieval culture

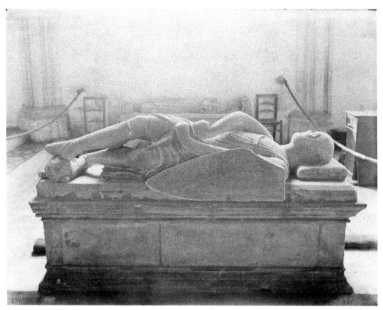

4.2   Effigy at Dorchester Abbey. Photograph by Henry W. Taunt (1890)

overlap. She works creatively with the critical archive of the Middle Ages and recognises the manner in which medieval survivals are mediated by their institutional, cultural and material histories.

As Tummers explains, although the effigy at Dorchester Abbey is the pinnacle of the tradition, there are around 200 other examples of the recumbent, sword-wielding effigy. The tradition flourished from the mid-thirteenth to the mid-fourteenth century and incorporates two-dimensional representations in stone and brass as well as sculptural bodies. Particularly noteworthy works in wood and brass remain largely intact at Danbury, Essex, and St Mary Redcliffe, Bristol. The popularity of the form qualifies and confirms the mystery of the precise meanings of their gestures. Tummers uses the term 'lively martial attitude' to describe their comportment;[8] Paul Binski suggests that the alert stance of the effigies may signify that the dead are soldiers of Christ, 'ever alert and ever ready to challenge the idea of eternal rest';[9] and both Tummers and Binski read the crossed legs as evocative of a calm, controlled and sophisticated social elite. There is also a suggestive echo between the legs of the effigies and the crossed legs of Christ on the cross. Rachel Dressler suggests that the placing of the

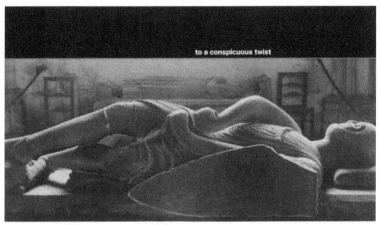

4.3   Still from Elizabeth Price, *The Woolworths Choir of 1979* (2012)

knight's hand on his sword is deliberately phallic but, like the crossed legs, it is fundamentally ambiguous and it is unclear even whether the swords are being drawn or sheathed.[10] For Price, as we will see, it is precisely the ambiguity of the gesture that generates its power.

The traditional interpretation of the crossed legs, however, is that they signify that the knight took part in the Crusades. The earliest association between the crossed legs and crusader identity is in Camden's *Britannia*, first published in 1594, when he writes of the monuments of Temple Church and notes that, 'Many noblemen were buried among them, whose images are to be seen in this Temple with their legs transverse in a cross: for, as I have heard, so all were buried, in that age, who had pledged themselves to the Holy War, or who (as was then said) had taken the Cross.'[11] The association is also picked up in John Stow's *Survey of London*, first published shortly after *Britannia* in 1598, when he explains of the Temple Church effigies that 'eight of them are Images of armed knights, five lying crosse legged as men vowed to the holy land, against the infidels and unbeleeving Jewe'.[12] Although this association is now discredited, it survives in churches and guidebooks.[13] The effigies at Danbury, for instance, are labelled 'crusader knights'. While there is no firm evidence to support this reading of the crossed-leg gesture, it is valuable because it reveals one way in which meanings of the body depend on ideas of similarity and difference. As Stow recognised, the effigies' gestures distinguished themselves. They offer an image of a desirable, stable, continuing subject position and functioned as a means of marking other, absent bodies, as abject.

Another valuable insight offered by the traditional association of the crossed-legged effigies with crusader knights is that it makes it clear that, while it is impossible to read the gestures individually – it is unclear exactly what they might mean – it is possible to read them collectively. Indeed, Tummers goes so far as to claim that, 'It may be said that the English cross-legged knightly effigies are class-conscious products.' For Tummers, the effigies suggest the existence of a self-aware knightly class. The similarities and differences among the effigies are, as Tummers writes, 'a sign of the individualism of the people belonging to this knightly class. All these thirteenth-century effigies stress the realistic, worldly outlook of a class of people that was becoming more and more conscious of itself.'[14] So, while the effigies initiate complex interactions with the bodies of viewers, they also speak eloquently to other remembered and reimagined bodies, both desired and feared. The effigies, no less than Stow's reference to 'infidels and unbeleeving Jewe(s)', sought to secure collective identities and social hierarchies.

Despite Stow and Camden's interpretative work, the ambiguity of the gestures cannot be divorced from their meanings or effects. As with the nationalist readings of *Beowulf* encountered in Chapter 3, it is the ambiguities of the effigies that enable and condition their appropriation. The overall effect of the gestures is, however, clear: they record the presence of the deceased man through a language of gesture that generates a sense of vital, perfected, animated life. The effigies invoke a way of remembering these men, a continued existence for them, that is corporeal and material as well as spiritual. They therefore recall elements of theological approaches to resurrection that exerted a strong influence on the culture of the Middle Ages. Caroline Walker Bynum's work on medieval Christian philosophies of resurrection and identity has demonstrated how, in the Middle Ages, the dead were often understood to be corporeal beings, even in the afterlife. Bynum notes that the discourses of resurrection were dominated by two metaphors – of the seed and of the statue.[15] In discussions of resurrection that followed the metaphor of the statue, emphasis was placed on bodily perfection in a manner which recalls the impressive physicality of the effigy at Dorchester. In St Augustine of Hippo's *Enchiridion*, for instance, he writes that 'the bodies of the saints will rise again free from defect, free from deformity, free from any corruption or burden or difficulty'.[16] As Roberta Gilchrist suggests, 'Right up to the end of the Middle Ages the archaeological evidence for medieval burial demonstrates an emphasis on preserving the material continuity of the body.'[17] In this context, the martial effigies offer a meditation on the perfected materiality of the body and express a privileged spiritual being. This perfection is also socially coded, however, as the eloquent expression of the materiality of the knight's body is achieved through the material out of which the effigy is made. At Dorchester, for instance, the Corfe stone, a valued and prestigious material, allows delicate carving, generating a more powerful sense of presence than the wood from which the effigy at Danbury is made.[18] So the knight's social identity and indeed the image of privilege the effigy conjures depends on the geological facticity of the matter from which it is constructed and the financial means necessary to purchase such valuable material.

Nevertheless, although a visitor to Dorchester Abbey may be struck by the cold, forceful and enduring materiality of the stone, it is the gestures of the effigy that communicate most powerfully. Erin Manning's work offers a way to interrogate the suggestions of movement evoked by the gestures. Manning examines moments of almost-movement, or preacceleration as she terms it, and offers a way to think through the coming together of viewer and effigy and effigy and effigy, the dynamic production of meaning that relies on the possibility of two bodies working together and possibly moving together. Manning writes that:

> There are always at least two bodies. These two stand close, facing one another, reaching-toward an embrace that will signal an acceleration of the movement that has always already begun. The movement within becomes a movement without, not internal-external, but folding and bridging in an intensity of preacceleration. This means you are never stopped. To move is to engage the potential inherent in the preacceleration that embodies you. Preaccelerated because there can be no beginning or end to movement. Movement is one with the world, not body/world, but body-worlding. We move not to populate space, not to extend it or to embody it, but to create it.[19]

Manning's thoughts point in two directions. First of all, she invites us to consider how the gestures of the effigies 'create' space, how the twin movements and makings of the effigies generate a feeling of fear in the viewer and how they speak with one another to generate what Tummers reads as a sign of class-conscious individualism. The movements of the viewer are engaged, or directed, by the gestures of the effigy. Secondly, then, Manning encourages us to think about how space is created through the interaction of two

bodies: the effigy and the viewer. That is to say that the effigy deter-
mines the manner in which the viewer occupies the space around
it. As the viewer leans in to examine the effigy, or moves around to
make sense of the comportment and dimensions of the body, 'the
potential inherent in the preacceleration' of the two bodies – the
knight and the viewer – is engaged. What is key here is repetition,
the repetition and refinement of the different gestures on the effi-
gies and the threat of repeated violence of the gestures, but also the
repeated interrogations of the viewer. A single glance is not enough
to comprehend any work of art, but these effigies invite the viewer
to move around the body, to examine the sculptured voids that give
movement to the legs and arms, to measure the power present in
the forms of those limbs, to return time and again to the threat of
movement generated by the pose.

This multiplicity, doubleness and self-referentiality of gesture
is central to the power of the effigies and brings to mind Giles
of Rome's tautological explanation of the relationship between
knightliness and the body. For Giles, in John Trevisa's fourteenth-
century translation, a knight is 'well desposed in his body whanne
his body is suche as nedeth for a knight's office'.[20] Giles' circular
thinking is persuasive: a knight is a knight because his body is that
of a knight and he does what a knight does. As this suggests, and
as the effigies confirm, control over one's body was a powerful con-
tributor to masculine identity. As Derek Neal writes, in late medi-
eval courtesy literature it is not enough for a man to display power
and strength: 'The movements of the body must be governed mod-
erately.'[21] The importance of bodily governance and comportment
is explored in numerous medieval works by, for instance, Albertus
Magnus and Thomas Aquinas, which agree that the outer body
reflects and constitutes the inner body so that, as J. Allan Mitchell
puts it, 'The properly ruled body reveals innermost qualities of
character ("soule"), and inner and outer man become isometric.'[22]
In these accounts, the body is double: signifier and signified. Outer
body reflects inner body, just as the inner body controls the outer.

The doubleness of gestures, the fact that they can at once be sin-
gular and multiple, individual and collective, internal and external,
is picked up by Augustine in *De doctrina christiana*, where he draws
a distinction between what he calls natural signs and given signs.
Augustine writes:

> Natural signs are those which without a wish or any urge to signify
> cause something else besides themselves to be known from them,
> like smoke, which signifies fire … The expression of an angry or

depressed person signifies an emotional state even if there is no such
wish on the part of the person who is angry or depressed, and like-
wise any other emotion is revealed by the evidence of the face even
if we are not seeking to reveal it.

...

Given signs are those which living things give to each other,
in order to show, to the best of their ability, the emotions of their
minds, or anything that they have felt or learnt ... When we nod,
we give a sign just to the eyes of the person whom we want, by
means of that sign, to make aware of our wishes. Particular move-
ments of the hands signify a great deal. By the movement of all their
limbs, actors give certain signs to the cognoscenti and converse with
the spectators' eyes, as it were; and it is through the eyes that flags
and standards convey the wishes of military commanders. All these
things are, to coin a phrase, visible words.[23]

Augustine's emphasis on the need of gestures to be read is signifi-
cant – the actors need the cognoscenti, the visible words of gestures
need to converse with the spectators' eyes – and provides another
means of thinking through the meeting between viewer and effigy.
Without the viewer's full participation, the meanings of the effi-
gies are compromised. To put it another way, the effigies consist of
and offer given signs – deliberate movements – that are designed
to generate natural signs in the viewer – perhaps an opening of
the eyes to suggest fright, or a lean backwards to suggest wariness.
This is how the effigies instigate a conversation across time com-
municated in the language of gesture.

Vilém Flusser's work can bring Augustine and Manning
together. He suggests that, 'Gestures are movements of the body
that express being. The gesticulating person's way of being in the
world can be read in them.'[24] Drawing on Tummers, Manning,
Augustine and Flusser, it becomes clear that that the effigies are
very keen to assert their way of being in the world, but that this
assertion depends on the participation of the viewer. Returning to
Nagel and Wood's language, we can say that the effigies 'instigate
a conversation across time' communicated in the language of ges-
ture. Nagel and Wood suggest that an interest in anachrony, what
they describe as a work of art's hesitation to locate itself precisely
in time, is an important characteristic of the art of the Renaissance,
but these medieval effigies demonstrate a similar hesitation. The
moment they are interested in is the moment of interaction – they
exist in a long now rather than a single, precise moment in time,

an ongoing moment, waiting for a viewer to participate in their language of gesture. Their meanings cannot be limited to a single context. They invite their viewers to think about duration rather than period. The knight is waiting for something – judgement day, perhaps – but the visitor interrupts that pause and becomes a witness to the knight's continuing life.

These bodies gather other bodies. The effigies speak eloquently to one another across time through their shared form, but they also gather other, living, bodies to them. To use Judith Butler's language, this 'gathering signifies in excess of what is said'.[25] An encounter between a viewer and a sculpture is, indeed, likely to be silent, but it nevertheless is loaded with signification. It conveys a message of male, martial identity which may attract or repel, but it also conveys an embodied sense of being that has the potential to transform the viewer's own sense of being-in-the-world. As Roberta Gilchrist suggests, this speaks of broader truths of medieval culture. 'The medieval life course began with the myriad strategies surrounding conception and pregnancy, and ended with the myriad strategies that aimed to ensure memory of the dead and their well-being in the afterlife', Gilchrist writes. 'The dead were regarded as a separate social group or even age grade: they were an age cohort perceived to continue their social existence in a parallel plane to the living.'[26] These sculptures take the possibility of affective relations between living and dead as a given. But these possibilities are transformed by their duration. To encounter these bodies in the twenty-first century is to encounter a new way of imagining and experiencing the existence of the body in time.

Tummers begins his study of the effigies by speculating on the reasons for their survival. He notes that 'two waves of iconoclasm have destroyed a great deal of English medieval sculpture' and suggests that the effigies may have survived because 'English iconoclasts like Cromwell only destroyed what they considered to be superstitious. They left intact the non-ecclesiastical effigies, which they considered to commemorate men worthy of their country.'[27] This contributes another layer of temporal complexity to the objects, another sense of doubleness, another set of meetings and coming-togethers, another kind of conversation across time. It also generates another insight into the importance of masculinity to these effigies, for it is not merely that they were created to memorialise a certain ideal of the masculine, but that they survived in part because that ideal remained culturally esteemed. So while part of the power of these effigies relies on their suggestion of change – the possibility that they will in fact come to life – their power and their existence also relies on continuity, particularly the continuing cultural significance of masculine violence. They record the desires of the knights to be remembered and the masculine forms they desired for themselves, but also the desire of later viewers for this perfected, outsized, impossible vision of masculinity.

In his otherwise sober study of medieval British sculpture, Lawrence Stone writes that the effigies display an 'alarming sense of power and vitality'.[28] It is worth pausing to ponder exactly what is alarming about the effigies. It is, first of all, the threat that the body might spring to life; but this depends on the clarity and communicative ability of the effigies' language of gesture. So the alarm might be generated in part by the manner in which the effigies reveal the continuing presence, the duration, of the forms of masculinity they celebrate. What is alarming is the fact that the language of the effigies remains contemporary, that they speak so eloquently in a historical context so far removed from the moment of their production. Jacques Lacan put it slightly differently when he suggested that, 'It's never, in any way whatever, by another person's excesses that one turns out, in appearance at least, to be overwhelmed. It's always because their excesses happen to coincide with your own.'[29] What is alarming, or overwhelming, about the excesses of the effigies is that they coincide with an image of masculinity that continues to be desired and feared. As we will see in the next section, for Elizabeth Price, the effigies reveal one of the key structures that determine human experience.

Elizabeth Price's *Woolworths Choir of 1979*: form and structure, gesture and collectivity

Like the effigy at Dorchester and *St Erkenwald*, *The Woolworths Choir of 1979* is a meditation on time, the body and collective identity.[30] The film is an assemblage of three distinct bodies of material: digital images of twentieth-century photographs of medieval architecture taken from the National Monuments Record; clips taken from internet archives of pop performances; and news footage and archival records of a fire in a Woolworths department store in Manchester in 1979 in which ten people died.[31] Price has described her video work as 'fabulations'.[32] Her films draw on the social histories of objects, ideas, archives and events to explore the processes of social assembly. She explains that 'I don't want to transcend material. I'm interested in, and part of, a world made up of unredeemed, sensual debris', and that in her work, 'I reorganise objects by recognising contingent properties that might link them. I find a materialist premise for a departure into fantasy, so that both social history and fiction are employed in knowing the past.'[33] The disparate things, narratives and histories out of which Price creates her films are brought together not just visually, in the way she seeks unities and echoes between form and material, but also verbally as Price composes a narration that is delivered textually and invokes what she has termed a 'manifold voice'.[34]

Price's earliest video work, *A Public Lecture and Exhumation* (2006), formed part of a larger project that sought to execute the terms of a bequest made by Alexander Chalmers to the London Borough of Stoke Newington in 1927. This project, which was also recorded in a book and a series of artist's commissions, appropriated the bureaucratic language of administrative process to reveal the complex relations that govern institutions and objects.[35] Price's 2009 work *User Group Disco* continued her interrogation of objects, archives and identities and staged a study of outdated, kitsch and apparently unwanted consumer goods. These objects – pet food dispensers, whisks, mass-produced sculptural objects and gadgets – are animated in the film to constitute what the narration calls 'a Hall of Sculptures'.[36] As the film begins, the narration unfolds in a manner reminiscent of a corporate or educational PowerPoint presentation, but in a stylised language that suggests invisible structures, beings, institutions and processes: 'Let Us show you / We are the Human Resource / We are singular and manifold / We are the sum total / of the ways in which we divide our labour / into distinct tasks / and achieve coordination amongst them'. There is an eroticism, an intimacy and sensuality to the film's gaze as Price brings together fantasy and documentary. There is humour, too, as the soundtrack, which begins as an aggressive and rhythmic beat becomes a light, airless rendition of A-Ha's 'Take on Me'. As the film progresses, the objects are placed on a turntable to rotate and move in the darkness. *User Group Disco* insists that these objects cannot be reduced to their relations and Price's videos practise what Manuel DeLanda terms a 'flat ontology'. For DeLanda, a flat ontology is one that is not 'based on relations between general types and particular instances', but one which approaches relations 'in terms of interacting parts and emergent wholes'. Price's films bring together, in DeLanda's words, 'unique, singular individuals, differing in spatio-temporal scale but not in ontological status'.[37] Price's work offers a radical, egalitarian politics that seeks to unpick the structures of power that confine the living and dead – the human and nonhuman – and reveal the potential for affective contact across time and media.

The Woolworths Choir of 1979 evinces an interest in being, mediation and assembly and retains a commitment to interrogating the social and political structures which form, and are formed by, the objects, spaces and bodies Price examines. Throughout the film, there is no footage in which material is directly filmed. Instead Price works from photographic archives, digital, video and textual sources. The structure of the film is defined by connections between language, gesture and form. As the word choir tells us and as the narration of the film makes clear, Price is interested in how ideas, bodies, histories can come together across space and time. Price's own handclaps and fingersnaps punctuate the film, sometimes synched with the footage of pop performances, sometimes marking cuts between shots, which gives a sense of embodied time. The image that unites the three movements of the film is a gesture of the hand, the 'conspicuous twist of the right wrist' that Tummers detected in the effigies, which Price situates in relation to the choreographed movements of twentieth-century pop performers and a waving hand in Manchester appealing for help through the barred windows of a burning building.

As I explained above, the film begins with a study of the architecture of the medieval choir. The camera pans across archival images, scholarly studies and digital reconstructions of medieval church architecture as the 'manifold voice' of the narrator delivers an introduction to the power relations embedded in the forms and structures. Text describes the spatial arrangement of the choir, explains how it is separated from the nave by the rood screen, illustrates the common formal patterns of the trefoil, quatrefoil and ogee, defines the difference between the 'chorus abbatis' and 'chorus prioritis' and finally notes 'how the stalls encircle the space'. Price has suggested that the choir is 'an architecture built to house people' and the film illustrates the hierarchies its material forms generate and sustain.[38] As the film progresses, attention turns to the central space of the choir. Text informs the viewer that, 'on the floor of the choir / and in the nave and transepts / there are other secular images / sepulchral effigies and monuments / here they are', as the camera presents images of the effigies in Temple Church, Dorchester Abbey, Jervaulx and other sites, taken from the National Monuments Record and Tummers' appendix of images in *Early Secular Effigies in England*. The narration tells the

viewer that these, often fragmented, forms are 'whole human fig-
ures / which lie recumbent / but with an animated attitude / the
greatest expression confined / to a conspicuous twist / to a twist /
of the right wrist'.

The sustained examination of the wrists of the effigies brings
in the transition to the next body of material, which is drawn from
the digital archive of twentieth-century pop performers recorded
on YouTube. Excerpts from the Shangri-Las' pop song 'Out in
the Street' are heard briefly throughout the film, but from the
eighth minute onwards, after a period of hiss, crackle and distor-
tion, the song is played in full along with the video of its perfor-
mance.[39] As they perform the song, the Shangri-Las execute what
Price has described as a 'sombre, enigmatic dance'[40] in which they
make synchronised, suggestive and apparently ritualised gestures.
The performers execute a movement in which their arms move
upwards with their palms outwards facing the viewer's gaze, as if
in greeting, supplication or worship and then, following a twist of
the wrists which turns their palms downwards, their arms move
down again, away from the viewer, as if in retreat or dismissal.
Next, the performers move their left hand swiftly but smoothly to
their side, almost in a shrug, before their bodies shift to their right,
turning away from the viewer and suggesting self-protection and
concealment. Price has described this performance as 'sardonic',
and there is a sense that the performers are aware of a meaning that
is lost on the viewers, that the viewers are participants in a perfor-
mance that they don't quite understand.[41] As the song reaches its
climax, the performers clap their hands and snap their fingers to
generate a sense of urgency and energy. This sense is confirmed by
the song's lyrics, which tell a story of doomed young love in which
the object of the narrator's affections is lost because 'His heart is
out in the streets'.

The footage of the Shangri-Las is intercut with numerous clips
of other pop performances by female performers that also contain
expressive yet ambiguous twists of the wrist and movements of the
arms. Images pass by very quickly, so it is very difficult to identify
the performers. What emerges instead is an accumulated archive,
a complex, entangled group of images and gestures that speak to
one another, like the medieval effigies, in an explicitly formal yet
mysterious language. Finally, Price turns to the fire in Manchester.
At this point the tempo slows and the music stops. The images are
punctuated only by Price's fingersnaps and the occasional shake
of a tambourine. Multiple interviews with survivors of the fire

are interwoven and repeated, spliced between clips from pop per-
formances, news reports and archival material relating to the fire,
while the narration records the words of the silent interviewees: 'it
all went up / in a matter of minutes / and we saw the smoke / right
here / we went down / but it was full of smoke / we just couldn't
see / smoke was in our eyes / in a matter of minutes / it was eve-
rywhere / and we just couldn't see / smoke was in our eyes / so we
just / we came out at the bottom / and saw all the flames coming
up / we saw all the flames'. The words tell the story of the fire, as
well as give an account of the experience of it. The repetition of
the interviewees' words, combined with Price's insistent, staccato
cutting between images creates a rhythm that coils and pulses and
generates a sense of claustrophobia and urgency. The interviewees
all share a language of gesture as they give form to the rising smoke
or point up towards the burning building with their hands. A sin-
gle arm is seen waving frantically for help from a smoking window.
These 'conspicuous twists' of the wrist carry a sense of panic and
fear and, like the gestures of the medieval effigies, also give form to
a shared experience and constitute a trace of a collective identity in
the historical record.

Price explained her interest in the gesture of the twisted wrist as
related to the manner in which it alludes 'to an emergence, a transi-
tion from one state to another', which she thought she could use 'in
order to shift us from one archive to another and also to populate
or inhabit the church with the idea of this emergence into life or
falling into death'.[42] So she uses this gesture as a point of con-
nection that enables the transition between moments in time. This
again then is a conversation across time enabled by the language of
gesture. And again, like Tummers, Price is interested in how the
repetition of this gesture creates a collective identity, how bodies
converse with one another across time and space.

For Price, the temporal diversity of her material enables her
to interrogate what she suggests are consistently self-reproducing
structures, structures that define the collective identities she exam-
ines and evokes. The three bodies of material – the effigies, the pop
performances and the Woolworths fire – are each defined by their
existence within structures of class and gender. It is self-evident
how the effigies and pop performances relate to these structures,
but in the case of the Woolworths fire, Price's footage demon-
strates that if you were a woman you were more likely to be near
the centre of the fire, while if you were a man, you were more
likely to be involved in combatting it or assessing it. Price's film

demonstrates how gender and class position individuals in space and time. Like the effigies, Price is interested in how gestures generate ideas of time and collective identities in a way that confounds traditional habits of historical periodisation and offer new, useful and productive ways of thinking about how time is organised and experienced. As Rebecca Schneider suggests, this interest in gesture demonstrates how it is possible to 'drag something of the no longer now, the no longer live, into the present, or drag the present into the no longer now'.[43] Price demonstrates the presence of the no longer now in modernity, but the effigies demonstrate the presence of the no longer now, and the not yet now, in medieval culture. What these texts also share is a conviction in the possibility of change, liberation and redemption, and the belief that this is achieved through collective action in, through and across time. What Price drags out of this multitemporal archive is a figure of the subject caught between structural forces, cultural and historical, struggling for self-determination and preservation in the realm of memory.

St Erkenwald: social and temporal structures

The most striking medieval account of an interaction with an ancient tomb survives in the Middle English poem *St Erkenwald*, which was likely composed around the year 1400 but looks back to the seventh century and the very beginnings of Anglo-Saxon Christianity. It is a text fascinated by the past, by artistry, affect and reading and begins with a brief history of the process of conversion in London. The poem imagines a diverse, pre-Christian past and explains that, 'Þat ere was of Appolyn is now of Saynt Petre; / Mahon to Saynt Margrete, oþer to Maudelayne'[44] (What was earlier Apollo's was now St Peter's, Mahomet's was St Margaret's or Magdalene's) and 'Þe Synagoge of þe Sonne was sett to oure Lady; / Jubiter and Jono to Jhesu oþer to James' (21–2, The synagogue of the sun was set to Our Lady, Jupiter and Juno's to Jesus or to James). These lines express a faith in a progressive model of historical change – a conversionary, linear model, in fact – which sees the past superseded by the present and ethnic and social difference defeated by white Christianity. But, as Jonathan Hsy suggests, the presence of those remembered names reminds the reader that the past may be passed but is not forgotten and the poem conceives the city as what he terms a 'complex multitemporal entity'.[45] For Seeta Chaganti, this is also a question of form, as the alliterative lines of the text reinforce 'a pattern of vestigiality'.[46] In *St Erkenwald* there is a truth to be discovered beneath the surface. The past remains present and requires unravelling. The presence of cultural difference makes this an urgent matter, as it suggests that the past holds a threat to the self-identity and coherence of the present.

The presence of the past, and its continuing meaning, is demonstrated by the discovery of an ancient tomb while builders are at work rebuilding St Paul's Cathedral:

> Þai founden fourmyt on a flore a ferly faire toumbe;
> Hit was a throghe of thykke ston, thryuandly hewen,
> With gargeles garnysht a-boute, alle of gray marbre.
> The speke of þe spelunke þat spradde hit o-lofte
> Was metely made of þe marbre and menskefully planede,
> And þe bordure enbelicit with bryȝt golde lettres;
> Bot roynyshe were þe resones þat þer on row stoden.

(46–52, They found in the floor a wonderfully fashioned tomb, its thick stone very skilfully carved, with gargoyles to garnish the grey marble. The canopy of the coffin, covering it on top, was finely made of grey marble smoothly planed and the border was embellished with bright gold letters – mysterious they stood, in sentences obscure.)

The tomb is a beautiful object – it is lavishly decorated, skilfully carved out of grey marble – but the 'bryȝt golde lettres' that decorate the border are mysterious. Like the gestures of the effigies at Dorchester and elsewhere with which I began, they are visible but illegible. Further, like the effigies, the affective power of this tomb relies on its indecipherability. Indeed, this affective power is so acute that the tomb's discovery threatens disturbance and indiscipline. Like the effigies, it gathers bodies:

> Quen tithynges token to þe ton of þe toumbe-wonder,
> Mony hundrid hende men highide þider sone;
> Burgeys boghit þer-to, bedels ande othire,
> And mony a mesters-mon of maners dyuerse.
> Laddes laften hor werke and lepen þiderwardes,
> Ronnen radly in route wyt ryngande noyce;
> Þer commen þider of alle kynnes so kenely mony,
> Þat as alle þe worlde were þider walon with-in a honde-quile.

(57–64, When news of the wondrous tomb came to the town, many hundreds of worthy men immediately hurried there. Burgesses, beadles and others turned there, and many members of craft guilds, of all sorts. Apprentices left their work and sprang, running quickly, in a disorderly, clamouring crowd. So many of all kinds came there eagerly, as if all the world were welling up there in an instant.)

Regardless of social role or rank, the men of the city are drawn to the tomb. While I suggested that the effigies with which I began might emphasise the precise contours of a social identity, one of the effects of this tomb is the dissolution of social differences: 'alle þe worlde' is brought together, as one. Or, rather, almost 'alle þe worlde' is brought together, as one, because women are not included in *Erkenwald*'s vision. The poem seems willing and able to contemplate social breakdown, but refuses to imagine the presence of women. As in Chapter 3, the reader is offered a fantasy of wholeness and exclusion, although in this case exclusion is dependent on gender rather than nation, ethnicity or race. To return to Butler's language, the Londoners' gathering 'signifies in excess of what is said' because it reveals unspoken and perhaps unspeakable assumptions, desires and social rules.

It is also significant, as Frank Grady suggests, that the 'roynyshe' figures, which stand at the centre of the crisis, 'are never deciphered or translated in the poem'. The poem insists on the ultimate mystery of the letters so that it can enforce its own sovereignty over the past. As Grady writes, the poem 'supplies the deficiencies of chronicles and corrects the failures of memory that render the letters unreadable'.[47] As with the accounts of Edward and Eleanor's performance at Glastonbury we encountered in the previous chapter, *St Erkenwald* is fascinated by the mediation of the past. The 'roynyshe' letters are its equivalent to Gerald of Wales' account of the lock of Guinevere's hair. *Erkenwald* insists that, without the correct authority, no access to the past will be possible. The past will be lost, as will the ties that bind communities together.[48]

The opening of the tomb does not soothe the anxieties generated by its discovery, however. The body of the man enclosed inside is apparently unchanged by the time he has spent in the tomb. His 'blisfulle body' is 'Araide on a riche wise, in rialle wedes' (77, arrayed richly, in rich clothes). Indeed, he looks 'As he in sounde sodanly were slippide opon slepe' (92, As if he soundly and suddenly had slipped into sleep). He looks, perhaps, like a thirteenth-century martial effigy. The people are puzzled that they have no knowledge of this man, they can find no trace of who the corpse might be in their histories and they wonder how 'Hit my3t not be

bot suche a mon in mynde stode longe' (97, it might not be but
such a man stood long in memory).

The bishop, Erkenwald, is away from London on pastoral duties
but is called back and begins to supervise the disinterment of the
man and soothe 'the troubulle in þe pepul' (109). He is as puzzled
as everyone else and prays that the corpse might speak. Speak it
does, and the corpse explains that he is a pagan judge who lived
in pre-Roman London. Again, the shock generated by the corpse
brings people together:

> Quil he in spelunke þus spake þer sprange in þe pepulle
> In al þis worlde no worde, ne wakenyd no noice,
> Bot al as stille as þe ston stoden and listonde,
> With meche wonder forwrast, and wepide ful mony.

> (217–20, When he in the stone coffin spoke thus, there came no
> word in the people in all the world, nor arose any noise; but all stood
> as still as the stone and listened, seized by great wonder, and very
> many wept.)

As they listen, there is complete silence and the crowds stand as
still as stone. Chaganti notes that in these lines, 'The language of
the poem renders indeterminate the boundary between the stone
tomb and the astonished audience, so that both fill the positions
of either a material thing or an occasion of spectacle.' The view-
ers are, for Chaganti, 'interactive participants in a scene of per-
formance blending spectacle, ceremony, and architecture'.[49] Again,
then, the poem asks its readers to think about participation, col-
lectivity and difference. When the people of London converge on
the tomb first of all their differences dissolve; now, as the figure in
the tomb speaks, their very humanity is questioned. Agency and
animation is transferred from the living to the dead and the people
of London are rendered as stone. As with the natural signs gener-
ated by the effigies, the poem is thinking about how viewers can be
caught up in, changed, transformed, by participation in a meaning-
making process.

The judge tells his story but explains very little. When he is
asked when he lived, he replies with a garbled riddle claiming that
he lived,

> After þat Brutus þis burghe had buggid on fyrste
> Noȝt bot (aght) hundred ȝere þer aghtene wontyd –
> Before þat kynned ȝour Criste by cristen acounte
> (Þre hundred) ȝere and þritty mo and ȝet threnen aght.

(207–10, After Brutus first built this borough, it was not but eight hundred years less eighteen before your Christ was born, by Christian accounts, three hundred years and thirty more and yet threefold again.)

Like the 'roynyshe' letters of the tomb, these lines are very difficult to decipher. And like the martial effigies at Dorchester and elsewhere, the judge seems leery to locate himself too precisely in time.[50] As Philip Schwyzer frames it, 'the Londoners in the poem experience not simply the simultaneous failure of living and historical memory but also a collapse of the distinction between these two modes of memory'.[51] The dualism of past–present breaks down. To draw a link back to the effigies in Dorchester and elsewhere, this is a moment of affective contact across time and very literally a conversation across time.

The climax of the poem – and the closest past and present come to touching – is the moment when the Bishop's tears fall on the judge. The poem tells us that Erkenwald, 'To þe liche þer hit lay, wyt lauande teres' (314, Bowed towards the body, and bathed it in tears), while he prayed to God. The corpse speaks too, and tells the Bishop that 'For þe wordes þat þou werpe, and þe water þat þou sheddes, / Þe brȝt bourne of þin eghen, my bapteme is worthyn' (329–39, By the words you have used and the water you have shed, / By the bright stream of your eyes, my baptism is achieved'). The judge ascends to heaven as his body disintegrates and becomes 'blakke as þe moldes' (343, black as the earth). Erkenwald's tears and the baptism they generate resolve the disruption caused by the discovery of the tomb. They realign past and present and confirm the authority of the Church. It is this authority – in the form of Erkenwald's tears – that seals the past off from the present and re-establishes the boundaries of historical periods.

Cynthia Turner Camp has written on *St Erkenwald*'s interest in memory and periodicity. She writes that 'The desire for direct apprehension – to "touch" the past' is central to the poem and that it 'is born of the conviction that the past is needful to the present'.[52] She continues to suggest that the fact 'That this desirable past is revealed by its verbal touch is key; even though the past that speaks itself is exposed as a fantasy, that fantasy nevertheless reveals the transformative possibilities of unmediated access to the past.'[53] However, while Turner Camp emphasises the verbal touch of the conversation and the touch of Erkenwald's tear on the judge, the poem is also heavily invested in mediation and distance. Transformation is achieved through affective contact, mediated by the authority of the Church, but bodies do not touch. In this text the past is not unmediated – the poem is about, in John Scattergood's phrase, 'the custody of the past'.[54] And the past is not touched: what is desired is the ability to work with the past, respond to it, to move with it, govern it, define it on the terms of the present, and this is achieved only by respecting hierarchies of authority and only enabled by the body of the Bishop. The poem demonstrates that, to use Sara Ahmed's language, 'not all bodies are within reach. Touch … involves an economy: a differentiation between those who can and cannot be reached.'[55] The 'peple' of London gather around the tomb, but like Erkenwald they do not touch the judge. The poem enables contact with the past, but only mediated through the authority of the Church and the body of the Bishop.

Although the moment of baptism is the climax of the poem, it is not the only moment in which Erkenwald cries. In fact he cries throughout the poem. By the time Erkenwald arrives at the tomb and prays for the mystery to be revealed, he is already 'wepande' (122, weeping). While tears can be understood as a bodily function rather than a gesture, Erkenwald's insistence on a public performance suggests a communicative element and indicates that his tears can be understood as both 'natural' and 'given' signs. Like the gestures of the effigies, Erkenwald's tears are designed to reveal internal qualities as well as status and power. In Judith Kay Nelson's words, 'crying contradicts mind–body dualism' because 'When tears are shed for emotional reasons – and sometimes when they are suppressed – the body speaks.'[56] In its desire to speak with and save long-dead non-Christians, St Erkenwald offers a double moment of porosity, between mind and body and also between past and present.

Like the effigies, Erkenwald's tears engage a language of gesture and gather other bodies. While the effigies' gestures reveal secular concerns, Erkenwald's speak to a long history of Christian embodiment. Most explicitly, the events of St Erkenwald direct readers towards the earliest Life of Gregory the Great, produced in the eighth century by a monk or nun at Whitby Abbey.[57] The Life explains that, one day while walking in the Forum, Gregory saw something that tells the story of Trajan's charity towards a bereaved mother and was moved to 'lacrimarum fluenta' (floods of tears) by the Christian behaviour of the pagan emperor and these tears secured Trajan's place in the kingdom of Heaven.

Quidam quoque de nostris dicunt narratum a Romanis, sancti
Gregorii lacrimis animam Traiani imperatoris refrigeratam vel
baptizatam, quod est dictu mirabile et auditu. Quod autem eum
dicimus babtizatum, neminem moveat: nemo enim sine babtismo
Deum videbit umquam: cuius tertium genus et lacrimę. Nam die
quadam transiens per forum Traianum, quod ab eo opere mirifico
constructum dicunt, illud considerans repperit opus tam elemosi-
narium eum fecisse paganum ut Christiani plus quam pagani esse
posse videret.[58]

(Some of our people also tell a story related by the Romans of how
the soul of the Emperor Trajan was refreshed and even baptized by
St Gregory's tears, a story marvellous to tell and marvellous to hear.
Let no one be surprised that we say he was baptized, for without
baptism none will ever see God; and a third kind of baptism is by
tears. One day as he was crossing the Forum, a magnificent piece of
work for which Trajan is said to have been responsible, he found on
examining it carefully that Trajan, though a pagan, had done a deed
so charitable that it seemed more likely to have been the deed of a
Christian than of a pagan.)

Like Erkenwald's, Gregory's tears have the effect of causing bap-
tism, so in a sense are supercharged, but tears functioned in a vari-
ety of ways in medieval Christian life.[59] In the Rule of St Benedict
tears function as a sign of humility and devotion. In his Life of
St Cuthbert, Bede writes that: 'Tantum autem conpunctioni erat
deditus, tantum coelestibus ardebat desideriis, ut missarum sollen-
nia celebrans, nequaquam sine profusione lacrimarum implere pos-
set officium' (He was so full of penitence, so aflame with heavenly
yearnings, that when celebrating Mass he could never finish the ser-
vice without shedding tears).[60] Beyond Anglo-Saxon England, tears
continued to hold great currency. In Sermon 26 of his commentary
on the Song of Songs, for instance, Bernard of Clairvaux wishes his
tears would 'Exite, exite' (flow on, flow on) so they might erupt like
a 'fontes' (fountain).[61] Erkenwald's tears are part of this tradition,
which goes back to Gregory, so generate a complex temporality. In
the poem, the moment of baptism is a moment of porosity between
past and present as the ancient pagan is rescued and sent to heaven,
but it is also a moment of porosity in terms of how Erkenwald's
gestures repeat Gregory's. This repeated gesture not only repeats
the outcome but, as with the effigies, it generates a collective iden-
tity, not of knights but of weeping holy men.

Margery Kempe offers an interesting counter-example of
the meaning of public tears. Margery's autobiography, probably

written in the late 1430s, records numerous moments when her bodily piety overwhelmed and disturbed those who were witness to it. Her 'boisterous' tears frequently drew disapproval from many of her witnesses. When, for instance, Margery is overcome with 'habundawnt teerys of hy deuocyon' (abundant tears of devotion) as she thinks of heaven, her neighbours tell her: 'ʒe haue not be þer no more þan we' (you haven't been there any more than we have).[62] Karma Lochrie and Santha Bhattachargi among others have explored the precedents, such as Marie d'Oignies and the Virgin Mary herself, that informed Margery's conduct. In Lochrie's words, Kempe's tears 'are proclamations of her own privileged reading of Christ's body'.[63] As proclamations of privilege, however, they were frequently challenged, in a marked contrast to Erkenwald's tears, which were accepted without question.

The work of performance theory offers valuable insights into the ethics and temporalities of Erkenwald's tears. To describe the Bishop's tears as a performance is not to question their sincerity, but merely highlights their complex temporality, and following Richard Schechner's work, we can understand Erkenwald's tears as a form of 'restored behaviour'. For Schechner, 'Performance means: never for the first time. It means: from the second to the nth time. Performance is "twice-behaved behaviours".'[64] According to Schechner's thinking, any man crying in a religious environment in public could be said to be enacting a form of restored behaviour, in so far as their gestures recall those gestures that preceded them, and it is important to recognise that it is not only behaviour that Erkenwald restores. Following the disruption caused by the discovery of the tomb, his behaviour restores order, as it secures the Church's control over the past and the 'peple'. If we return to Augustine's natural and given signs, we might locate Gregory's and Erkenwald's tears between these categories, in that they are an apparently natural product of the body, but their meaning is determined by the environment of the gesture. Erkenwald could of course step away from the corpse and not weep all over him. Because he doesn't, his body initiates a conversation with Gregory's body, a conversation that takes place across time.

Erving Goffman's thoughts on the parameters of performance are also helpful here. Goffman writes:

A 'performance' may be defined as all the activity of a given participant on a given occasion which serves to influence in any way any of the other participants. Taking a particular participant and his performance as a basic point of reference, we may refer to those who contribute to the other performances as the audience, observers, or co-participants.[65]

This returns us to the question of participation. I have already suggested that participation is key to the effigies. But the same can be said of *St Erkenwald* – the poem brings the Londoners in as participants in the saint's performance and the whole poem can be thought of as a performance of ecclesiastical authority. If we can think of the effigies as relying on the participation of the viewers, or perhaps co-performers or co-participants, the same could be said of the readers of *St Erkenwald*. The Londoners, like the readers, are invited to read Erkenwald's performance and see the relationship that is created between his body and Gregory's. They are invited to witness the power and authority of his body. As E. Gordon Whatley suggests, the poem 'presents the story in such a way as to magnify the role and prestige of the bishop and the visible sacramental church, which together turn out to be vital to the salvation of the heathen soul, regardless of his matchless justice'.[66] As the text invites its readers to acquiesce with its structures of power, so it invites its readers to share its temporal logic. It presents the past as mysterious, threatening, out of the present's control – without, that is, the assistance of the Church. This reading is supported by the alliterative patterns of the verse but also the manner in which the text tells the story of London's past, with the non-Christian temples becoming churches. As with the effigies, the poem thinks about duration rather than period, or at least it does so until Erkenwald's tears baptise the judge and historical order is restored. So, like the effigies, the poem allows for the possibility of participation, but on the condition that this participation follows its own structural logic, a logic bound up in the male body and the male power of the judge.

Michael Landy's *Saints Alive*: touch and destruction

Michael Landy's 2013 exhibition *Saints Alive* was a response to the medieval cultures of hagiography of which *St Erkenwald* forms a part. Landy's work consisted of seven kinetic sculptures that were operated by viewers and a selection of related drawings and collages. The sculptures represented figures and stories from the lives of saints that circulated in the Middle Ages and were assembled from sculptured details taken from paintings in the National Gallery's collection combined with recycled machinery. So Landy's sculpture of St Jerome, for instance, is an assemblage of three distinct works of art, animated by a complex – and apparently less than safe – motor engine (see Figure 4.4). The statue is headless but stands at an outsized height of 3 metres, resting on legs Landy replicated from Cima da Conegliano's early sixteenth-century painting *Saint Jerome in a Landscape*. Above the engine, Landy reproduces Jerome's chest from Ercole de' Roberti's *The Dead Christ*, from about 1490. When a visitor activates the sculpture's mechanism and presses the button in front of the sculpture,

4.4   Michael Landy, *Saint Jerome* (2012)

the statue's arm, taken from Cosimo Tura's *Saint Jerome* (*c.* 1470), strikes its chest with the rock it holds in its hand. The contact between rock and chest is executed with shocking violence. It is noisy and the rickety machine seems to be at risk of flying out of control. Another of Landy's sculptures, of St Francis of Assisi, takes the form of a donation box. The upper half of Francis' body, taken from Sandro Botticelli's *Saint Francis of Assisi with Angels* (1475–80), sits on the box and, when a visitor makes a donation, the statue strikes its head with the cross clasped in its hands. Again, the sculpture is a multi-sensory spectacle that can prompt shock as well as delight. The sculptures are therefore intrinsically multitemporal objects. They are assemblages of diverse sources, animated by the presence of the viewer, but are also auto-destructive, so as soon as the viewer participates and animates the sculpture, they become aware of their inevitable future disintegration. Like the effigy at Dorchester Abbey, the viewer is deeply implicated in the sculpture's meaning-making process.

A number of Landy's art works are marked by his interest in destruction and performance. Most famously, his 2001 work *Break Down* consisted of the destruction of every one of his personal possessions. Landy catalogued each of his items, from his passport, clothes and his toothbrush to professional equipment and his car. In a disused commercial unit in London's Oxford Street, Landy set up a dis-assembly line and, over fourteen days and with a number of assistants, sorted his possessions and systemically reduced them to dust. *Break Down* is most often read as a meditation on consumer culture, but it is also clearly interested in the relationship between memory, identity and material culture.[67] Like *Saints Alive* it examines the manner in which the boundaries between human and nonhuman, subject and object, are breached. Landy's next major work, *Semi-Detached*, installed at Tate Britain in 2004, brought these interests into tighter focus. *Semi-Detached* was a life-sized replica of Landy's parents' house, placed in Tate Britain's Duveen Galleries.[68] The house was divided into two halves, with films projected onto the back panels of each part. These films documented Landy's father's life in the house. John Landy suffered life-limiting injuries as a result of an industrial accident he experienced at the age of thirty-seven and was forced to take early retirement. As Judith Nesbitt has explained, the accident was a defining moment in the lives of Landy's family and the intimacy of the portraits Landy produced 'might leave viewers struggling to define the boundaries between prurience and personal reflection'.[69] As with

Break Down, Semi-Detached documents frayed edges of self-hood, moments at which subjecthood is threatened and explores how the artist and the viewer are implicated in the making of art.

One final context of *Saints Alive* is Landy's long-standing interest in the work of the Swiss artist Jean Tinguely (1925–91).[70] Tinguely produced auto-destructive automata, anarchic sculptures that juddered into unpredictable life when activated by viewers. His most celebrated piece of work is *Homage to New York* (1960), which destroyed itself after only twenty-seven minutes, although by bursting into flames rather than the actions it was expected to execute. As Rosalind Krauss writes, while Tinguely's sculptures might have looked like 'little more than animated junk', they can be thought of 'as actors in specific performances'.[71] As in *Saints Alive*, the viewers are implicated in this performance and so are required to think through their participation in the destruction of art. This sense of the agency of sculpture speaks eloquently to the power of the effigy at Dorchester and has a similarly unsettling effect.

Saints Alive adapted Tinguely's methodology to transform pictures of saints into auto-destructive automata animated by the viewer. Landy's sculpture *Multi Saint*, for instance, consists of physiological elements drawn from paintings by Carlo Crivelli and Hans Memling. Installed, the sculpture looms over the viewer. A button sits on the floor of the gallery, in front of the sculpture and when a viewer steps on it, the sculpture judders into life. The viewer's touch is required to animate the art. This participation of the viewer requires the willingness of the viewer to cross the threshold, the fourth wall, which governs most modern engage-ment with art. Like the effigies discussed above, the power of Landy's sculptures literally depends upon the viewer's desire to engage with them. As with the effigies, there is a charged sense of ethics encoded in this engagement. To take another example, in the sculpture that responds to the life of St Catherine, the viewer is asked to spin a massive Catherine wheel. Although the saint is absent, the viewer is required to put themselves in the position of the torturer. The wheel is inscribed, however, with text that speaks directly to the saint and in fact invites the viewer to iden-tify with her: 'You will convert the Roman guards, who will then be punished by being decapitated and thrown to the dogs.' 'You are beautiful loved and admired by everyone.' So there is no easy way for the viewer to extricate themselves from the conversations the sculpture instigates. In other sculptures the participation of the viewer is figured differently, but still loaded with ethical meaning. This is because the engagement of the viewer guarantees the destruction of the sculptures. The outsized figure of St Apollonia pulls a tooth from her mouth when the viewer presses the button, but also slowly defaces herself. *Doubting Thomas*, a fragmented chest which is jabbed violently by a finger when prompted by the viewer, suffered visible damage during the exhibition, as did *Saint Jerome*. Just as the Life of a saint necessarily brings the sacrifice of Christ into the present of both the saint and the reader, so the sculptures offer a powerful sense of the multitemporality of art. Landy's work insists that the meanings of the saints are activated by the viewers, but also that the martyrdom of the saint is inextricably woven through that engagement, in the form of the eventual self-destruction of the sculpture.

While Landy's transformation of the saints into automata may have appeared to some viewers to be anachronistic, his work actually speaks with a long-established fascination with automata in medieval culture. The Rood of Grace, for instance, was a mechanised figure of Jesus mounted on a crucifix that was kept at Boxley Abbey and was destroyed as part of the iconoclasm of the Reformation. Its abilities ranged, according to different accounts, from moving its eyes and opening and shutting its mouth to weeping, nodding its head and even foaming at its mouth. As we saw with the Eleanor Crosses in Chapter 2, it seems that the power of the Rood's mechanical feats depended on the puritanical fervour of the viewer.[72] E. R. Truitt has explored the history of automata in the Middle Ages and reveals how mechanical expertise was developed in medieval Britain as a result of sustained exchange with the cultures of the Byzantine regions and the Islamic world. The history of medieval automata reveals a cosmopolitan Middle Ages and, as Truitt writes, 'also that the turn toward mechanism – to using mechanical models to explain and understand the body, the universe, and the laws that govern both – which is usually taken as one of the hallmarks of modernity of seventeenth-century natural philosophy, stretches back to antiquity'.[73] Truitt's work challenges common perceptions of the medieval world as uninterested in technology and lacking in creative thinking, but also illustrates the cultural exchange that informed many aspects of medieval culture. Her work demonstrates that although Landy's sculptures may appear to be post-modern responses to medieval sources, they can also be understood as engaging with medieval traditions of innovation, performance and devotion.

Sarah Salih has drawn a link between Landy's sculptures and John Capgrave's Life of St Catherine, in which the saint refuses the Emperor Maxentius' offer to have a statue made of her. 'But this wolde I knowen, er we þis thing make, / Of what mater shal my leggis bee?' Katherine asks, incredulous. 'What-maner werkman is he that dar vndirtake / To make hem meve and walke in her degree?'[74] Catherine is steadfastly opposed to the worship of images and remains unconvinced even after Maxentius instructs fifty philosophers to debate doctrine with her. It is her resistance to the worship of idols that guarantees her martyrdom. Salih, however, notes that 'Many of Capgrave's readers would have loved a St Katherine robot, and would have stoutly defended it as a stimulus to devotion'.[75] There is a fascinating division here, then, between the apparent authority of Capgrave's text and the lived experience of his fifteenth-century readers. As Sarah Stanbury suggests, the text 'performs a commentary on the seduction of images, drawing on visual cultic practice to discipline the reader'.[76] The reader is taught that images may form part of devotional practice, but that their worship needs to be moderated and governed. As with Landy's work, the text explores how borders of the self are determined by institutional governance, borders of time and borders of culture.

In the exhibition and the exhibition catalogue that accompanied *Saints Alive*, Landy reflected that his working method, 'taking body parts from the paintings in the Gallery and kind of putting them back together again', was 'not unlike what happened to saints' bodies in the past'.[77] Landy and his curators further emphasised the historicity of his practice by acknowledging the importance of *The Golden Legend* to his work and copies of William Granger Ryan's translation of the text were available for viewers to purchase in the gallery shop.[78] The brief lives which make up the *Legend* all begin with an investigation of the significance and meaning of the saint's name. In the case of St Jerome, for instance, the reader is told that:

> The name is also construed as meaning vision of beauty, or one who judges speech. Beauty is manifold. First of all, there is spiritual beauty, which is in the soul, secondly, moral beauty, which consists in propriety of conduct, thirdly, intellectual beauty, which is the beauty of the angels, fourthly, supersubstantial beauty, which is divine, fifthly, celestial beauty, which is the beauty of the saints in heaven. Jerome had this fivefold beauty and saw it in himself – the

spiritual in the variety of his virtues, the moral in the propriety of his way of life, the intellectual in the excellence of his purity, the supersubstantial in the ardor of his love, the celestial in his eternal and excellent charity. He judged speech, whether his own or that of others, his own by carefully weighing his words, that of others by confirming what was true, refuting what was false, and exposing what was dubious.[79]

The Life of the saint was simultaneously a means of interpreting the world, an example to follow and a means of celebrating the joys of heaven. It provided a guide to the physical and spiritual worlds and revealed its truth through meditative study and performed action. Both texts and images offered possibilities of reflection and action. Thomas Aquinas similarly offered three justifications for the use of images by the Church:

[T]o instruct the illiterate, who learn from them as if they were books; so that the mystery of incarnation and the example of the saints may be brought to mind more often, being represented before our eyes every day; thirdly to stir up the feeling of devotion, which is aroused more powerfully by seeing than by hearing.[80]

Like medieval images and stories of saints, Landy's sculptures breach the borders of the self. Their physical presence prompts reflection and meditation on deeper matters. Like the Life of St Jerome and the thoughts of Thomas Aquinas, the sculptures insist that participation is at the root of community. As with the effigies, *St Erkenwald* and Price's film, they ask what happens when temporality is replaced by desire as the governing structure of cultural life. While the Lives of saints are predicated on the possibility of joining the community of the saved in heaven, Landy's sculptures offer the viewer little reassurance about their ultimate destination. Like the saints, the sculptures demand to be brought into the viewer's present, but their ragged, unpredictable, apparently ungoverned movements seem to undermine rather than enforce established structures of authority and practice, whether that practice is the interpretation of art or religious texts and images. Landy's work encourages the viewer to examine their own participation in, resistance to or consumption of, the texts and traditions of the Christian Church. But *Saints Alive* also asks how contemporary culture forms ideas of the Middle Ages and how the cultural traces of the Middle Ages participate in the construction of the now.

The Middle Ages in motion

What is the duration of a gesture? How do structures of time enclose and limit meaning?

In the earliest text encountered in this chapter, Pope Gregory the Great sees something in the Roman Forum – maybe Trajan's Column, maybe a sculptured frieze or some other work of art – and that moment of affective contact between past and present, that willingness to be changed by an encounter with the past is the gesture that unites all the other texts encountered in this chapter. But what does that phenomenological encounter between past and present generate? For Gregory, for the effigies and for Erkenwald, it generates an identity and it reveals the multitemporality of subject formation and the reliance on others, on participation, in that formation. It demonstrates, in Stuart Hall's words, how 'the different ways we are positioned by, and position ourselves within the narratives of the past' create our social identities.[81] These structures and narratives might relate to gender, or class, or time, or violence, or power, as in the effigies and Erkenwald. What Price and Landy show, like *Erkenwald* in fact, is that those narratives remain open, but that when we engage with them, when we participate in them, we may well be supporting structures that close down the futures available to us. Landy and Price offer creative and critically astute models for engagement with medieval culture and insist that the narratives of the past remain open, but also recognise that not everyone enjoys equal access to them. By using their engagement with the past to undermine normative structures rather than reinforce them, the artists reveal the emancipatory potential of medievalist thinking. They emphasise shared humanity rather than difference, possibility rather than stricture, care for the future rather than nostalgia for the past. They create a hybrid Middle Ages, an assemblage formed through and across time, that is open and relational rather than closed and stable. Their medievalist thinking makes a shared future possible. A future based on difference and exchange rather than similarity and exclusion.

Notes

1 Alexander Nagel and Christopher Wood, *Anachronic Renaissance* (New York: Zone Books, 2010), p. 12.
2 Elizabeth Valdez del Alama and Carol Stamatis Pendergast, 'Introduction', in Elizabeth Valdez del Alama and Carol Stamatis

Pendergast (eds), *Memory and the Medieval Tomb* (Aldershot: Ashgate, 2000), p. 1–15, p. 1.

3 The most sustained study of gesture in the Middle Ages is J. C. Schmitt, *La raison de gestes dans l'occident médiéval* (Paris: Éditions Gallimard, 1990). See also J. A. Burrow, *Gestures and Looks in Medieval Narrative* (Cambridge: Cambridge University Press, 2002). See also Jody Enders, 'Of miming and signing: The dramatic rhetoric of gesture', in Clifford Davidson (ed.), *Gesture in Medieval Drama and Art* (Kalamazoo, MI: Medieval Institute Publications, 2001), pp. 1–25 and Carol L. Robinson, 'Gesture', in Elizabeth Emery and Richard Utz (eds), *Medievalism: Key Critical Terms* (Woodbridge: D. S. Brewer, 2014), pp. 79–85.

4 See warburg.library.cornell.edu/. Accessed 20 December 2017.

5 Christopher D. Johnson, *Memory, Metaphor, and Aby Warburg's Atlas of Images* (Ithaca, NY: Cornell University Press, 2012), pp. 9–10. See further Philippe-Alain Michaud, *Aby Warburg and the Image in Motion*, trans. Sophie Hawkes (New York: Zone Books, 2004) and E. H. Gombrich, *Aby Warburg: An Intellectual Biography, With a Memoir on the History of the Library by F. Saxl* (Oxford: Phaidon, 1986).

6 Jan Assmann, *Religion and Cultural Memory* (Stanford: Stanford University Press, 2006), pp. 94–5.

7 See H. A. Tummers, *Early Secular Effigies in England* (Leiden: Brill, 1980), p. 131. The National Monuments Record is now known as the Historic England Archive. See https://historicengland.org.uk/images-books/archive/ accessed 20 December 2017.

8 Tummers, *Early Secular Effigies*, p. 125. See also Judith W. Hurtig, *The Armored Gisant before 1400* (New York: Garland Publishing, 1979), pp. 109–67.

9 Paul Binski, *Medieval Death* (London: British Museum, 1996), p. 101.

10 Rachel Dressler, *Of Armor and Men: The Chivalric Ethic of Three English Knights' Effigies* (Aldershot: Ashgate, 2003), p. 102.

11 See William Camden, *Britannia* (London, 1594), p. 321. Translation by Oliver D. Harris, 'Antiquarian attitudes: Crossed legs, crusaders and the evolution of an idea', *Antiquaries Journal* 90 (2010), 401–40, p. 411.

12 John Stow, *Survey of London: Reprinted from the text of 1603, with introduction and notes by Charles Lethbridge Kingsford* (Oxford: Clarendon Press, 1908), vol. 2, pp. 50–1.

13 At, for instance, Danbury, where the effigies are identified as 'crusader knights'.

14 Tummers, *Early Secular Effigies in England*, p. 126.

15 Caroline Walker Bynum, *The Resurrection of the Body in Western Christianity, 200–1336* (New York: Columbia University Press, 1995), pp. 6–7.

16 *Saint Augustine's Enchiridion, or Manual to Laurentius Concerning Faith, Hope, and Charity*, trans. Ernest Evans (London: SPCK, 1953), p. 78.

17 Roberta Gilchrist, *Medieval Life: Archaeology and the Life Course* (Woodbridge: Boydell Press, 2012), p. 21.

18 On the narratives and materiality of stone see further Jeffrey Jerome Cohen, *Stone: An Ecology of the Inhuman* (Minneapolis: University of Minnesota Press, 2015).

19 Erin Manning, *Relationscapes: Movement, Art, Philosophy* (Cambridge, MA: MIT Press, 2009), p. 13.

20 Giles of Rome, *Governance of King's and Princes: John Trevisa's Middle English Translation of the* De Regimine Principum *of Aegidius Romanus*, ed. David Fowler, Charles Briggs and Paul Remley (New York: Garland Publishing, 1997), p. 242.

21 Derek Neal, *The Masculine Self in Late Medieval England* (Chicago: University of Chicago Press, 2008), p. 155.

22 J. Allan Mitchell, *Becoming Human: The Matter of the Medieval Child* (Minneapolis: University of Minnesota Press, 2014), p. 67.

23 St Augustine, *On Christian Teaching*, trans. R. P. H. Green (Oxford: Oxford University Press, 1997), pp. 30–1.

24 Vilém Flusser, *Gestures*, trans. Nancy Ann Roth (Minneapolis: University of Minnesota Press, 2014), p. 55.

25 Judith Butler, *Notes towards a Performative Theory of Assembly* (Cambridge, MA: Harvard University Press, 2015), p. 8.

26 Gilchrist, *Medieval Life*, p. 1.

27 Tummers, *English Secular Effigies*, p. 2.

28 Lawrence Stone, *Sculpture in Britain: The Middle Ages*, The Pelican History of Art 29 (Harmondsworth: Penguin, 1955), p. 150.

29 Jacques Lacan, *The Seminar of Jacques Lacan, Book XVII: The Other Side of Psychoanalysis*, ed. Jacques-Alain Miller, trans. Russell Grigg (New York: Norton, 2007), p. 12.

30 A short clip from the film is available to view online: www.theguardian. com/artanddesign/video/2012/dec/04/elizabeth-price-woolworths-choir-video, accessed 24 October 2017. The full film can be viewed by subscribing to the Lux collection at https://lux.org.uk/.

31 For information on the fire see www.bbc.co.uk/news/uk-england-manchester-20598600, accessed 24 October 2017.

32 Elizabeth Price, lecture at 'Art Out of Time: Challenging Periodization' conference at Oxford University, 27 June 2014.

33 Paul O'Neil, 'Mad love: An interview with Elizabeth Price', *Art Monthly* 326 (2009), 2–7.

34 Elizabeth Price, lecture at Focal Point Gallery, Southend, 14 November 2013.

35 See Elizabeth Price (ed.), *Small Gold Medal* (London: Bookworks, 2001).

36 Elizabeth Price, *User Group Disco* (-2009).

37 Manuel DeLanda, *Intensive Science and Virtual Philosophy* (New York: Continuum, 2002), p. 51.

38 Price, lecture at Focal Point Gallery, Southend.

39 The video is viewable online: www.youtube.com/watch?v=ZK1-u0yHNSU, accessed 24 October 2017.

40 *Elizabeth Price Here Exhibition Guide*, Baltic Centre for Contemporary Arts (Gateshead: Baltic, 2012), n.p. Available online: http://baltic-plus.uk/elizabeth-price-here-exhibition-guide-c20491/, accessed 24 October 2017.

41 Price, lecture at Focal Point Gallery, Southend.

42 Elizabeth Price, 'Private Utopia', a British Council Japan Artist Talk, 27 January 2014. Available online: www.youtube.com/watch?v=eC-Ss4fZhjE, accessed 24 October 2017.

43 Rebecca Schneider, *Theatre and History* (Basingstoke: Palgrave Macmillan, 2014), p. 45.

44 *St Erkenwald*, ed. Israel Gollancz, Select Early English Poems 4 (London: Oxford University Press, 1922), lines 19–20, p. 1. Further references given in text by line number.

45 Jonathan Hsy, 'City', in Marion Turner (ed.), *A Handbook of Middle English Studies* (Chichester: Wiley-Blackwell, 2013), pp. 315–29, p. 318.

46 Seeta Chaganti, *The Medieval Poetics of the Reliquary: Enshrinement, Inscription, Performance* (Basingstoke: Palgrave Macmillan, 2008), p. 67. See also Monika Otter, '"New werke": *St. Erkenwald*, St. Albans, and the medieval sense of the past', *Journal of Medieval and Renaissance Studies* 24 (1994), 387–414 and Eric Weiskott, *English Alliterative Verse: Poetic Tradition and Literary History* (Cambridge: Cambridge University Press, 2016), pp. 127–47.

47 Frank Grady, *Representing Righteous Heathens in Late Medieval England* (Basingstoke: Palgrave Macmillan, 2009), p. 4.

48 On the social consequences of the interpretation of the tomb see further D. Vance Smith, 'Crypt and decryption: *Erkenwald* terminable and interminable', *New Medieval Literatures* 5 (2002), 59–85.

49 Chaganti, *Medieval Poetics of the Reliquary*, p. 53. See also Ruth Nisse, '"A coroun ful riche": The rule of history in *St. Erkenwald*', *ELH* 65 (1998), 277–95.

50 See further Grady, *Representing Righteous Heathens*, p. 40 and Ruth Morse (ed.), *St Erkenwald* (Cambridge: D. S. Brewer, 1975), p. 72.

51 Philip Schwyzer, 'Exhumation and ethnic conflict: From *St. Erkenwald* to Spenser in Ireland', *Representations* 95 (2006), 1–26, p. 7.

52 Cynthia Turner Camp, 'Spatial memory, historiographic fantasy, and the touch of the past in *St. Erkenwald*', *New Literary History* 44 (2013), 471–91, p. 482.

53 Turner Camp, 'Spatial memory', p. 484. On 'touching' the past see Carolyn Dinshaw, *Getting Medieval: Sexualities and Communities, Pre- and Post-Modern* (Durham, NC: Duke University Press, 1999).

54 John Scattergood, *The Lost Tradition: Essays on Middle English Alliterative Poetry* (Dublin: Four Courts Press, 2000), pp. 179–99.

55 Sara Ahmed, *Queer Phenomenology: Objects, Orientations, Others* (Durham, NC: Duke University Press, 2006), pp. 106–7.

56 Judith Kay Nelson, *Seeing through Tears: Crying and Attachment* (New York: Brunner-Routledge, 2005), p. 131. On crying and the Christian tradition see E. M. Cioran, *Tears and Saints*, trans. Ilinca Zarifopol-Johnston (Chicago: University of Chicago Press, 1995).

57 On the meanings of medieval tears see, among others, Mary Carruthers, 'On affliction and reading, weeping and argument: Chaucer's lachry-mose Troilus in context', *Representations* 93 (2006), 1–21; Katherine Harvey, 'Episcopal emotions: tears in the life of the medieval bishop', *Historical Research* 87 (2014), 591–610; and André Vauchez, *Sainthood in the Later Middle Ages*, trans. Jean Birrell (Cambridge: Cambridge University Press, 1997), pp. 438–9. See also Thomas Dixon, *Weeping Britannia: Portrait of a Nation in Tears* (Oxford: Oxford University Press, 2015).

58 'Latin life and translation', in Bertram Colgrave (ed. and trans.), *The Earliest Life of Gregory the Great by an Anonymous Monk of Whitby* (Cambridge: Cambridge University Press, 1968), pp. 72–139, pp. 126–7.

59 See further Thomas O'Loughlin and Helen Conrad O'Brian, 'The baptism of tears in early Anglo-Saxon sources', *Anglo-Saxon England* 22 (1993), 65–83 and E. Gordon Whatley, 'The uses of hagiogra-phy: The legend of Pope Gregory and the Emperor Trajan in the Middle Ages', *Viator* 15 (1984), 25–63.

60 'Bede's life of St Cuthbert', in Colgrave (ed. and trans.), *Two Lives of Saint Cuthbert*, pp. 212–13.

61 Bernard of Clairvaux, 'Sermones super Cantica Canticorum', in J. Leclercq, C. H. Talbot and H. M. Rochais (eds), *Sancti Bernardi opera* (Rome: Editiones Cistercienses, 1957), vol. 1, p. 176.

62 *The Book of Margery Kempe*, ed. Barry Windeatt (Cambridge: D. S. Brewer, 2004), p. 11.

63 Karma Lochrie, *Margery Kempe and Translations of the Flesh* (Philadelphia: University of Pennsylvania Press, 1991), p. 196. See also Santha Bhattacharji, 'Tears and screaming: Weeping in the spir-ituality of Margery Kempe', in Kimberley Christine Patton and John Stratton Hawley (eds), *Holy Tears: Weeping in the Religious Imagination* (Princeton: Princeton University Press, 2005), pp. 229–41.

64 Richard Schechner, *Between Theater and Anthropology* (Philadelphia: University of Pennsylvania Press, 1985), p. 28.

65 Erving Goffman, *The Presentation of Self in Everyday Life* (London: Penguin, 1990), p. 72.

66 E. Gordon Whatley, 'Heathens and saints: *St Erkenwald* in its legendary context', *Speculum* 61 (1986), 330–63, p. 333.

67 See Jen Harvie, 'Witnessing Michael Landy's *Break Down*: Metonymy, affect, and politicised performance in an age of global consumer capitalism', *Contemporary Theatre Review* 16 (2006), 62–72.

68 See Imogen Racz, 'Michael Landy's *Semi-Detached* and the art of making', *Journal of Visual Art Practice* 10 (2012), 231–43 and Judith Nesbitt and John Slyce, *Michael Landy: Semi-Detached* (London: Tate Publishing, 2004).

69 Judith Nesbitt, 'Everything must go', in *Michael Landy:Semi-Detached*, p. 15.

70 On Tinguely and Landy see Laurence Sillars (ed.), *Joyous Machines: Michael Landy and Jean Tinguely* (Liverpool: Tate Liverpool, 2009). On Tinguely see David Antin, 'Jean Tinguely's new machine', in *Radical Coherency: Selected Essays on Art and Literature, 1966–2005* (Chicago: University of Chicago Press, 2011), pp. 31–4 and Marcia Brennan, 'Studies in self-creation and creative destruction: Jean Tinguely', in *Curating Consciousness: Mysticism and the Modern Museum* (Cambridge, MA: MIT Press, 2010), pp. 138–67.

71 Rosalind E. Krauss, *Passages in Modern Sculpture* (London: Thames and Hudson, 1977), p. 220.

72 See Kara Reilly, *Automata and Mimesis on the Stage of Theatre History* (Basingstoke: Palgrave Macmillan, 2011), pp. 19–23 and Leanne Groeneveld, 'A theatrical miracle: The Boxley Rood of Grace as puppet', *Early Theatre* 10 (2007), 11–50.

73 E. R. Truitt, *Medieval Robots: Mechanism, Magic, Nature, and Art* (Philadelphia: University of Pennsylvania Press, 2015), p. 2.

74 John Capgrave, *Life of St Katherine*, ed. Karen Winstead (Kalamazoo, MI: Medieval Academy, 1999), v. 449–52.

75 Sarah Salih, 'Review of Michael Landy, *Saints Alive*, National Gallery, London, 23 May–24 November 2013', *International Centre of Medieval Art Newsletter* (2014), 6–7.

76 Sarah Stanbury, *The Visual Object of Desire in Late Medieval England* (Philadelphia: University of Pennsylvania Press, 2008), pp. 39–40.

77 Colin Wiggins, with Richard Cork and Jennifer Sliwka, *Michael Landy: Saints Alive* (London: National Gallery and Yale University Press, 2013), p. 52.

78 See Wiggins, Cork and Sliwka, *Saints Alive*, pp. 65–77.

79 'Saint Jerome', in Jacobus de Voragine, *The Golden Legend: Readings on the Saints*, trans. William Granger Ryan, with an introduction by Eamon Duffy (Princeton: Princeton University Press, 1993), pp. 597–602, pp. 597–8.

80 Translation by Robert Bartlett, in *Why Can the Dead Do Such Great Things? Saints and Worshippers from the Martyrs to the Reformation* (Oxford: Oxford University Press, 2013), p. 496.
81 Stuart Hall, 'Cultural identity and diaspora', in Jonathan Rutherford (ed.), *Identity: Community, Culture, Difference* (London: Lawrence and Wishart, 1990), pp. 222–37, p. 225.

Afterword: Migrations

The past is always contemporary.

Derek Jarman[1]

This book has traced a series of movements across time, space, form and media. It has attempted to reveal and accommodate the diversity of the archive of the Middle Ages and demonstrate how forms of cultural memory produced in or inspired by the Middle Ages define subject positions, collective identities and visions of the future. It has offered a series of micro-histories that illustrate the intimate connections between ideas of 'the modern' and 'the medieval' and outline some of the cultural possibilities produced by medievalist thinking.

Caroline Bergvall's 2014 work *Drift* tells the story of a long-term creative engagement with the Old English poem known as *The Seafarer*. This is, though, only one of the stories it tells. Bergvall's translations and reworkings of the poem structure a broader and deeper reflection on time, power, the body and geography. As she writes in the 'log' that charts her working process and forms part of the published text of *Drift*, 'the project is not an exercise in translation', however closely it relates to *The Seafarer*, but rather uses the Old English text as a 'template for writing. And for excavating language. For finding the teeth of my own text, for locating its workable memory trails.'[2] As well as *The Seafarer*, Bergvall drew on various medieval accounts of sea travel to explore the temporalities of language, journeys and community. In her 'log' she meditated on the meanings of medieval and modern migrations and journeys, explored how shared routes might form a kind of shared knowledge across time and how the experience of space is always determined by precise historical context:

> These days travelling great distances by sea is mainly done for luxurious leisure, or as a last resort. It is the last option. How many

overfilled open boats fleeing war zones and political oppression have resorted to dangerous, clandestine crossings of the Mediterranean Sea, of the Sicily Channel, of the Aegean Sea, of the Caribbean Sea, of the Red Sea, of the Gulf of Thailand, of the South China Sea.[3]

The locus of her contemporary reflections is the case of the 'left-to-die boat'. In March 2012 seventy-two migrants were forced into a boat by Libyan soldiers in Tripoli and set course for Lampedusa. The boat was allowed to drift across the Mediterranean Sea for fourteen days, under the gaze of the NATO naval blockade of Libya and numerous other military and commercial ships. After they ran out of fuel and lost their satellite phone, the passengers in the boat were washed up again on Libya's cost, although only eleven survived the journey and two died shortly after.[4]

Drift therefore traces trajectories of bodies as well as texts, histories and languages. Bergvall uses the medieval history of the *Seafarer* to reposition the modern subjects of the 'left-to-die boat'. They, like the poet and narrator of the Old English poem, are anonymous. That is to say that their identities are bound by structures or institutions outside of their own control, their agency is compromised by the political and social contexts of their lives.

Drift opens with lines intimately related to the Old English *Seafarer* but moves in and around the text, sometimes translating, sometimes rewriting. What emerges from this process is an untimely language that refuses to reveal a singular source or meaning as Bergvall leaves the ambiguities of the poem and its language unresolved:

> Let me speak my true journeys own true songs
> I can make my sorry tale right soggy truth
> sothgied sodsgate some serious wrecan my ship
> sailing rekkies tell Hu ic how ache wracked from
> travel gedayswindled oft thrownabout bitterly
> tested gebanging head keeling at every beating
> waves What cursed fool grimly beshipped
> couldnt get signs during many a nightwacko
> caught between whats gone ok whats coming
> on crossing too close to the cliffs Blow wind
> blow, anon am I[5]

Bergvall's reworkings of *The Seafarer* tell a story of how language and history can subsume as well as give form to a self. The relationship between source text and target language is slippery and Bergvall draws on medieval and modern Scandinavian languages as well as English. In her lyrical accounts of seafaring, which recall medieval narratives of travel as well as the 'left-to-die boat', Bergvall's language fragments and re-forms as crises unfold and traces of life and memory are lost and found:

> Then the wind ddrope and the were beset by w inds from then orth and fog for manyd ays they did not know where they were sailing Thef air wind f ailed and they wholly l ost their reck their reckoning did not not know from what direction D riven here and there The f og was sodense they they l ost all ss ense of dirrrtion and l ost thr course at sea There was much fog and the w inds were light and unf and unfavourable They driftedf ar and wide on the high sea Mo stof those onboard completely l ost l ost l ost their reckoning Th ec rew had no idea in which direction they were ststeering A thick fo g which d i d n o t l ift for days The sh ip was driven offf course tol and They were ossted about astea for a longt time and f iled to each their destination We mbarkt and sailed but a fog so th but a fog so th but a fog so th th th th thik k overed us that we could scarcely see the poop or the prow of the boa t[6]

Bergvall's broken lines manage to capture the difficulty and ambiguity of medievalist thinking, but unlike many of the works encountered in this book, *Drift* attempts to trace the process of thought through the result of it: Bergvall doesn't gloss over the workings out or the intuitive and affective leaps that define her work. There is an ethic to Bergvall's refusal of meaning: these lines are honest about the uncomfortable confusion and power-lessness that might be felt by someone attempting to imagine a long-passed historical moment, or someone witnessing the passage of refugees escaping war from the comfort of a prosperous country. The experience of the refugees is evoked but not defined; it is left unknowable and unimaginable. But *Drift* suggests that the untimeliness of the Middle Ages can speak to and with the untimeliness of the modern subject, particularly those modern subjects who are marked as undesirable, feared, out of place and out of time, even as it refuses to speak for those subjects. *Drift* produces a deterritorialised Middle Ages, an open and relational site of cultural potential and potential affective bonds, a means of initiating contact and belonging across time and space without dissolving difference. Bergvall's Middle Ages at once recognises the ideological weight of its legacies and offers a means of navigating, reimagining and undoing those legacies.

Visions and Ruins has traced a number of trajectories of texts and ideas, across time and space. It has mapped some of the ways in which the idea of the Middle Ages and the remaining traces of the medieval cultural record offer resources, templates and means of excavating our own and others' places in the world, and the workable memory trails that constitute those places. It has also shown how artists, writers and communities have used the Middle Ages as a means to reimagine and remake their own place in the world. The material explored in this book shares a conviction that the Middle Ages is not over, that the past is not out of date and might, in fact, offer a means of securing attachments in the present and future. But it has also recorded the ideological work cultural memories are put to, in both medieval and post-medieval culture. The Middle Ages offers a valuable point of origin to those who insist that not all cultures, or people, are equal or deserve equal access to the future. Cultural memories of the Middle Ages have been an effective means of restricting the distribution of power and prestige. This means that the work of medievalist cultural memory often carries a contemporary urgency.

The medieval may be open and relational, but it is always located at intersections of competing ideological interests. Bergvall weaves a number of medieval histories and narratives of North Atlantic journeys through *Drift*, including the Vinland Sagas, the Poetic Edda, the Voyage of St Brendan and the voyages of Ohthere and Wulfstan. Perhaps the most famous medieval migrants, however, are Hengist and Horsa, the brothers who supposedly led the Germanic tribes to Britain in the fifth century. Their exploits are recorded in Bede's *Historia ecclesiastica*, the Anglo-Saxon *Chronicles* and numerous other sources and became a fulcrum of cultural memory from the Middle Ages onwards.[7] While Bergvall reworks histories of medieval travel to unsettle the normative structures of time, period and social and ethnic history, stories of the Germanic migration to Britain are more often employed to entrench myths of singular racial origin.

One such event occurred in 1949, in the direct aftermath of the Second World War, when the story of Hengist and Horsa was the prompt for a remarkable act of medievalist cultural memory in which a Viking longboat was rebuilt and sailed from Denmark to England to mark the fifteen-hundredth anniversary of the arrival of Hengist and Horsa and to recognise the contribution Britain made in defeating the Nazi occupation of Scandinavia. The boat, named the *Hugin*, was a replica of the Gokstad ship, a ninth-century vessel, 24 metres long, which was found in a burial mound in Sander, Norway, in 1880. In 1949 it was manned by a crew of fifty-three men who sailed it from Esbjerg on the Jutland peninsula to Broadstairs in Kent. Their arrival was marked by a series of celebrations and numerous civic activities, including recitals of the British and Danish national anthems and the performance of a historical play. Geoffrey Fisher, the Archbishop of Canterbury, and Prince Georg of Denmark were among the crowds who greeted them.[8] The celebrations are recorded in contemporary newsreel footage and the *Hugin* was later bought by the *Daily Mail* newspaper and given as a gift to the people of Kent. It remains on display near Cliffs End, the putative site of Hengist and Horsa's arrival in the fifth century (see Figure A.1).[9]

The story of the 1949 Vikings constitutes the obverse to the story of the 'left-to-die boat'. Here a boatload of people sailed across a dangerous sea not to secure their freedom but to celebrate it. Their association with the medieval past reveals the cultural prestige of their journey, not their lack of agency. It is also worth noting the role played by the *Daily Mail* in this performance of cultural memory, a newspaper famously wary of immigration, diversity and cultural change, and keen to promote explicitly racialised

A.1   *The Hugin*, Cliffs End

myths of Britain's, and particularly England's, national past.[10] The journey of the *Hugin* told a story of a stable, singular, racially pure point of origin for modern England, which disregarded indigenous British culture and the broader history of migration and settlement that defines the country's history and culture. To imagine that the history of England begins with a single journey from Denmark to the coast of Kent is to purposefully forget the influence of indigenous Celtic and British culture, as well as Irish culture, Roman culture, the Normans, as well as the Jewish communities who arrived after the Norman Conquest only to be expelled 200 years later, among many other arrivals.[11] The political meaning of the *Hugin* is perhaps most clearly expressed when it is situated alongside the arrival of another vessel that docked in Tilbury, Essex, the year before: HMT *Empire Windrush*, which brought one of the first large groups of West Indian migrants to the UK. The history of the *Hugin* is another example of medievalist double consciousness: an event that celebrates the cultural memory of the medieval past on the condition that that past is singular, familiar and over. In this context, medievalist cultural memory functions to migrate questions of social and cultural hierarchy and inequality, identity and belonging to a realm that is conditioned as prepolitical and therefore beyond dispute.

An alternative perspective on migration and medievalist cultural memory is offered by the *Refugee Tales* project, organised by the Gatwick Detainees Welfare Group. The project began with a series of walks across southeast England in the summer of 2015 and a book was published to mark the events in 2016. The organisers described the walks as acts 'in Solidarity with Refugees, Asylum Seekers and Detainees' and participants on the walks included refugees, asylum seekers, activists and writers.[12] The walks followed the route of the North Downs Way and the Pilgrims' Way, and the events and book used the structure of Chaucer's *Canterbury Tales* as their guide. The organisers' aim was to make visible 'people who are hidden by and from the culture, rendered invisible by the procedures of the state', and at the end of each day's walk, two tales were told: one, the story of an asylum seeker, refugee or former immigration detainee; the other, the story of working with asylum seekers in the UK, told by a lawyer, translator or volunteer.[13] The medievalist contexts of the project were important. As David Herd, one of the organisers of the project and a co-editor of the collection, writes, 'Deep within the *Refugee Tales* project is a proposal that the language of national space be re-read, that we read back through to find the expression that gestures outwards.'[14] Unlike the journey of the *Hugin*, then, *Refugee Tales* used medieval culture as a resource that might expand, rather than limit, the possibilities of the present. Like *Drift*, *Refugee Tales* demonstrates how engagement with medieval structures might radically disrupt modern habits and assumptions.

In his theorisation of the migrant, Thomas Nail explores how the migrant subverts many of the assumptions of modern citizenship. As he writes, 'Place-bound membership in a society is assumed as primary; secondary is the movement back and forth between social points.' The migrant, however, Nail suggests, 'more than any other political figure … is the one least defined by its being and place and more by its becoming and displacement: by its *movement*'.[15] Nail's theorisation of movement brings to mind Paul Zumthor's work on *mouvance*, which speaks of what he describes as 'the essential instability' of medieval texts and explores how medieval textuality subverts modern notions of authority and authenticity.[16] For Zumthor, the search for original medieval texts disregards the importance of circulation, adaptation and reinvention to medieval textual culture. Zumthor therefore argued that medieval texts such as the *Chanson de Roland* should not be viewed as stable, finished or complete. Instead, Zumthor writes, 'The "work" floats, offering not a fixed shape of firm boundaries but a constantly shifting nimbus.'[17] The same might be said of the Old English *Seafarer*. Even though only a single copy survives, it is no doubt only one iteration in a long textual tradition and, as I demonstrated in the opening chapter of this book, many Old English texts sit, or float, at the centre of networks of influence and exchange that extend across the Middle Ages and through modernity.

Together Nail and Zumthor encourage us to reflect on the question of orientation. Nail asks what happens if we reorient our understanding of the subject as fundamentally mobile, if we privilege journeys rather than origins, while Zumthor similarly asks what the consequences of a focus on movement might enable in cultural criticism and production. As Sara Ahmed writes, 'orientations involve different ways of registering the proximity of objects and others. Orientations shape not only how we inhabit space, but how we apprehend this world of shared inhabitation, as well as "who" or "what" we direct our energy and attention toward.'[18] Part of the power of Bergvall's *Drift* is derived from the manner in which it suggests that the cultural artefacts of the Middle Ages, in all their fragmented, neglected and ambiguous glory, can speak to and with the untimeliness of the undesirable, the feared and the neglected. Bergvall uses the medieval history of the *Seafarer* to reorient the modern subjects of the 'left-to-die boat'. Literally cast adrift from the modern West, anonymous, without power, but not without significance, not without meaning, not necessarily without a place in the future. The journey of the *Hugin*, however, performs migration as chronology and insists on a singular orientation. The ambiguities of the story of Hengist and Horsa are artfully ignored in favour of a coherent and singular narrative that documents the emergence of cultural hegemony. *Refugee Tales*, in contrast, uses the archive of the Middle Ages to attempt to disrupt contemporary political discourse.

As this book has demonstrated, medievalist acts of cultural memory often rely on an idea of the Middles Ages as singular, closed-off and stable, but nevertheless demonstrate its multiplicity, openness and indeterminacy. So they offer a prompt to reorient our apprehension of time and culture, an opportunity to reassess how we share our time and culture with objects and others, present or absent, near or distant. Acknowledging the diversity of the archive of the Middle Ages – from early modern iconoclasm to Victorian monuments and twenty-first-century art – recognises the diverse cultural work the idea of the Middle Ages has been put to and the manner in which the medieval is folded through later historical periods. It recognises the multiplicity and diversity of those times and places we identify as 'the Middle Ages' and offers valuable tools for rethinking the multiplicity and diversity of the present, too. The untimeliness of the Middle Ages should be celebrated rather than mourned. Its difference is not a problem or embarrass-ment but a hopeful reminder of the potential for cultural change. The Middle Ages offers indeterminacy but brings with it oppor-tunity. Its archive offers new models of cultural production, new possibilities of subject formation, new horizons of experience and new ways of imagining the future.

Notes

1 Simon Field and Michael O'Pray, 'Imaging October, Dr Dee and other matters: An interview with Derek Jarman', *Afterimage* 12 (1985), 55.
2 Caroline Bergvall, *Drift* (New York: Nightboat Books, 2014), pp. 151–2.

3 Bergvall, *Drift*, p. 148.
4 On the 'left-to-die boat' see www.forensic-architecture.org/case/left-die-boat/, accessed 24 October 2017, and Bergvall, *Drift*, pp. 132–5. See also Eyal Weizman, *Forensic Architecture: Violence at the Threshold of Detectability* (Cambridge, MA: MIT Press, 2017).
5 Bergvall, *Drift*, p. 25. A short clip of Bergvall's performance of *Drift* is available to view online: https://vimeo.com/87724392, accessed 24 October 2017.
6 Bergvall, *Drift*, p. 37.
7 See Nicholas Brooks, *Anglo-Saxon Myths: State and Church, 400–1066* (London: Hambledon Press, 2000), pp. 37–46; Fabienne L. Michelet, 'Lost at sea: Nautical travels in the Old English *Exodus*, the Old English *Andreas*, and accounts of the *adventus Saxonum*', in Sebastian I. Sobecki (ed.), *The Sea and Englishness in the Middle Ages: Maritime Narratives, Identity and Culture* (Cambridge: D. S. Brewer, 2011), pp. 59–79; Patrick Sims-Williams, 'The settlement of England in Bede and the *Chronicle*', *Anglo-Saxon England* 12 (1983), 1–41. See also Nicholas Howe, *Migration and Mythmaking in Anglo-Saxon England*, 2nd edn (Notre Dame, IN: University of Notre Dame Press, 2001).
8 One of the crew published a memoir of the journey, illustrated with images of the celebrations and media coverage. See Jørgen Røjel, *The 1949 Cruise of the Viking Ship Hugin*, trans. Holger Brønnum (Copenhagen: Samlerens Forlag, 1949).
9 The newsreel is available online: www.britishpathe.com/video/kent-greets-viking-invaders/query/landing+craft, accessed 24 October 2017.
10 On the discourses of immigration perpetrated by the *Daily Mail* see 'Space and the migrant camps of Calais: Space-making at the margins', in Einar Thorsen, Daniel Jackson, Heather Savigny and Jenny Alexander (eds), *Media, Margins and Civic Agency* (Basingstoke: Palgrave Macmillan, 2015), pp. 131–48; Nick Davies, *Flat Earth News: An Award-Winning Reporter Exposes Falsehood, Distortion and Propaganda in the Global Media* (London: Vintage, 2009), pp. 371–9; and Adrian Addison, *Mail Men: The Unauthorized Story of the 'Daily Mail', the Paper that Divided and Conquered Britain* (London: Atlantic Books, 2017).
11 See further www.englandsimmigrants.com, accessed 24 October 2017.
12 David Herd, 'Afterword: Walking with "Refugee Tales"', in David Herd and Anna Pincus (eds), *Refugee Tales* (Manchester: Comma Press, 2016), pp. 133–43, p. 133. The project is also archived online at http://refugeetales.org/, accessed 24 October 2017.
13 Herd, 'Afterword', p. 134.
14 Herd, 'Afterword', p. 139.
15 Thomas Nail, *The Figure of the Migrant* (Stanford: Stanford University Press, 2015), p. 3.

16 Paul Zumthor, *Toward a Medieval Poetics*, trans. Phillip Bennett (Mi
nneapolis: University of Minnesota Press, 1992), p. 45. See also Bella
Millet's explanation of *mouvance* at www.southampton.ac.uk/~wpwt/
mouvance/mouvance.htm, accessed 24 October 2017.

17 Zumthor, *Toward a Medieval Poetics*, p. 46.

18 Ahmed, *Queer Phenomenology*, p. 3.

Select bibliography

Editions

Adami de Domerham Historia de rebus gestis Glastoniensibus, ed. Thomas Hearne. 2 vols. Oxford: E Theatro Sheldoniano, 1727.

Æthelweard. *The Chronicle of Æthelweard*, ed. and trans. A. Campbell. London: Thomas Nelson and Sons, 1962.

Alcuin. 'De clade Lindisfarnensis monasterii', in E. Duemmler (ed.), *Poetae latini aevi Carolini*, MGH, Poetarum latinorum medii aevi 1. Berlin: Weidmann, 1881, pp. 229–35.

Alcuin. *The Bishops, Saints and Kings of York*, ed. and trans. Peter Godman. Oxford: Clarendon Press, 1982.

The Anglo-Saxon Poetic Records, ed. George P. Krapp and Elliott van Kirk Dobbie, 6 vols. New York: Columbia University Press, 1931–53.

Annales Monastici, vol. 3: *Annales prioratus de Dunstaplia and Annales monasterii de Bermundeseia*, ed. Henry Richards Luard. London: Longmans, Green, Reader, and Dyer, 1866.

Augustine. *Saint Augustine's Enchiridion, or Manual to Laurentius Concerning Faith, Hope, and Charity*, trans. Ernest Evans. London: SPCK, 1953.

Augustine. *On Christian Teaching*, trans. R. P. H. Green. Oxford: Oxford University Press, 1997.

Bede. *Bede's Ecclesiastical History of the English People*, ed. and trans. Bertram Colgrave and R. A. B. Mynors. Oxford: Clarendon Press, 1969.

Beowulfes Beorh, eller Bjovulfs-Drapen, ed. and trans. N. F. S. Grundtvig. Copenhagen: Schönberg, 1861.

Cædmon's Metrical Paraphrase of Parts of the Holy Scriptures, in Anglo-Saxon, ed. Benjamin Thorpe. London: Society of Antiquaries of London, 1832.

Codex Exoniensis: A Collection of Anglo-Saxon Poetry, ed. Benjamin Thorpe. London: Society of Antiquaries of London, 1842.

The Dream of the Rood, ed. Michael Swanton. Exeter: University of Exeter Press, 2000.

The Earliest Life of Gregory the Great by an Anonymous Monk of Whitby, ed. and trans. Bertram Colgrave. Cambridge: Cambridge University Press, 1968.

The Exeter Anthology of Old English Poetry: An Edition of Exeter Dean and Chapter MS 3501, ed. Bernard J. Muir, 2 vols. Exeter: University of Exeter Press, 2000.

The Exeter Book of Old English Poetry, R. W. Chambers, Max Förster and Robin Flower. London: P. Lund, Humphries & Co., 1933.

Gildas. *The Ruin of Britain and Other Works*, ed. and trans. Michael Winterbottom. London: Phillimore, 1978.

Giles of Rome. *Governance of King's and Princes: John Trevisa's Middle English Translation of the* De Regimine Principum *of Aegidius Romanus*, ed. David Fowler, Charles Briggs and Paul Remley. New York: Garland Publishing, 1997.

Giraldus Cambrensis opera, ed. J. S. Brewer *et al.*, 8 vols. London: Eyre and Spottiswood, 1891.

Johannis de Trokelowe et Henrici de Blaneforde, monachorum S. Albani, necnon quorundam anonymorum chronica et annales, regnantibus Henrico tertio, Edwardo primo, Edwardo secundo, Ricardo secundo, et Henrico quarto, ed. Henry Thomas Riley. London: Longmans, Green, Reader, and Dyer, 1866.

Kempe, Margery. *The Book of Margery Kempe*, ed. Barry Windeatt. Cambridge: D. S. Brewer, 2004.

Klaeber's Beowulf and the Fight at Finnsburg, 4th edn, ed. R. D. Fulk, Robert E. Bjork and John D. Niles. Toronto and London: University of Toronto Press, 2008.

The Luttrell Psalter: A Facsimile, ed. Michelle Brown. London: British Library, 2006.

The Old English Elegies, ed. Anne Klinck. London: McGill-Queen's University Press, 1992.

Registrum epistolarum Fratris Johannis Peckham, Archiepiscopi Cantuariensis, 3 vols, ed. C. T. Martin. London: Longman, 1882–85.

St Erkenwald, ed. Israel Gollancz. Select Early English Poems 4. London: Oxford University Press, 1922.

Sermo Lupi ad Anglos, ed. Dorothy Whitelock. Exeter: University of Exeter, 1976.

Sources and Analogues of Old English Poetry: The Major Latin Texts in Translation, ed. Michael J. B. Allen and Daniel G. Calder. Totowa, NJ: Rowman and Littlefield; Cambridge: D. S. Brewer, 1976.

The Toronto Dictionary of Old English Corpus in Electronic Form, ed. Cameron Angus, Ashley Crandell Amos, Antonette diPaolo Healey *et al.* Toronto: Dictionary of Old English Project, 1981–.

Two Lives of St Cuthbert, ed. Bertram Colgrave. Cambridge: Cambridge University Press, 1985.

Walter of Guisborough. *The Chronicle of Walter of Guisborough, Previously Edited as the Chronicle of Walter of Hemingford or Huemingburgh*, ed. Harry Rothwell. London: Royal Historical Society, 1957.

William of Malmesbury. *Gesta pontificum anglorum: The History of the English Bishops*, vol. 1: *Text and Translation*, ed. and trans. Michael Winterbottom, with the assistance of R. M. Thomson. Oxford: Clarendon Press, 2007.

Wynn, Sir John. *The History of the Gwydir Family and Memoirs*, ed. and trans. J. Gwynfor Jones. Llandysul: Gomer, 1990.

Early printed books

Cheap-side crosse censured and condemned by a letter sent from the vice-chancellour and other learned men of the famous Universitie of Oxford. London: Printed by A. N. for I. R., 1641.

Dering, Edward. *A briefe and necessary catechisme or instructio(n). Very need-full to be known of al housholders. Wherby they may teach & instruct ther famelies, in such pointes of Christian religion as is most meete. With prayers to the same adioyning*. Middelburg: Printed by Richard Schilders, 1590.

The Downe-fall of Dagon, or, The taking downe of Cheap-side crosse this second of May, 1643. London: Printed for Thomas Wilson, 1642.

Overton, Richard. *Articles of high treason exhibited against Cheap-side crosse. With the last will and testament of the said crosse. And certaine epitaphs upon her tombe. By R. Overton. Newly printed and newly come forth; with his holinesse priviledge, to prevent false copies*. London: Printed for R. Overton, 1642.

Pameach, Ryhen (Henry Peacham) *A dialogue between the crosse in Cheap, and Charing Crosse. Comforting each other, as fearing their fall in these uncertaine times*. London, 1641.

Secondary

Abel, John. *Memorials of Queen Eleanor, Illustrated by Photography: with a short account of their history and present condition*. London: Published for the Proprietor, 1864.

Abram, Chris 'In search of lost time: Aldhelm and the *Ruin*', *Quaestio* 1 (2000), 23–44.

Adorno, Theodor. *Minima Moralia: Reflections from Damaged Life*, trans. E. F. N. Jephcott. London: NLB, 1978.

Agamben, Giorgio. *Infancy and History: The Destruction of Experience*, trans. Liz Heron. London: Verso, 1993.

Ahmed, Sara. *Queer Phenomenology: Objects, Orientations, Others*. Durham, NC: Duke University Press, 2006.

Alexander, Jonathan and Paul Binski, eds. *Age of Chivalry: Art in Plantagenet England*. London: Royal Academy of Arts, 1987.

Alexander, Michael. *The Earliest English Poems*. Harmondsworth: Penguin, 1966.

Anderson, Benedict. *Imagined Communities: Reflections on the Origin and Spread of Nationalism*. London: Verso, 2006.

Arany, János. *Balladák*, ed. Földes Tamás. Budapest: Akkord Kiadó, 2009.

Assmann, Jan. 'Collective memory and cultural identity', *New German Critique* 65 (1995), 125–33.

Assmann, Jan, *Religion and Cultural Memory*. Stanford: Stanford University Press, 2006.

Bal, Mieke. *Quoting Caravaggio: Contemporary Art, Preposterous History*. London: University of Chicago Press, 1999.

Beaston, Lawrence. '*The Ruin* and the brevity of human life', *Neophilologus* 95 (2011), 477–89.

Berend, Iván. *History Derailed: Central and Eastern Europe in the Long Nineteenth Century*. Berkeley: University of California Press, 2003.

Bergvall, Caroline. *Drift*. New York: Nightboat Books, 2014.

Berkhout, Carl T. and Milton McCormick Gatch, eds. *Anglo-Saxon Scholarship: The First Three Centuries*. Boston, MA: G. K. Hall and Co., 1982.

Bhabha, Homi. *The Location of Culture*. London: Routledge, 1994.

Bildhauer, Bettina. *Filming the Middle Ages*. London: Reaktion, 2011.

Binski, Paul. *Medieval Death: Ritual and Representation*. London: British Museum Press, 1996.

Bjork, Robert E. and Taylor Corse. 'Grímur Jónsson Thorkelin's Preface to the first edition of *Beowulf*', *Scandinavian Studies* 68 (1996), 291–320.

Boellstoff, Tom. 'When marriage falls: Queer coincidences in straight time', *GLQ: A Journal of Lesbian and Gay Studies* 13 (2007), 227–48.

Brand, Paul. 'Jews and the law in England, 1275–90', *English Historical Review* 115 (2000), 1138–58.

Bynum, Caroline Walker. *The Resurrection of the Body in Western Christianity, 200–1336*. New York: Columbia University Press, 1995.

Bynum, Caroline Walker. *Metamorphosis and Identity*. New York: Zone Books, 2001.

The Cædmon Memorial. Being a description of the cross, with explanation of lettering and figures thereon. Whitby: Horne & Son, 1899.

Camille, Michael. *Mirror in Parchment: The Luttrell Psalter and the Making of Medieval England*. London: Reaktion, 1998.

Camille, Michael. *The Gargoyles of Notre Dame: Medievalism and the Monsters of Modernity*. Chicago: University of Chicago Press, 2009.

Camp, Cynthia Turner. 'Spatial memory, historiographic fantasy, and the touch of the past in *St. Erkenwald*', *New Literary History* 44 (2013), 471–91.

Carruthers, Mary. *The Book of Memory: A Study of Memory in Medieval Culture*. Cambridge: Cambridge University Press, 2008.

Carruthers, Mary and Jan M. Ziolkowski, eds. *The Medieval Craft of Memory: An Anthology of Texts and Pictures*. Philadelphia: University of Pennsylvania Press, 2002.

Carte, Thomas. *A General History of England: An account of all public Transactions from the Accession of Henry II, A.D. 1216, to the Death of Henry VII, April 22, A.D. 1509*. London: Printed for the Author, at his House in Dean's Yard, Westminster, 1747.

Caruth, Cathy. *Unclaimed Experience: Trauma, Narrative, and History*. London: Johns Hopkins University Press, 1996.

Chaganti, Seeta. *The Medieval Poetics of the Reliquary: Enshrinement, Inscription, Performance*. Basingstoke: Palgrave Macmillan, 2008.

Chakrabarty, Dipesh. *Provincializing Europe: Postcolonial Thought and Historical Difference*. Princeton: Princeton University Press, 2008.

Chickering, Howell. 'Lyric time in *Beowulf*', *Journal of English and Germanic Philology* 91 (2004), 489–509.

Cohen, Jeffrey Jerome, ed. *The Postcolonial Middle Ages*. New York: Palgrave, 2000.

Conner, Patrick W. *Anglo-Saxon Exeter: A Tenth-Century Cultural History*. Woodbridge: Boydell Press, 1993.

Conybeare, John Josias. *Illustrations of Anglo-Saxon Poetry*, ed. William Daniel Conybeare. London: Harper and Lepard, 1826.

Dailey, Patricia. 'Questions of dwelling in Anglo-Saxon poetry and medieval mysticism: Inhabiting landscape, body, and mind', *New Medieval Literatures* 8 (2006), 175–214.

Davies, Norman. *The Isles: A History*. London: Macmillan, 2000.

Davies, R. R. *The Age of Conquest: Wales 1063–1415*. Oxford: Oxford University Press, 2000.

Davis, Kathleen. *Periodization and Sovereignty: How Ideas of Feudalism and Secularization Govern the Politics of Time*. Philadelphia: University of Pennsylvania Press, 2008.

Delanty, Greg and Michael Matto, eds. *The Word Exchange*. London: Norton, 2011.

Derrida, Jacques. *Mémoires: For Paul de Man*, trans. Cecile Lindsay, Jonathan Culler, and Eduardo Cadava. New York: Columbia University Press, 1986.

Derrida, Jacques. *Memoirs of the Blind: The Self-Portrait and Other Ruins*, trans. Pascale-Anne Brault and Michael Naas. London: University of Chicago Press, 1993.

Dillon, Brian. *Ruin Lust: Artists' Fascination with Ruins from Turner to the Present Day*. London: Tate, 2014.

Dinshaw, Carolyn. *How Soon is Now? Medieval Texts, Amateur Readers, and the Queerness of Time*. Durham, NC: Duke University Press, 2012.

Dolar, Mladen. *A Voice and Nothing More*. Cambridge, MA: MIT Press, 2006.

Doubleday, James F. '*The Ruin*: Structure and theme', *Journal of English and Germanic Philology* 71 (1972), 369–81.

Dressler, Rachel. *Of Armor and Men: The Chivalric Ethic of Three English Knights' Effigies*. Aldershot: Ashgate, 2003.

Du Bois, W. E. B. *The Souls of Black Folk*, ed. Henry Louis Gates, Jr. and Terri Hume Oliver. New York: Norton, 1999.

Duffy, Maureen. *Environmental Studies*. London: Enitharmon, 2013.

Eaton, Tim. *Plundering the Past*. Stroud: Tempus, 2000.

Eco, Umberto. *Faith in Fakes: Travels in Hyperreality*, trans. William Weaver. London: Vintage, 1998.

Emory, Elizabeth and Richard Utz, eds. *Medievalism: Key Critical Terms*. Woodbridge: D. S. Brewer, 2014.

Erll, Astrid. *Memory in Culture*, trans. Sara B. Young. Basingstoke: Palgrave Macmillan, 2011.

Evans, Ruth, Helen Fulton and David Matthews, eds. *Medieval Cultural Studies in Honour of Stephen Knight*. Cardiff: University of Wales Press, 2006.

Fabian, Johannes. *Time and the Other: How Anthropology Makes its Subject*. New York: Columbia University Press, 2002.

Fanthorpe, U. A. *Queueing for the Sun*. Calstock: Peterloo Poets, 2003.

Felski, Rita. *The Limits of Critique*. Chicago: University of Chicago Press, 2015.

Fradenburg, Aranye. 'Living Chaucer', *Studies in the Age of Chaucer* 33 (2011), 41–64.

Fradenburg, Louise O., ed. *Women and Sovereignty*. Edinburgh: Edinburgh University Press, 1992.

Frantzen, Allen J. *Desire for Origins: New Language, Old English, and Teaching the Tradition*. New Brunswick: Rutgers University Press, 1990.

Freedman, Paul and Gabrielle Spiegel. 'Medievalisms old and new: The rediscovery of alterity in North American medieval studies', *American Historical Review* 103 (1998), 677–704.

Freud, Sigmund. *The Standard Edition of the Complete Psychological Works of Sigmund Freud*, trans. and ed. James Strachey in collaboration with Anna Freud, assisted by Alix Strachey and Alan Tyson, vol. 11. London: Hogarth Press and the Institute of Psycho-analysis, 1957.

Freud, Sigmund. *The Standard Edition of the Complete Psychological Works of Sigmund Freud*, trans. and ed. James Strachey in collaboration with Anna Freud, with the assistance of Alix Strachey and Alan Tyson, vol. 6. London: Hogarth Press and the Institute of Psycho-analysis, 1960.

Frow, John, 'On midlevel concepts', *New Literary History* 31 (2010), 237–52.

Fry, Christopher. *One More Thing, Or, Caedmon Construed*. London: King's College London, 1986.

Garner, Lori Ann. *Structuring Spaces: Oral Poetics and Architecture in Early Medieval England* (Notre Dame, IN: University of Notre Dame Press, 2011).

Geary, Patrick J. *The Myth of Nations: The Medieval Origins of Europe*. Princeton: Princeton University Press, 2002.

Gellner, Ernest. *Thought and Change*. London: Weidenfeld and Nicholson, 1964.

Gilchrist, Roberta. *Medieval Life: Archaeology and the Life Course*. Woodbridge: Boydell Press, 2012.

Godden, Malcolm and Michael Lapidge, eds. *The Cambridge Companion to Old English Literature*. Cambridge: Cambridge University Press, 1991.

Goffman, Erving. *The Presentation of Self in Everyday Life*. London: Penguin, 1990.

Gray, Thomas. *The Complete Poems of Thomas Gray*, ed. H. W. Starr and J. R. Hendrickson. Oxford: Clarendon Press, 1966.

Grazia, Margreta de. 'The modern divide: From either side', *Journal of Medieval and Early Modern Studies* 37 (2007), 453–67.

Greenfield, Stanley. *Hero and Exile: The Art of Old English Poetry*. London: Hambledon Press, 1989.

Grosz, Elizabeth. *The Nick of Time: Politics, Evolution, and the Untimely*. Durham, NC: Duke University Press, 2004.

Hahn, Thomas, ed. 'Race and ethnicity in the Middle Ages', *Journal of Medieval and Early Modern Studies* 31 (2001), 1–165.

Hall, John A., Ove Korsgaard and Ove K. Pedersen, eds. *Building the Nation: N. F. S. Grundtvig and Danish National Identity*. Montreal: McGill-Queen's University Press, 2015.

Hall, Stuart. 'Cultural identity and diaspora', in *Identity: Community, Culture, Difference*, ed. Jonathan Rutherford (London: Lawrence and Wishart, 1990), pp. 222–37.

Harris, Jonathan Gil. *Untimely Matter in the Time of Shakespeare*. Philadelphia: University of Pennsylvania Press, 2009.

Harris, Jonathan Gil. 'Four exoskeletons and no funeral', *New Literary History* 42 (2011), 615–39.

Heaney, Seamus. *The Spirit Level*. London: Faber and Faber, 1996.

Hell, Julia and Andreas Schönle, eds. *The Ruins of Modernity*. Durham, NC: Duke University Press, 2010.

Heng, Geraldine. 'The invention of race in the European Middle Ages I: Race studies, modernity, and the Middle Ages', *Literature Compass* 8 (2011), 315–31.

Heng, Geraldine. 'The invention of race in the European Middle Ages II: Locations of medieval race', *Literature Compass* 8 (2015), 332–50.

Higham, N. J. *King Arthur: Myth-Making and History*. London: Routledge, 2009.

Hobsbawm, Eric and Terence Ranger, eds. *The Invention of Tradition*. Cambridge: Cambridge University Press, 1983.

Howe, Nicholas. *Writing the Map of Anglo-Saxon England: Essays in Cultural Geography*. New Haven: Yale University Press, 2008.

Hume, Kathryn. 'The ruin motif in Old English poetry', *Anglia* 94 (1976), 339–60.

Hunter, Michael. 'Germanic and Roman antiquity and the sense of the past in Anglo-Saxon England', *Anglo-Saxon England* 3 (1974), 29–50.

Hurtig, Judith W. *The Armored Gisant before 1400*. New York: Garland Publishing, 1979.

Ingham, Patricia Clare. '"In contrayez straunge": Colonial relations, British identity, and *Sir Gawain and the Green Knight*', *New Medieval Literatures* 4 (2001), 61–93.

Jones, Chris. *Strange Likeness: The Use of Old English in Twentieth-Century Poetry*. Oxford: Oxford University Press, 2006.

Jones, Chris. 'The Ruin (after the Anglo-Saxon)', *The Reader* 28 (2007), 46–7.

Karkov, Catherine E. 'The body of Saint Æthelthryth: Desire, conversion and reform in Anglo-Saxon England', in *The Cross Goes North: Processes of Conversion in Northern Europe, AD 300–1300*, ed. Martin Carver. Woodbridge: Boydell Press, 2005, pp. 397–411.

Karkov, Catherine E. *The Art of Anglo-Saxon England*. Woodbridge: Boydell Press, 2011.

Kinoshita, Sharon. 'Deprovincializing the Middle Ages', in *The Worlding Project: Doing Cultural Studies in the Era of Globalization*, ed. Rob Wilson and Christopher Leigh Connery. Santa Cruz, CA: New Pacific Press, 2007, pp. 61–75.

Latour, Bruno. *Reassembling the Social: An Introduction to Actor-Network-Theory*. Oxford: Oxford University Press, 2007.

Lees, Clare A., ed. *The Cambridge History of Early Medieval English Literature*. Cambridge: Cambridge University Press, 2013.

Lees, Clare A. and Gillian R. Overing. *Double Agents: Women and Clerical Culture in Anglo-Saxon England*. Cardiff: University of Wales Press, 2009.

Levertov, Denise. *Breathing the Water*. Newcastle: Bloodaxe Books, 1988.

Littler, Jo and Roshi Naidoo, eds. *The Politics of Heritage: The Legacies of 'Race'*. London: Routledge, 2005.

Liuzza, R. M. 'The Tower of Babel: *The Wanderer* and the ruins of history', *Studies in the Literary Imagination* 36 (2003), 1–35.

Longfellow, Henry Wadsworth. *The Poets and Poetry of Europe with Introductions and Biographical Notes*. Philadelphia: Porter and Coates, 1871.

Lowenthal, David, *The Past is a Foreign Country*. Cambridge: Cambridge University Press, 1985.

Macaulay, Rose. *Pleasure of Ruins*. London: Thames and Hudson, 1953.

McCarthy, Mike. *Roman Carlisle and the Lands of the Solway*. Stroud: Tempus, 2002.

Manning, Erin. *Relationscapes: Movement, Art, Philosophy*. Cambridge, MA: MIT Press, 2009.

Marsden, Richard. *The Cambridge Old English Reader*. Cambridge: Cambridge University Press, 2004.

Massingham, Harold W. 'The Ruin (after the Anglo-Saxon)', *Times Literary Supplement* 2264 (18 August 1966).

Masterman, Neville. 'The massacre of the Bards', *Welsh Review* 7 (1948), 58–66.

Matthews, David. *Medievalism: A Critical History*. Cambridge: D. S. Brewer, 2015.

Momma, Haruko. *From Philology to English Studies: Language and Culture in the Nineteenth Century*. Cambridge: Cambridge University Press, 2013.

Morgan, Edwin. *Collected Poems, 1949–1987*. Manchester: Carcanet, 1990.

Morris, Marc. *A Great and Terrible King: Edward I and the Forging of Britain*. London: Windmill Books, 2009.

Nagel, Alexander. *Medieval Modern: Art Out of Time*. London: Thames and Hudson, 2012.

Nagel, Alexander and Christopher Wood. *Anachronic Renaissance*. New York: Zone Books, 2010.

Nail, Thomas. *The Figure of the Migrant*. Stanford: Stanford University Press, 2015.

Niles, John D. *The Idea of Anglo-Saxon England 1066–1901: Remembering, Forgetting, Deciphering, and Renewing the Past*. Chichester: Wiley-Blackwell, 2015.

Niles, John D. and Allen J. Frantzen, eds. *Anglo-Saxonism and the Construction of Social Identity*. Gainesville: University Press of Florida, 1997.

Ó Carragáin, Éamonn. *Ritual and Rood: Liturgical Images and the Old English Poems of the Dream of the Rood Tradition*. London: British Library, 2005.

Odney, Paul. 'Thomas Gray's daring spirit: Forging the poetics of an alternative nationalism', *CLIO: A Journal of Literature, History, and the Philosophy of History* 28 (1999), 245–60.

Orton, Fred and Ian Wood, with Clare A. Lees. *Fragments of History: Rethinking the Ruthwell and Bewcastle Monuments*. Manchester: University of Manchester Press, 2007.

Parsons, David, ed. *Eleanor of Castile 1290–1990: Essays to Commemorate the 700th Anniversary of her Death, 28th November 1290*. Stamford: Paul Watkins, 1991.

Parsons, John Carmi. *Eleanor of Castile: Queen and Society in Thirteenth-Century England*. London: Macmillan, 1995.

Polley, Jacob. *The Havocs*. London: Picador, 2012.

Prescott, Sarah. *Eighteenth-Century Writing from Wales: Bards and Britons*. Cardiff: University of Wales Press, 2008.

Reading, Peter. *Last Poems*. London: Chatto & Windus, 1994.

Robinson, Fred. C. *The Tomb of Beowulf and Other Essays on Old English*. Oxford: Blackwell, 1993.

Røjel, Jørgen. *The 1949 Cruise of the Viking Ship Hugin*, trans. Holger Brønnum. Copenhagen: Samlerens Forlag, 1949.

Russell, Peter. *Visions and Ruins*. Aylesford, Kent: St Albert's Press, 1964.

Scala, Elizabeth and Sylvia Federico, eds. *The Post-Historical Middle Ages*. Basingstoke: Palgrave Macmillan, 2009.

Schechner, Richard. *Between Theater and Anthropology*. Philadelphia: University of Pennsylvania Press, 1985.

Schneider, Rebecca. *Theatre and History*. Basingstoke: Palgrave Macmillan, 2014.

Serres, Michel, with Bruno Latour. *Conversations on Science, Culture, and Time*, trans. Roxanne Lapidus. Ann Arbor: University of Michigan Press, 1995.

Shippey, T. A. and Andreas Haarder, eds. *'Beowulf': The Critical Heritage*. London: Routledge, 1998.

Simpson, James. 'Ageism: Leland, Bale and the laborious start of English literary history, 1350–1550', *New Medieval Literatures* 1 (1997), 213–35.

Simpson, James. *Reform and Cultural Revolution, 1350–1547*. Oxford: Oxford University Press, 2002.

Simpson, James. *Under the Hammer: Iconoclasm in the Anglo-American Tradition*. Oxford: Oxford University Press, 2010.

Spivak, Gayatri Chakravorty. *Outside in the Teaching Machine*. New York: Routledge, 2009.

Stodnick, Jacqueline and Renée R. Trilling, eds. *A Handbook of Anglo-Saxon Studies*. Oxford: Wiley-Blackwell, 2012.

Strohm, Paul. 'Historicity without historicism?', *Postmedieval: A Journal of Medieval Cultural Studies* 1 (2010), 380–91.

Swanton, Michael. *English Poetry before Chaucer*. Exeter: Exeter University Press, 2002.

Thornbury, Emily V. 'Admiring the ruined text: The picturesque in editions of Old English verse', *New Medieval Literatures* 8 (2006), 215–47.

Thornbury, Emily V. *Becoming a Poet in Anglo-Saxon England*. Cambridge: Cambridge University Press, 2014.

Trigg, Dylan. 'The place of trauma: Memory, trauma, and the temporality of ruins', *Memory Studies* 2 (2009), 87–101.

Trilling, Renée R. *The Aesthetics of Nostalgia: Historical Representation in Old English Verse*. Toronto: University of Toronto Press, 2009.

Trumpener, Katie. *Bardic Nationalism: The Romantic Novel and the British Empire*. Princeton: Princeton University Press, 1997.

Tummers, H. A. *Early Secular Effigies in England*. Leiden: Brill, 1980.

Turner, Marion, ed. *A Handbook of Middle English Studies*. Oxford: Wiley-Blackwell, 2013.

Turner, Sharon. *The History of the Anglo-Saxons, from their first appearance above the Elbe, to the death of Egbert*. London: T. Cadell, 1799.

Venuti, Lawrence. 'Translation as cultural politics: Regimes of domestication in English', *Textual Practice* 7 (1993), 208–23.

Warton, Thomas. *The History of English Poetry, from the Close of the Eleventh to the Commencement of the Eighteenth Century*. London: J. Dodley, 1774.

Whitaker, Cord J., ed. 'Making race matter in the Middle Ages', *Postmedieval: A Journal of Medieval Cultural Studies* 6 (2015): 1–110.

Wiggins, Colin, with Richard Cork and Jennifer Sliwka. *Michael Landy: Saints Alive*. London: National Gallery and Yale University Press, 2013.

Williams, Raymond. *Marxism and Literature*. Oxford: Oxford University Press, 1977.

Wollenberg, Daniel. 'The new knighthood: Terrorism and the medieval', *Postmedieval: A Journal of Medieval Cultural Studies* 5 (2014), 21–33.

Wood, Ian. *The Modern Origins of the Early Middle Ages*. Oxford: Oxford University Press, 2013.

Woodward, Christopher. *In Ruins*. London: Chatto & Windus, 2001.

Žižek, Slavoj. *The Sublime Object of Ideology*. London: Verso, 2008.

Znojemská, Helena. '*The Ruin*: A reading of the Old English poem', *Litteraria Progensia* 8 (1998), 15–33.

Zukowsky, John. 'Montjoies and Eleanor Crosses reconsidered', *Gesta* 13 (1974), 39–44.

Zumthor, Paul. *Toward a Medieval Poetics*. Minneapolis: University of Minnesota Press, 1992.

Online resources

BoB: Learning on Screen: https://learningonscreen.ac.uk/ondemand.

British Newspaper Archive: www.britishnewspaperarchive.co.uk.

Historic England Archive: https://historicengland.org.uk/images-books/archive/.

Lux: https://lux.org.uk/.

Prosopography of Anglo-Saxon England: www.pase.ac.uk.

University of Toronto Dictionary of Old English: A–G Online: http://tapor.library.utoronto.ca/doe/.

University of Toronto Old English Corpus: http://tapor.library.utoronto.ca/doecorpus/.

Index

CPSIA information can be obtained
at www.ICGtesting.com
Printed in the USA
LVHW04*1648270818
588268LV00010B/128/P

9 781526 125934